Marx and
the new individual

Marx and
the new individual

Ian Forbes

London
UNWIN HYMAN
Boston Sydney Wellington

Published by the Academic Division of

Unwin Hyman Ltd
15/17 Broadwick Street, London W1V 1FP, UK

Unwin Hyman Inc.,
8 Winchester Place, Winchester, Mass. 01890, USA

Allen & Unwin (Australia) Ltd
8 Napier Street, North Sydney, NSW 2060, Australia

Allen & Unwin (New Zealand) Ltd in association with the
Port Nicholson Press Ltd,
Compusales Building, 75 Ghuznee Street, Wellington 1, New Zealand

First published in 1990

British Library Cataloguing in Publication Data

Forbes, Ian
  Marx and the new individual.
  1. Political ideologies: Individualism. Marxist theories, history.
  I. Title
  320.512

  ISBN 0-04-445432-5

Library of Congress Cataloging-in-Publication Data

Forbes, Ian.
  Marx and the new individual / Ian Forbes.
    p. cm.
  Includes bibliographical references.
  ISBN 0-04-445432-5
  1. Individualism. 2. Communism and individuals. 3. Marx, Karl.
  1818–1883. I. Title.
  HM136.F65 1990
  302.5'4—dc20
                                  90–31142
                                    CIP

Typeset in 10 on 11 point Bembo
Printed by Billing and Sons
London and Worcester

To my parents,
and to Connie and Kate

Contents

Foreword

Ian Forbes's discussion of Marx as a theorist of individuality could not come at a more apposite time. In many ways the 1980s were marked (many would say scarred) by the dominance of a narrow individualism in much thinking about economics, politics and society. Indeed in some quarters even society itself was notoriously declared non-existent, legitimate social science being left to deal with rationally self-centred individuals "choosing" in the context of a free market. The dominance of these emaciated individuals of classical liberal economic theory has in turn emaciated the societies in which they stalk. With the collapse of the Communist regimes in Eastern Europe many have come to wonder whether the Marxist tradition has any better conception of individuality to offer. It has been widely thought that Marxism derogates the individual by subsuming her/him under some species of class analysis, a feature of class-divided societies to be transcended under communism. Recently the rational-choice theory of what has come to be known as "analytical" Marxism has tried to effect a compromise between socialist ideas and the dominant ethos of capitalist societies. Ian Forbes's work on Marx is bolder: he shows that at the origin of the Marxist tradition, in the work of Marx himself, there lies an all-pervasive and far richer concept of individuality. Forbes demonstrates that Marx, with his developmental view of human nature, assumed that humankind could expand its individuality to such an extent that individuals themselves would constitute a force powerful enough to break down social institutions that had hitherto prevented that individuality from realising its full potential. On Forbes's account, Marx's consideration of the individual can generate not only a radical critique of contemporary society but also a vision of an alternative of which both East and West stand in such evident need.

David McLellan
December 1989

Introduction
The puzzle of the individual

Is the individual a central feature of Marx's account of social existence, or something to be transcended? This is the question this book examines, with specific reference to the role in Marx's thought of the concepts of human nature and historical development. The issue of the individual warrants close analysis for a number of reasons. First, for the Marxian critique of contemporary society and explanation of historical change to be more potent as a theory and more responsive to political and social developments, a more complete understanding of the individual is vital. It is, therefore, important to demonstrate that Marx's thought, in its structure and interest, has more potential significance for explanations of the individual in society than theories which explicitly purport to provide such explanations.

Second, individuality is contrasted with individualization and with individualism. Individualization describes the process whereby society gives rise to and 'forms' the individual. Here the environmental context is of interest and importance for a theory of society, not individuals themselves. Individualism, however, focuses on the notion of the individual in order to derive accounts of politics and society. The significance of the individual for any theory of society, then, is contentiously bound up with issues like the content of the individual as a representative of human nature and the form that individuals take in actual societies. Individuality denotes a richer and more accurate way of understanding the individual, in so far as the individual is taken to be neither a blank sheet nor the fundamental unit of analysis. That is, the concept of individuality locates the individual in a critical theory of society in a way that is consistent with Marx's thought, even though this aspect has not yet been fully acknowledged.

Third, Marx is conventionally understood to be antagonistic to theories in which the individual is of theoretical and practical importance. He is said to make individuals entirely subject to historical processes rooted in material needs, to conceive only of collectivities and to place historical significance on class antagonisms which are the material expression of development arising out of objective (but not yet fully human) social forces. Furthermore, consciousness of the true nature of society and the real basis for proper human existence apparently relate to and spring from class experience, not individual existence. Each of these claims comes under direct and critical scrutiny.

The puzzle of the individual is approached in the following way. It will be argued that Marx's analysis of the individual in society is composed of a strong critique of individualism as well as an insight into the importance of true individuality. The approach is theoretical and historical, focusing first on the critique of individualism that Marx's thought provides, and then concentrating more deeply on the understanding of individuality which can be gained from his thought as a whole. This involves three things: (1) an analysis of his view of human nature in respect of history, society and the individual; (2) the use of his account of the history of productive activity through successive historical epochs to explain progress and generate a developmental account; (3) the application of Marx's historical materialist method to the development, not of productive activity, but of *individuality* in successive historical epochs. This means that the individual is viewed dialectically, as expressing at the same time the partiality of all pre-communist existence as well as the latent all-sidedness which makes possible the movement toward the realization of true individuality in communism.

Implicitly and explicitly, there is a series of challenges to conventional wisdom in this approach. The major difference is a downgrading of the importance of class analysis. It is not disputed that history hitherto is the history of class struggle, but there are serious problems in the class conflict explanation of the transition to communism. In such accounts, the move from class to non-class existence has no historical precedent to draw upon, and the theoretical arguments that can be unearthed are tenuous. Put another way, Marx believes in individuals but must reject individualism. In terms of the major interpretations of Marx, the Althusserian insistence on the primacy of economic determination is misleading, as is the related notion that humanist interpretations of Marx are fundamentally flawed. However, ethical Marxist interpretations do not thereby stand, since such arguments are not in any event decisive, and consideration of them would lead in a quite different direction. Most controversially, the individual is regarded as an historical agent of considerable importance for future transitions from one form of society to another. The basis of individual agency has already been developed, and has become a part of fundamental human nature.

In the first two chapters, theoretical issues are tackled, before the evidence concerning the nature of individual existence, as Marx understood it, under various historical epochs - feudalism, capitalism and communism - is examined.

Chapter 1 discusses the relationship between the individual and Marxian thought. The first concern is with the argument that there is no place for the individual in Marx's theory, and the claim that individualism's only role is as ideology. Althusser is the major thinker in this respect, and he sees Marx's thought as a science of history, wherein entities such as the individual have no role whatsoever. This view is particularly antagonistic to a serious consideration of the individual. Therefore, the Althusserian perspective is discussed in order to highlight the relevant flaws in this strongly determinist position. Having dealt with this criticism from within Marxism, there is a consideration of the modes of individualism that abound in social theory, all of which are explicitly or implicitly critical of the Marxian enterprise, however it is defined. This involves separating out different notions of, or ways of thinking about, the individual. Establishing that there are numerous forms of the argument over the role of the individual in explanations and critiques of society brings to light different modes of individualism and pinpoints the individualist thinking which has most relevance to Marx's thought. It will be found that Marx's critique is very corrosive of certain kinds of individualism and that individuality can be distinguished from the various types of individualism. Elster's interpretation of Marx as a methodological individualist is explicitly rejected. Finally, it will be shown how Marx's theory relates to these modes of individualism by discussing the concept of human nature, which proves to be a key construct, and the connection between it, autonomy and history. This prepares the way for a discussion of Marx's theory of change.

Building on the possible interpretations of the individual in theoretical terms, Chapter 2 focuses on the issue of historical change and the place of the individual in descriptions and explanations of such change. It is shown that the historical materialist account offered by Marx and Engels did not foreclose on the possibility of non-economic forces having a vital role in historical change. The first section thus refers to the conflict between views of human action and agency derived on the basis of assumptions of determinism versus autonomy, highlighting the contrast between the 'puzzling individual' and the mass of humankind. A firm commitment to the ubiquity and variety of change in history is noted, and the section concludes that Marx should not be associated with a monocausal view of constant historical change. In order to provide an alternative to an economically determined source of change in society, it is argued that the relationship between history and human nature deserves particular attention. It is these features of his thought which are capable of being used to theorize the theme of constancy of change in Marx's thought.

This leads on to a specific application of the idea of human nature. The introduction of a distinction between a *conception of human nature* and a *notion of human nature* enables reference respectively to a transhistorical nature, and to a nature as it emerges under specific circumstances. These are taken to be different on both theoretical and practical levels, yet linked to a progressive movement of history. The application of this distinction is a fruitful way to conceive of the individual in society expressing fundamental human nature as well as being the result of earlier social formations and developments. In other words, both human nature and history 'produce' the individual, but the individual which results is not reducible to either factor.

The final section on social change and individuality shows how this relationship should differ from one historical epoch to another. Using this as a basis, the core argument of the book is derived. It is argued that, if Marx saw the movement from one mode of production to another as development, then the principle of development might equally apply to the individuals who filled, sustained and transcended those epochs. Therefore, individuals in pre-capitalist, capitalist and then communist societies theoretically represent a succession of expressions of basic human nature. This constitutes a series, within which each description produces a notion of human nature – how it is possible to be an individual under this or that form of social organization.

A detailed examination of how Marx characterized individual existence under these kinds of societies, then, will reveal a number of insights. First, it will be possible to judge whether Marx did see individuality developing through successive stages, and whether the emergent individual might develop to the point at which the making of historical destiny is the task of human agents. Second, the contrast between capitalist modes of individuality and the nature of individual existence in other social formations will shed light on his critique of individualism.

Chapter 3 is the first of the chapters which put this theoretical scheme into operation. The review of Marx's thoughts on primitive social existence sees the reiteration of the basic principles of his conception of human nature, just as they reveal the reasons why that nature will express itself differently under differing circumstances. Moreover, he emphasized the qualities of primitive existence which were to be important for his vision of the future. This chapter shows, as does the next, that Marxian thought is never backward-looking. His observations tend to have relevance in both the present and the future. Feudalism is important to Marx's work because it was a mode of production that he could analyse in its final death throes as capitalism came to dominate productive relations. Feudalism was in many ways a complete contrast with his own society, yet it was the society which gave birth to historic opportunities. The life of the individual under feudalism is a confined and limited one, and Marx has little sympathy for its passing. His critique of the possibilities, however, reveals his belief in the progress of humankind throughout history. Crucially, he saw history as the emergence of the individual out of a mass or herd-like existence. That individual was developing independence from the natural associations that came to define existence less and less. The individual is of particular interest in late feudalism. Marx viewed that expression of individuality with interest and referred to the changes that were occurring in the relationship of humans to their natural and social environment. It was these changes, it is argued, that constituted a force for change to a new society.

Chapter 4 has the most complex set of issues with which to deal, because Marx was involved with developing all aspects of an account of capitalism. His work on pre-capitalist society laid the foundation for an explanation of the transition from feudalism to capitalism, which Marx saw as a victory for a superior mode of production, one which was more in tune with the capacities and abilities of human nature. Early capitalism, in its dynamic phase, is an expression of the enormous creative ability and energy of humankind, for which it receives high praise.

In general, this chapter focuses on the way that capitalism brings about an unprecedented expansion of human capacities and needs, and shows that this is crucial in a number of ways for Marx's concept of a developing individuality. Marx's critique of capitalism is constructed, he thought, at the turning point of history, in respect of a major change in how history was made, and in respect of capitalism specifically. His criticisms, therefore, take on a special significance, because they are predicated on the understanding that capitalist society was about to collapse, and that all movement and change in that society was preparation and development for the next stage. His piercing criticisms of the reality of productive and social relations, for example, provide a wealth of insights to the nature of the development that he thought was taking place, what that development could lead to, and the speed at which it was taking place. At the same time, he was aware of the individualist alternative to his social explanation, and his social critiques give an opportunity to analyse the connections he saw and distinctions he made between capitalism, individualism and individuality. Bourgeois individuality is something that Marx was able to praise yet show to be partial and inadequate as an expression of human nature, and this reiterates the argument that Marx's thought, above all, establishes that the unique achievement of capitalism is the development of individuality to such an extent that it is possible to conceive of a completely new social formation.

Chapter 5 looks forward to communist society, to draw out Marx's perception of individual existence after the ultimate resolution of class conflict and examine the formation of a society based on real human needs. This is a subject about which Marx was relatively coy, but there proves to be sufficient material to make some interesting conclusions. First, communism as the end of classes is discussed, where it is pointed out that the absence of class calls for a qualitatively different way of conceiving of people. The evidence suggests that Marx thought communism would enable people to express human faculties under conditions of social freedom of their own making.

The character of such communist individuals is explored, in order to note the differences between this form of individuality and all those that have gone before. This is followed by an analysis of the claims that must accompany this vision of individual existence. It is suggested that the vision of the future offered by Marx is based on the individual becoming a universal being, which means that, in communism, the conception of human nature fully realizes itself in its individual and specific expression. In other words, the *notion of human nature* under communism is equivalent to Marx's *conception of human nature*. As such, society for the individual under communism changes quite substantially. It is not the *social* individual that communism allows for the first time, but the transcendence of that individual.

The conclusion gathers together the contributions that the studies of different epochs have to make concerning the nature and extent of the development of individuality. It is proposed that to label Marx as a theorist of individuality is not to insult his work or misuse his method. One of his central concerns was the existence that individuals could have in societies under different modes of production. He seems to have assumed that humankind could become developed to such a degree that this constituted a powerful enough historical force for the destruction of social organizations which restricted the full realization of human capacities and abilities. At times Marx assumed that this demonstration of a possibility of humankind amounted to a moral as well as historical imperative for the changes which he thought desirable. It not only *would* happen, it *should* happen. There are weaknesses in this kind of reasoning, but that does not affect a further conclusion: that Marxian thought can be used to generate a searching and radical analysis of contemporary existence, and a powerful vision of the future, on the basis of a consideration of the individual rather than the conventional categories of class, economics, and their associated political assumptions and purviews.

Political theory has long sought the appropriate way to conceive of the relationship between the individual and the state. Marx's thought transcends this problematic with the concept of the withering away of the state. There remains, however, the other side of that pairing, the individual. By removing, in theory at least, the state from the agenda of the politically inescapable, it is generally assumed that the individual no longer needed to be theorized, except in so far as s/he was also to disappear. The following chapters seek to show that the individual is not necessarily a derivative of the state, the creation of state-centred theories, or idealism.

Individuals remain, it will be argued, at the centre of Marx's thought. He discussed them in his historical work, in his critical analysis of capitalism and in his vision of the future. It is demonstrated that he dispensed with the understanding of the individual that dominated the ideologies of his day, but he did not jettison his interest in an individual existence of a radical kind. This entailed a developmental view of human nature and therefore individuality. Far from individuals ceasing to exist with the withering away of the state, he saw a history unfolding where individuals could truly and freely exist. Moreover, the flowering of human capacities and their individual expression was, for him, the unfolding of that history. Individuals, that is, are the subjects and agents of Marxian historical change.

Of the many individuals who have assisted me in the writing of this book, I would like to thank in particular John Street, Raymond Plant, Terrel Carver, Steve Smith, Graeme Duncan, David McLellan and Albert Weale for their comments and encouragement; Gordon Smith's editorial team has ensured that any remaining errors are mine alone.

1 The individual, political theory and Marx's thought

This book is about the existence, nature and relevance of the individual in Marx's thought. It argues that the individual is a central feature of Marx's theory and that he made important contributions to the study of the role of individualism, individuality and human nature in social explanation. There are schools of thought which regard these claims as controversial and this kind of project as doomed. It is necessary, therefore, to tackle such arguments and models of explanation at the outset.

Louis Althusser's claim that Marx's science of history has no place for such an entity as the individual is the starting point. The theoretical treatment of the individual is a key indicator of the difference between two competing modes of Marxist interpretation: the humanist tradition, which recognizes and values the individual in history; and deterministic accounts, which reject the notion of an historical subject. Althusser sets himself squarely against the humanist tradition. He brands that approach idealist, and tries to transcend *all* humanisms with the development of an interpretation of Marx's mature thought as a theoretical anti-humanism. This is an attempt to generate a truly scientific socialist analysis, but has the effect of removing the individual from political analysis altogether.

The account of the dispute between idealists and scientists (so-called) within Marxism is followed by a section on modes of individualist theory. Here there is a contrasting stress on the importance of the individual in social theories which are less controversially understood as idealist. They, too, are critically analysed, since they see in any version of Marxism a fundamental threat to the sanctity of the individual and claim to have successfully grounded social explanation in various conceptions of the individual. Third, the immediate nature of the conflict between individualist thought and the contribution of Marx is examined. This leads to a discussion of different notions of, or ways of thinking about, the individual, and

1

the manner in which Marx's own theory relates to them. Finally, the difference between Marx's perceptions of individualism and individuality is outlined, and the method for studying the historical nature of his views on the individual is presented.

The individual in humanism and theoretical anti-humanism

Marx is often accused of ignoring the fundamental importance of the individual in society. There is, for example, the suggestion that the individual is held to be only of secondary significance to the determination of social structures and forces. In his defence, however, are those Marxists who have regularly and confidently pointed to those features of Marx's thought which rebut attacks bemoaning the loss of individuality in the social order. These rebuttals have rejected the accusations both in terms of arguments used and conclusions reached.

While the central figure (or non-figure) of this internal Marxist argument is the individual, the centrepiece of the theoretical dispute concerns the status of the concept of humanism. Humanism has become a pivotal term and is often used as a convenient shorthand to convey a general and complex epistemological orientation in Marxist thought. Yet it does retain meaning outside that specialist ambit. The concept of humanism can also be used to demonstrate the connections between Marx's thought and individualist thought. It attaches theoretical and practical significance to the individual in society, just as Marx's thought does. Arguments about the validity of humanism, therefore, will have a direct bearing on the assessment of Marx in this respect.

It is important, then, to see how the evolution of the concept of humanism came to contribute to a certain kind of Marxist (socialist) explanation of the individual and society. Renaissance humanism, it is generally agreed, is primarily based on the Protagorean notion that the person is the measure of all things. This understanding represented a secularization of the study of human cultural and political achievements, but did not necessitate or involve the rejection of belief in a god. Instead, the focus merely shifted from an interest in the divine to an interest in human activity. It was not until the eighteenth century that humanism began to amount to a direct, and negative, response to religion. Here the individual became the sole and sufficient source of all values – a strand of humanism that persists into this century. Raymond Williams, however, detects a third historical development in the nineteenth century, when humanism also came to incorporate an Hegelian belief in history as human self-development and self-perception (Williams, 1976, pp. 122–3).

Taken together, humanism can be summed up as a theory, doctrine, or ideology which concerns itself more with humans than with something other than humans. There are two things to observe here. First, this definition seems to echo the claim and purpose of most individualisms (and particularly methodological individualism), where individuals are deemed to be the prime consideration. This implies a rejection of structuralism, and seems to suggest that the 'out with God' development has been followed by an 'out with structure' movement. Second, then, the history of the development of humanism appears to be closely linked to the birth and subsequent transformations of individualism as the basis of theories of society, and in terms of the self-perceptions of social beings. Lukes sees a progression taking place, from religious individualism to ethical individualism, with an associated increase in the moral autonomy and valuational power of the individual human being (Lukes, 1973b, pp. 101–3).

One of the questions to keep in mind, therefore, is whether a defence of Marx on *humanist* grounds necessarily implies an appeal to both, or either, methodological and ethical individualism. In other words, is humanism a form of individualism? From this, other questions arise. Is Marx's socialism a humanism, or vice versa? If so, to what extent, and does this mean that Marx's socialism has important connections with individualism? The question then becomes whether Marx should be seen as part of this trend toward individualist-humanism, or as a vehement opponent of it who effectively wanted to replace religious determinism with structural determinism.

Althusser is one who certainly thinks that the latter is the case. For him, 'precisely in the couple "humanism–socialism" there is a striking theoretical unevenness: in the framework of the Marxist conception, the concept "socialism" is indeed a scientific concept, but the concept "humanism" is no more than an ideological one' (Althusser, 1969, p. 223). 'Ideological' here means a concept that reflects an 'unconscious relation ... between men and their world' (ibid., p. 229). Since that relation is unconscious, the ideological concept is philosophical in that it precedes a scientific reformulation based on knowledge. Thus Althusser addresses directly the question of the status of humanism in Marx's thought and is

3

uncompromising in his response. First, and quite correctly, he denies that *philosophical* humanism of the kind outlined above can ever be consistent with Marx's materialistic methodology. However, Althusser also wishes to claim that Marx, in realizing this, became an anti-humanist not only in a philosophical, but in a theoretical sense as well (ibid., p. 229).

In 1845, Marx broke radically with every theory that based history and politics on an essence of man. This unique rupture contained three indissociable elements.

(1) The formation of a theory of history and politics based on radically new concepts: the concepts of social formation, productive forces, relations of production, superstructures, ideologies, determination in the last instance by the economy, specific determination by other levels, etc.

(2) A radical critique of the *theoretical* pretensions of every philosophical humanism.

(3) The definition of humanism as an *ideology*. (ibid., p. 227)

The new scientific conception constitutive of this 'epistemological break' is particularly corrosive of both philosophical humanism and methodological individualism. The inadequacy of these assumptions had already been established by Marx in the Sixth Thesis on Feuerbach, when he wrote that 'the human essence is no abstraction inherent in each single individual. In its reality it is the ensemble of social relations' ([1845] 1968, p. 29). Althusser, however, takes this critique much further, and raises it to a theoretical principle that rejects *every* humanism, on the basis that an ideology cannot employ ethics and still remain a theoretical concept. In general terms, this means that 'the subject', so crucial for all forms of individualism, was no longer useful, since the subject could no longer be said to exist. Marx, he argues:

drove the philosophical categories of the *subject*, of *empiricism*, of the *ideal essence*, etc., from all the domains in which they had been supreme. Not only from political economy (rejection of the myth of *homo economicus*, that is, of the individual with definite faculties and needs as the *subject* of classical economy); not just from history (rejection of social atomism and ethico-political idealism); but also from philosophy itself: for Marx's materialism excludes empiricism of the subject (and its inverse: the transcendental subject) and the idealism of the concept (and

4

its inverse: the empiricism of the concept). (Althusser, 1969, pp. 228–9)

According to this account, both methodological and ethical individualism, because they are based on social atomism and ethico-political idealism respectively, must be theoretically inadequate. That is, they are 'unscientific'. Moreover, it is just these forms of individualism that Althusser takes to be implicit in Marx's humanism, at least in the early works and in philosophical humanism generally. In so far as 'bourgeois humanism made man the principle of all theory' (ibid., p. 237), humanism is no more than an ideology. Such a definition, however, is not just a blanket term of denigration, since 'ideology is not an aberration or contingent excrescence of History: it is a structure essential to the historical life of societies' (ibid., p. 232). Therefore, it is important not merely to understand the underpinnings of this particular ideology, which at one level leads Althusser to adopt a theoretical anti-humanism, but also to comprehend the appropriate way to respond to the very existence of humanism.

> Marx's philosophical anti-humanism does provide an understanding of the necessity of existing ideologies, including humanism. But at the same time, because it is a critical and revolutionary theory, it also provides an understanding of the tactics to be adopted towards them; whether they should be supported, transformed or combatted. And Marxists know that there can be no tactics that do not depend on a strategy – and no strategy that does not depend on a theory. (ibid., p. 241)

Here humanism is downgraded to being the subject of a political strategy, since it has no foundation in theory, and therefore in reality. Yet Althusser is aware that 'in the real world philosophies of man are found after Marx as often as before, and today even some Marxists are tempted to develop the themes of a new theoretical humanism' (ibid., p. 231). It follows that scientific socialism must have a two-pronged response. On the level of tactics, humanism as ideology may or may not be supported according to the specific conjuncture, while on a strategic level, Althusser recognizes the need to develop the notion of a 'real-humanism'.

> Real-humanism is scientifically defined by its opposition to unreal humanism, ideal(ist), abstract, speculative humanism and so on. This *reference* humanism is simultaneously invoked as a reference and rejected for its abstraction, unreality, etc, by the

5

new real-humanism. So the old humanism is judged by the new as an abstract and illusory humanism. Its illusion is to aim at an unreal object, to have as its content an object which is not the real object. (ibid., p. 242)

Thus real-humanism would not need to, indeed could not, exist without 'old' humanism. The aim is, strategically, to dispose of the intrusion of the concept of the abstract individual, but this involves the theoretical articulation of scientific socialism.

It means that to find the reality alluded to by seeking abstract man no longer, it is necessary *to turn to society*, and to undertake an analysis of the ensemble of social relations. (ibid., p. 243)

This is the point at which the individual and any associated notions of human nature, autonomy and free will are ultimately jettisoned. These are crucial claims for this study. If human nature, autonomy and free will are simply redundant explanatory and descriptive terms and approaches, then Marx, and Marxist thought, cannot be said to have a structure and interest which in any way relate to explanations of the individual, much less offer a superior form of understanding of the individual in society. Althusser's claim is that Marx's superiority as a thinker lies in showing that understanding is not to be focused *at all* on the individual. Further, turning to society should not be conceived as a means to the end of reaching a humanist understanding of society, since society is to be regarded as the complex totality of *practices*, not as an Hegelian expressive totality of any inner essence:

a knowledge of concrete (real) men, that is, a knowledge of the ensemble of social relations is only possible on condition that we do completely without the theoretical services of the concept of man ... In fact, this concept seems to me to be useless from a scientific viewpoint, not because it is abstract! – but because it is not scientific. To think the reality of society, of the ensemble of social relations, we must put into effect a radical *displacement*, not only a spatial displacement (from the abstract to the concrete) but also a conceptual displacement (we change our basic concepts!). The concepts whereby Marx thought reality, which real-humanism pointed out, never again introduce as *theoretical* concepts the concepts of man or humanism; but other quite new concepts, the concepts of mode of production, forces of production, relations of production, superstructure, ideology, etc. (ibid., pp. 243–4)

There are several things to note about the claims that Althusser makes. First, he is describing a particular moment in the development of Marx's thought, with the proposition that there is a transition to be observed from idealist philosophy to scientific socialism. Therefore, to accept Althusser's version of the epistemological break is to conclude that Marx, beyond 1845, could not have made any positive contributions to the concepts of human nature, autonomy and the nature of individual existence in society as part of his larger explanatory model of society. This will be discussed in more detail later.

There *is* a crucial distinction to be made between social explanations that rely on a merely theoretical concept of an abstract human nature and those that focus only on social structure and forces. Without doubt, the latter methodology is not only more productive, but also confutes 'philosophical' humanism. The move from idealism to scientific socialism, then, is said to entail not merely a rejection of the *content* and *form* of humanist premisses concerning human nature, but crucially, such premisses, however derived, are not scientific, i.e. can *never* be part of a theory of society. Concepts of mode, forces and relations of production, superstructure and ideology are deemed not to need any conception of human nature and social relations in their descriptive/critical function. Nor can they be used to develop an enriched conception of human nature. Of course, this still amounts to a conception of human nature. To construct a theory where a role for human nature is denied is not to establish the unimportance of human nature.

Althusser also implies that philosophical humanism represents the pinnacle of idealist efforts to conceive of human nature and social relations as a basis for the development of social theory. Yet he provides no particular or strong proof that Marx confronted and found wanting the *pinnacle* of idealist thinking. In terms of individualist thought, Marx confronted only that which had been developed in his time, as both ideology and rhetoric. Moreover, it is not altogether clear that philosophical humanism must automatically include all modes of individualism, especially since developments have occurred in direct response to the challenge of Marx's thought. A successful attack on philosophical humanism, then, is not necessarily a refutation of all forms of humanist thought out of hand, nor does it mean that Marx is best described as a theoretical anti-humanist.

Althusser's formula for replacing the inadequacy of philosophical humanism with the strength and relevance of 'real-humanism' is as follows:

the 'real' is not a *theoretical slogan*; the real is the real object that exists independently of knowledge – but which can only be defined by its knowledge ... the real is identical to the means of knowing it, the real is its known or known-to-be structure. (ibid., p. 246)

Thus real-humanism, as a theoretical object in but not of knowledge, can only be conceived in the context of two preconditions:

that it can serve as a *practical, ideological* slogan in so far as it is exactly adequate to its function and not confused with a quite different function; that there is no way in which it can be abrogated the attributes of a *theoretical* concept. (ibid., p. 246)

There is no knowledge, then, to be gained concerning human nature. Again, this is in direct contrast to the view that a focus on the individual will lead to precisely this form of knowledge. Instead, an understanding of the ideological role of a concept of human nature can only be gleaned given the objective existence of structural features of society and practical theoretical knowledge of them. This implies a hard, though not vulgar, form of determinism. Althusser's real-humanism is a reflexive praxis theory which evacuates the subject from the notion of a process. Individuals, just as much as human nature, are mere words, lacking even an interesting descriptive content.

It is in these respects that Althusser's formulation comes under serious attack. His account of the notion of human nature cannot provide at the same time an account of the person or the individual in society and in history. There can be no doubt that Althusser correctly identifies Marx's break with philosophical humanism, and therefore the account of individuals as *abstract* individuals, but this by no means amounts to the quite different claim that the rejection of this one, unsatisfactory, answer to the question of the individual invalidates the question itself. As Lucien Sève asks:

Are the works of Althusser and his comrades still so convincing when they regard all humanism as necessarily philosophical and all use of the concept of man as ideological and assert that this rupture leads Marx to theoretical anti-humanism, as when they describe the birth of Marxism itself by the rupture with philosophical humanism? (1978, p. 162)

Part of Sève's answer is to demonstrate that the notion of the epistemological break is made to do far too much. For our purposes, 'doing too much' means invalidating a concern with the individual in society. Nor is it imagined that significant changes in the structure of Marx's thought never took place on any great scale. The development of Marx's thought and especially the articulation of historical materialist premisses certainly occurred, making it possible to see Marxism as a scientific and practical instead of merely philosophical enterprise. However, when the incidence of this development is applied and made to exclude any humanist overtones after the break, Althusser's account is faced with great difficulties. First, as Sève points out, there are 'those works of Marx which unquestionably belong to the mature period and which all, without exception, most clearly and invariably contain elements of what Engels calls 'the science of real men and their historical development' (ibid., p. 162). If this is so, then humanist concerns not only persist, but cannot be described as matters of ideology.

Alternatively, an insistence on the primacy of social relations can just as easily transform itself into a structuralism that precludes any other considerations and inputs. Althusser's 'real-humanism' is an example of this tendency, where individuals are evacuated of meaningful (i.e. revolutionary) content, and have no perception of other possibilities or the ability to initiate radical and emancipatory social action. However, in the denial that people can undertake revolutionary action that is not ultimately reducible to class analysis, old problems – like the contradiction of a revolutionary theory of human emancipation being brought about only by historically determined social forces – remain and new ones are created. Instead of human nature residing in and springing from the 'ensemble of social relations', the 'ensemble' no longer relates to the production and reproduction of our nature. That milieu is itself ideology; according to Althusser, 'the "lived" relation between men and their world' (Althusser, p. 233). Moreover, he argues that ideology is 'profoundly *unconscious*', only to be understood in terms of the structures that 'impose on the vast majority of men' (ibid., p. 227).

Althusser's notion of ideology is akin to a new form of idealism under the guise of Althusser's 'scientific' socialism. Freedom from those structures, which – it is implicit – only a few like Althusser can understand and to whose their ideological sway those few are immune, is as problematic as Marcuse's (1965) notion of repressive tolerance. Althusser and Marcuse both fail to answer the questions they have posed as the most important ones. How, collectively or individually, are distinctions to be made between real and unreal choices/ideologies, why should unreal choices *not* be preferred to none at all, and what is wrong with wanting to know about that which is presently unconscious? There is so great an emphasis on the social determinants of behaviour and order that no other determinants could ever break that hold.

An associated argument claims that anthropological categories have no theoretical status in any theory of society, and certainly not a Marxist theory (Sève, 1978, p. 863). Far from clinching the argument in favour of economic determination in the last instance, Connolly, for example, sees the relationship between ideology and structure as requiring above all an individual with an *independent* role and consciousness.

> My charge is this: without an anthropological dimension in theory, it is inexplicable why the role-bearers require ideology to bear the roles imposed by capitalism; with such an anthropology, the view that theory is not and cannot be made available to participants in ways that influence conduct must be revised profoundly. Structural theory does not eliminate, rather it suppresses, the anthropological dimension. And once the supposed premise is exposed, structural theorists must re-engage the very issues that they have sought to expunge from theory – issues such as the nature of human subjects; the relation between individual subjects and intersubjectivity; the structural limits to the emergence of self-consciousness; the connection between consciousness and political practice; and the moral inhibitions to both social control and revolutionary action. (Connolly, 1981, p. 50)

By drawing attention to the importance of the nature of human subjects and the problem of individual intersubjectivity, Connolly highlights the particular interests of the emergence of the new individual. His critique of Althusser's methodology and theoretical conclusions as a structural theory perceptively identifies the way in which the anthropological dimension is *suppressed* rather than overcome or shown to have no value. Connolly is doing more than criticizing a specific thinker, however, because he is also asserting that political theory must always deal directly with the nature of human subjects and the complexities of individual intersubjectivity. Any attempt to evade them, by whatever theoretical device, will ultimately lead to a renewed sense of their importance and intricacy.

If Connolly's representation of the nature and responsibility of political theory is accurate, and if Althusser's reading of Marx is accepted, then Marx is the thinker primarily responsible for suppressing the anthropological or humanist dimension. However, there are good reasons for rejecting the notion that Althusser represents the 'real' Marx. For example, the structuralist interpretation of Marx is subject to searching textual criticisms. The standard Althusserian response to this kind of criticism was to insist that Marx was never entirely free of his younger, philosophical, self. This claim is highly suspect when one considers the practice of distinguishing science from ideology via a 'symptomatic reading' – knowing the scientific theory before trying to grasp the real meaning of the texts which first set out and utilized that theory.

> In other words, one passes surreptitiously from the *break* which was initially presented to us as a real historical turning point in Marx's thought, separating a still philosophical 'before' and fully scientific 'after', to a demarcation among the texts of mature Marxism itself, which the anti-humanist interpreter authorizes himself to effect, between those texts which he agrees with and those which he rejects as being humanist. (Sève, 1978, p. 163)

The success, in Althusserian terms, of this manoeuvre cannot disguise the lack of clear argumentation to rule out altogether any form of humanism as a theoretical concept. Implicitly, Connolly's charge of suppression remains unrefuted, and Marx's rejection of the historical subject has not been substantiated. Althusser moves from one proposition, namely the view that Marx rejected *philosophical* humanism, to the proposition that humanism could *only* be philosophical. By contrast, Sève, and this writer, are prepared to accept the first point, but insist that Marx's historical materialism actually makes it 'possible to conceive scientifically the *existence* of individuals' (ibid., p. 166). Furthermore, Marx's mature work does more than just allow for non-philosophical humanism. In the *Grundrisse*, for example, Marx talked of the need for human beings to 'individuate' themselves in society, and of the production of 'social individuals' ([1857–8] 1980, pp. 84–5), while in *Capital*, Vol. I, he wrote of the practical and human need for 'the totally developed individual' ([1867] 1976, p. 618). That is, the Althusserian exegesis of Marx's critique of certain forms of individualist-humanist social theory can be separated from the claims about the proper trajectory of Marxian scientific socialism.

These kinds of criticisms, and more positive claims that Marx has important contributions to make concerning the development of individuals in history, have led Althusser to respond to that aspect of his thought which connects structuralist theoretical practice to theoretical anti-humanism. It is noteworthy that he has shifted his ground somewhat. Whereas, in his earlier works, the telling distinction was the clear superiority of science over philosophy, Althusser now presents theoretical anti-humanism as a *choice* between competing explanatory frameworks.

> Marx's theoretical anti-humanism means a refusal to root the explanation of social formations and their history in a concept of man with theoretical pretensions, that is, a concept of man as an *originating subject*, one in whom originate his needs, (*homo economicus*) his own thoughts (*homo rationalis*) and his acts and struggles (*homo moralis, juridicus and politicus*). (Althusser, 1976, p. 205)

In this passage, Althusser makes useful distinctions between the kinds of thought which might employ a concept of wo/man. His categories do not necessarily, however, coincide with the use of a concept of human nature, which need not be reducible to an originating subject in any of the reductionist senses he outlines. At the same time, the characteristics of possible originating subjects are not in conflict with assumptions inherent in the modes of individualism to be found in the next section. The similarities between individualist and humanist thought may be apparent, and the proximity of their concerns highlighted, but these things do not of themselves establish that the two kinds of approach are to all intents and purposes the same.

The key phrase in the passage is 'means a refusal to root the explanation', since it does imply that tactics are an important consideration. Choice between the models is not entirely based on the logical requirements and efficacies of a particular explanatory model. The choice, as Althusser presents it, is skewed markedly in favour of theoretical anti-humanism: the alternative is seen as a conglomerate of individualisms, involving once again the fundamental premiss of the ahistorical, abstract individual expressed in a variety of forms. Althusser accurately perceives the reliance on an abstract individual as a form of thinking most inimical to Marxist thought as well as the hopes of Marxists themselves, and wished all Marxists to stay well clear of this area. Unfortunately, humanism is once more misrepresented, which only serves further to weaken Althusser's argument, because he suggests that the choice between his version of the alternatives means a rejection of the weaker and an acceptance of that which remains. This happens to be theoretical anti-humanism.

Three conclusions can be drawn from this change of position. First, theoretical anti-humanism cannot be scientifically *correct*, since it is only to be preferred to a poorer alternative. Second, Althusser's structural theory no longer *entails* theoretical anti-humanism.

The individual, political theory and Marx's thought

Instead, that theory, or his representation of it, is transformed in that it now seems to need the *support* of theoretical anti-humanism to maintain its potency and viability. Finally, if it is compared, more realistically, with a non-individualistic humanism, then Althusser's preference may not have the 'correctness' he claims. In any event, the realm of the argument has certainly shifted from readings of Marx's works to a consideration of the strength of Althusser's propositions, which is not our main concern.

Nevertheless, the strong determinist account of scientific socialism has served an important function in Marxist thought. The issue of agency, the question of the historical subject, the nature of individuals and their social existence, have all been raised again, and in new ways. What has emerged is an awareness of the way in which a structuralist explanation presupposes a disjuncture between theory and ideology.

Thus Althusser's enterprise is no tiresome detour around the more interesting or substantive areas of investigation. Rather, he has caused a shift in the way that the anthropological dimension, so called, is approached, justified and utilized. Most crucial is that the commitment to historical-materialist method is retained and strengthened. Instead of the anthropological dimension being a collection of *assumptions* (some of them uncritically adopted and held), the issues are conceived in terms of questions or problems which must be answered scientifically. This greater critical awareness of an appropriate attitude to theory itself is a positive result of Althusser's claim that theoretical practice has a determining influence as a form of labour. To the extent that this is true, then, the form and content of a theory will have an important bearing on the unfolding of history. As such, the inadequacies and omissions in Marxist theory did and still can prove disastrous, and can undermine the very possibility of socialism. It is the responsibility of those who adopt Marx's fundamental theoretical premises to acknowledge the consequences of the theory as it was first developed, and not to explain them away by extending the theoretical construction.

One of the chief consequences is the fate of the individual in social explanation. An inability to produce an account of the person must count as a failure or lacuna of any social theory. Marxism can be held 'responsible' for a silence with respect to the individual if it is accepted that Althusser's rejection once and for all of the question of the individual, and his argument that scientific socialism should not have to provide any such account whatsoever, is appropriate. But this position is deeply flawed, in that it misrepresents Marx's enterprise as well as his actual thought. Marxism is nevertheless in danger of finding itself confined to a collectivistic and deterministic ghetto of its own making unless a credible theory of the individual is developed. Not only would Marxism be in danger of losing wider relevance, but it would not realize its creative potential.

Far from an abandonment of Marxian thought, a validation and examination of the human subject can be a legitimate concern within the Marxian tradition. Marxism, from this perspective, is a 'dangerous' method of social and political analysis, since outcomes are unpredicted and unpredictable. Nevertheless, it ought to be pursued in order to refresh and add to the cumulative store of knowledge, not in an accretive but a reflexive sense, such that knowledge changes not only what we want to know, but also how we want to come to know it. That is, the methods of that science must equally come under scrutiny, in order to highlight weaknesses in the way that individuals and society are understood and changed. Thus the rejection of theoretical anti-humanism means the acceptance of some form of humanism. The acceptance of a humanistic account is equivalent to accepting the existence and importance of the individual.

Individualism and social theory

Some social and political theories, of course, have always assumed that the individual is the fundamental unit of analysis. Their protagonists may well argue that Marxism is only just becoming aware of a pivotal reality long recognized and built upon by individualist thinkers. On this view, individualist theories claim to be naturally superior, and to understand the individual and society in a much deeper and more advanced fashion. More directly, Marx has always been the target of antagonism for these forms of individualism, since it is Marxist thought and practice which are held to be inimical to the values ascribed to the individual and the kind of society which permits their free enjoyment. This section will examine the various forms of individualism as they have developed and been in conflict with Marx's thought. The aims are several: to demonstrate the ways in which Marx distinguishes between individuals and individualism; to find the forms of individualism that Marx might accept or recognize; and to see in general whether the non-Marxist explorations of political and social theories grounded in the individual have yielded anything useful and coherent.

Although the term individualism was relatively new in Marx's time, the method of thought which underpinned it was not. Rather, individualism quickly became not just a word but a very flexible rubric in liberal thought, and its most successful rhetorical touchstone. Thus the term may be used to support different moral and political positions, and can be stated as a central metaphysical proposition from which the proper study of society as a whole can proceed. It is important to note at the outset, therefore, that it is as a *concept* that individualism causes some confusion, since it can have different and sometimes conflicting meanings for different people, times and purposes. Given its theoretical locations, it makes sense to distinguish, as Lukes (1973b) has done, between various modes of individualism. His study indicates that it is not possible to rely upon a single explanatory and/or descriptive framework of individualism, and highlights the aims and limitations involved in particular uses of the term individualism. His typology of distinctions of modes of individualism is the basis for the following analysis.

Notwithstanding his practice of turning first to the values and ideals of individualism, such predicates are of secondary importance, since they depend fundamentally on the conception of human nature employed – more specifically, on the appropriate way to conceive of the relationship between human beings and society. This is no small question: a complete answer must amount to a general theory of society. However, the principal concern must be with the manner in which certain key issues are addressed, such that the coherence of that treatment can be assessed. At the forefront is the question, what is the procedure when faced with the problem of defining what it is to be human? Individualism's first answer was clear, if lacking in depth, and is summarized by Lukes as the conception of the abstract individual.

> According to this conception, individuals are pictured abstractly as given interests, wants, purposes, needs, etc . . . The crucial point . . . is that the relevant features of individuals determining the ends which social arrangements are held to fulfil, whether these features are called instincts, faculties, needs, desires, rights, etc., are assumed as given, independently of a social context. (1973b, p. 73)

The independence of individuals with given properties from the social context is the defining difference between Marxist and individualist approaches, and warrants examination.[1] Even if the representation of the nature of individuals as fixed is true, of itself such a nature carries no particular weight, since it does not necessarily imply any one set of structural forms, and affords no special

15

protection for that nature.[2] Ruling out the social context effectively denies even a tactical redrawing of the boundaries to the individual that would incorporate, perhaps, some notion of sociability. Thus it becomes clear that the moral predicates of human dignity and autonomy and the ideals of privacy and self-development represent an attempt to give the human nature of individuals a status and form that cannot be sustained on the basis of its *a priori* content alone. That is, the normatively 'neutral' content of human nature is both protected from the possibility of social engineering and buttressed as a model for the good society by the strategic addition of prescriptive values.

Society is problematic for another reason. The denial of a formative social context means that society can be only the sum of its atomistic constituents. This summation requires that values and ideals cannot be the properties of society so defined, either in principle or in practice. Therefore, there is no power to those beliefs beyond the measure in which individuals organize themselves, or are forced to deny a part of their nature and invest in social coercion over themselves and others. The abstract individualist, to be consistent with first principles, must rely ultimately on social forces while rejecting the notion that they have any determining significance. Those forces are social in that they depend for their existence on co-operative or collective creation and observance, so constituting the real definition, status and possibility for individual agency. In short, the creation and adoption of values and ideals depends upon a prior *social* understanding.

Further support for the argument that the conception of human nature is the crucial aspect of individualist thought emerges when considering the pervasiveness and strength of moral and ideal notions of autonomy and primacy. By contrast, the weakness of the idea of the abstract individual, implicit even in the thought of Rousseau (Lukes, 1973b, p. 77), is borne out by its apparent unpopularity in subsequent individualist thought. On the one hand, there was a proliferation of modes of individualism in the last century, and on the other, a sharpening of the epistemological focus in this century. These two main developments represent attempts either to refine the explanations of social processes, or to enhance the explanations of individuals *qua* individuals.

The first approach enlarges upon the ways in which individuals can be conceived and articulates the means by which the relationship between the individual and society is to be understood. Here the idea of an abstract individual is disguised and driven underground somewhat. Nevertheless, the abstract individual remains central. The connections between individual and society are articulated either by the attribution of descriptive qualities to the individual, or the generation of the principles of the explanatory model as a whole. Both permit the development of much more sophisticated analyses of, for example, rights, obligation and justice. In this way, values and ideals can be accepted universally, and yet can still be dragooned into service to actualize the basic assumptions about individual human beings. Into such a group Lukes (1973b, pp. 138–45) places political, economic, epistemological and methodological individualism, but it might also include possessive, utilitarian and radical individualism.[3]

The second approach dispenses with the abstract individual altogether. Moral categories of human dignity and autonomy are not enlisted to support the notion of the individual in quite the same way, thereby allowing a reassessment of their force and logical and social status. Such values and ideals as are employed by the above doctrines are seen to be only provisionally acceptable as tenets of individual and social explanation. The appeal, therefore, to non-social universals is not considered tenable, because the values and ideals with respect to the moral primacy and autonomy of the individual depend for their existence on a specified view of an abstract human nature, but are also used to provide the necessary supports for that same view of an abstract human nature.

Ruling out the abstract individual, but retaining the individual as the basis of explanation, has definite ramifications for the propositions which make up the resultant individualist thought. The focus must shift from the qualities of human existence (uniquely deriving from our place in the moral universe) to the physical nature of existence – specifically, the structure of the mind and the nature of human behaviour. Instead of moral constructs dwelling in the consciousness of the individual, the operations of the mind, the way they are constructed, become the focus. Religious and ethical individualism are the relevant modes here.

It may be possible to add another form of individualism here: 'conservative' individualism. Conservative thought retains a robust awareness that the individual is a social creation. Once created, the individual is enlisted as the justification for the preservation of the conditions which are held to perpetuate the appropriate existence for that individual (Berry, 1983, p. 53). Unlike political and methodological individualism, etc., which attempt to explain social processes through individuals, ethical and 'conservative' individualisms seek to explain what the first set takes for granted – individuals themselves. Thus conservatives are especially attuned to

17

'historical and social influences on the individual mind', but do not concede that history and society are the wellsprings of motivation and causality (Lukes, 1973b, p. 140).

There is one similarity of particular importance between these two methods of individualist explanation. Both seek to acknowledge the significance of history and society, without undermining the claim that the individual remains the prime referent. This puts them in opposition to determinist or collectivist views of society, and it is in this respect that they are relevant to this study. If Marx is to be castigated for his collectivism, or alternatively accused of failing to consider the individualist dimension of his own thought, then it is crucial to identify those doctrines which bear most directly on these issues.

Of the doctrines mentioned so far, two have specific importance for this study; methodological individualism and ethical individualism. The former carries within it the notion of the abstract individual, yet it remains the most developed critique of Marx's method and prescriptions. According to Lukes' definition:

> Methodological individualism is a doctrine about explanation which asserts that all attempts to explain social (or individual) phenomena are to be rejected ... unless they are couched wholly in terms of facts about individuals. (ibid., 1973b, p. 110; 1973a, p. 180)

This states the position perhaps too baldly, because the doctrine is presented in its defensive and critical, rather than purposeful and positive, perspective. Methodological individualism might also be described as a social scientific approach which attempts to restrict as much as possible any reference to collectivities or institutions by focusing on the intentions and actions of individuals. This definition highlights two features that are not immediately obvious in Lukes' account. First, the doctrine has a clear element of conditionality and does not automatically exclude other forms of explanation. In a sense, this is a statement of *preference* for a certain way of describing the world, one which recognizes the difficulty of explaining everything, immediately, by the application of the doctrine. Such a form of explanation is at the same time a specific approach and a goal to be attained.

This conditionality is also displayed by J. W. N. Watkins's understanding of the precepts of methodological individualism: 'that social processes and events *should* be explained by being

deduced from (a) principles governing the behaviour of participating individuals and (b) descriptions of their situation' (1973,
p. 149). Here a distinction is being made between procedure and
forms of evidence. On the one hand the formation and treatment
of the approach to social events and processes are outlined, and
on the other hand the relevant 'facts' are identified and separated
from non-facts. The 'principles' of (a) are discoverable and examinable facts, even though they must incorporate judgements about
both basic human nature and behavioural patterns of individuals
in society. 'Descriptions' under (b) are not facts in the same
way, but *contexts* within which the facts must be placed and
analysis occur. These contexts may appear to have the strength
of facts, to be as discoverable and examinable as the principles
of (a). But a description may be flawed, incomplete and even
amended: a principle cannot be judged and discarded in the
same way.

Methodological individualism retains the abstract individual at
the core, but does not seek to explain individual actions and
intentions. Instead, a dialectical element is introduced at the
methodological level, in order to establish the form and content
of the mediating links between individual and society. In this way,
a *social* explanation can be the intent and result, overcoming the
objection that the conception of society has no substance or force
by arguing that the *impact* of society on individuals is the real
issue. Thus methodological individualism is distinct from a more
metaphysical account based on the absolute commitment to the
idea that the individual can be perceived and understood without
reference to society.

This produces an interesting contrast with ethical individualism, which is not a doctrine that purports to be an explanation on the level of grand social theory; it is 'a view of
the nature of morality as essentially individual' (Lukes, 1973b,
p. 99).

> According to this doctrine, the *source* of morality, of moral
> values and principles, the creator of the very criteria of moral
> evaluation, is the individual: he becomes the supreme arbi-
> ter of moral (and, by implication, other) values, the final
> moral authority in the most fundamental sense. (ibid., p.
> 101)

Although it may appear to do so, ethical individualism does
not rely upon a notion of the abstract individual. Morality
is a social phenomenon, and the individual is related to it as

19

both creative subject and responding object. As such, ethical individualism concerns an aspect of social reality, and is explanatory and prescriptive in only this limited respect. The key idea here is autonomy, not simply as a right or quality that is ascribed to human beings. The added dimension stems from a critical account of the *role* of morality as a form of social structure, if not determining, certainly circumscribing and directing human thought and action. It becomes possible, therefore, to explain what it is to be an individual in society, and to postulate an alternative that simultaneously presupposes and makes a reality the *autonomous* individual. Here the recommendatory aspect of individualism is most apparent. The individual is counterposed, not to society *per se*, but to this or that form of society.

The importance of this interpretation is based on two features of the explanation – one explicit, the other implicit. Explicitly, ethical individualism is deeply concerned with history. Its development as a doctrine, unlike the development of methodological individualism, is not the result of attacks on its legitimacy by other deterministic, collectivist *Weltanschauungen*. Ethical individualism does not take the individual as given, but regards the person as a cultural and social product – crucially, a product that emerges and changes in specific ways. Thus, for example, MacIntyre points to the disordered and partial 'social processes in transition' during and after the Reformation, such that, 'in every case, what emerges is a new identity for the moral agent' (1968, p. 24). For Nietzsche (1966), this was not only a pattern to be observed throughout history, but also a *process* with a specific end-product.

> If we place ourselves at the end of this tremendous process, where the tree at last brings forth fruit, where society and custom at last reveal *what* they have simply been the means to: then we discover that the ripest fruit is the *sovereign individual*, like only to himself, liberated again from morality of custom, autonomous and supramoral (for 'autonomous' and 'moral' are mutually exclusive), in short, the man who has his own independent, protracted will and the *right to make promises*. (ibid., II, 2)

Since the individual is a recent historical product, *conceptions* of the individual are equally historical. Thus the notion of autonomy, too, cannot be regarded as a universal ideal, but can be seen as an aspect of human social development (*vide* Nietzsche's sovereign individual and MacIntyre's (1968) moral agent).[4] Thus,

Lukes's statement that ethical individualism is 'the philosophical consequence of taking the idea of autonomy seriously and carrying it to its logical conclusion' simplifies a much more complex process (1973b, p. 101). Autonomy itself is not given, but derives its form and content from historically placed individuals. Indeed, the concepts of autonomy and the individual are complementary. Autonomy requires a subject in specific relation to society to make any sense. Similarly, the notion of the individual cannot exist without the (at least partially unfulfilled) faculty of autonomy, and an experience of it in society. Therefore, it is an *acquired* property of individuals, and the consequences of taking autonomy seriously are not merely philosophical.

The implicit feature of ethical individualism is an underlying naturalism. It is this which connects the view of the individual in society to specific prescriptions. On a general level, these emerge as suspicion of the collectivity and the demand that individuals should determine their own existence. What is entailed here is a naturalistic confidence in the ethical potential of individuals as much as a critique of existing impediments to human autonomy. Thus ethical individualism, too, is founded on an appeal to human nature (though not of an abstract kind), and argues for an appropriate way of responding to that which we come to know about individuals.

There is more than one 'individualism' with which Marx's thought can be compared, and the rejection of collectivist thought can be on a variety of grounds, not all of which are inimical to Marxian analysis. There are some important overlaps with the Marxian enterprise here. Central to the ethical individualist view of reality and the individual is the belief that it is indeed possible to 'come to know' about individuals. Marx offered a powerful means for generating such knowledge and for judging the strength and applicability of such knowledge. Also, the claims concerning autonomy have a direct bearing on the nature of the individual in Marx's thought. Autonomy, as will be seen, is related to the issue of human agency, whether the individual be in a feudal, capitalist, or communist society. Finally, the notion of potentiality has strong affinities with Marx's view of humans in society. These confluences suggest that Marx's thought cannot properly be defined as intrinsically hostile to all aspects of individualist thought. The next section pursues this claim, by examining further the methodologies of Marxism and individualism.

21

Marx and modes of individualism

Marx's own reaction to individualism is significant, and occurs at several levels. In the first place, his responses were in the main aggressive toward what he saw as an inferior social theory. His most powerful critique of individualistic thought has been carried forward into the debates over modes of individualism in the twentieth century by the Marxist tradition, but it has also permeated the structure of non-Marxist thinking. Second, Marx was also aware of its role in providing a most persuasive ideology for the ruling class. His theoretical and practical interests meant that he could not help but be involved in the intellectual conflict between individualistic and communitarian thought. Third, the presence of individualist rhetoric must have had an influence on the way that Marx felt able to present his own thought with regard to the individual in society. He could use the word 'individual' only with the utmost care, lest he reinforce the fundamental tenet of all individualist thought – the primacy of the (abstract) individual.

This underlying principle of individualism concerned Marx deeply. Ontologically at least, all modes of individualism share the premiss that the individual person may exist independently of or in opposition to society. Any reading of Marx shows him to be diametrically opposed to this notion, however it may be couched. However, his trenchant stand against such a supposition does not mean that he had no interest in or understanding of individual *persons*, nor does it establish that he was prepared to sacrifice individuals at the altar of social or historical necessity. As will become apparent in later chapters, it is not possible to impose any such crude lines of demarcation on Marx's social theory.

The real issue of interpretation lies in the claim that individualist thought expresses a significant as well as commonsensical truth about social and political analysis. Watkins states this notion quite simply, when he writes that 'it is people who determine history, however people themselves are determined' (1973, p. 179). It is interesting that this is considered a claim worth making. The intention, clearly, is to attack deterministic accounts of history and society, but it is not at all obvious that an appeal to 'people', 'however ... determined', achieves anything. Marx, for example, is one of the prime targets, yet he never sought to deny the role of people, though he was very concerned about how they were to be defined.

In the *German Ideology*, he was quite precise on this point. For him, the 'first premises of materialist method' were 'the real individuals, their activity and the material conditions under which they live, both those which they find already existing and those produced by their activity' ([1845–6] 1970,, p. 42).[5] These individuals are more than 'people'. Such individuals are recognizable as real only when the substance of their situation is given, revealing their existence as it actually is or might be.

Yet there is a great deal of difference between saying that people determine history and explaining the means of understanding them. For Watkins, people may be a mass of individuals, or represent a collectivity, or be defined by national or cultural boundaries, or by roles and positions in society. 'People' may be a genus, or actors, or the individual unit writ large. This conflict between the explanation of social processes through individuals (however constituted or determined) and the explanation of individuals themselves is connected to larger themes and underlying tensions between individualist and non- or anti-individualist accounts of society and history. Underpinning all the debates over detail, the major issue of free will versus determinism persists unresolved. On a practical level, as O'Neill argues:

> Once we attempt to specify the nature of the interaction between individual conduct and its institutional contexts, we are involved in disagreement about the instrumental, rational and value matrices of social action, particularly when it is recognized that we possess few universal generalizations about human nature and social structure. (1973, p. 4)

Indeed, the common ground is very difficult to discover and mark out. Freedom may be the central concern, but this may mean it is a value, an assumption, an ideal, or a practical goal, depending upon who is providing the definitions and labels. For example, O'Neill finds it 'a curiosity of scholarship that Hegel and Marx have come to be identified with a deterministic conception of history and the place in it of human freedom, whereas both conceived of history as the story of freedom' (ibid., pp. 12–13). This reading is confirmed by Allen Wood, when he notes that, far from denying the role of the individual in history, historical determinism represents the commitment to the practical realization of that very thing – the 'individual-in-history', as it were (1981, p. 102). Since Marx sought to demonstrate that it is individuals who *can* make society, but who are presently prevented from doing so, he is in conflict with individualism, no matter how sophisticated its form, because he claims to be able to incorporate and realize some of its key values, while demonstrating that individualist practice cannot.

Against this, individualistic accounts reiterate that the individual, not society, must be the prime referent, and that concepts such as freedom, and the proper form and experience of it, are to be based on such a presupposition. In other words, individualist thinkers want to establish that individuals do actively and actually 'make' society. But to do this, they have to be able to show that individuals were and are the ultimate determiners of history and society. However, their initial assumption forecloses the possibility of finally achieving anything but a circular argument. Moreover, if the required focus is the individual, then social behaviour must be extraneous phenomena, subject to non-individual categories of explanation. Indeed, as R. Bhaskar points out:

> the real problem appears to be not so much that of how one could give an individualistic explanation of social behaviour, but that of how one could give a non-social (that is strictly individualistic) explanation of individual, at least characteristically human, behaviour. (1979, p. 35)

The most recent and sustained attempt to do just that has come from Jon Elster; his *Making Sense of Marx* (1985) seeks to redefine the Marxian enterprise, restructure dominant interpretations of his thought and rescue Marxism from the obloquy of its bloody state socialist history. The rudiments of his schema are based on re-reading Marx as a methodological individualist and employing rational-choice theory to transcend the inadequacies of a functionalist and teleological account of human history. According to Elster, Marx relied too heavily on a concept of humanity 'as a collective subject whose inherent striving towards full realization shapes the course of history', and that 'Marx was also committed to methodological individualism, at least intermittently' (ibid., p. 7). Both of these claims misrepresent the substantive positions that Marx adopted in respect of humanity and methodology, and ignore the provisional nature of the logical and historical connections that Marx saw between human history and individual existence.

Elster has contributed to a lively debate on the virtues and relevance of rational-choice theory to Marx's thought (Roemer, 1986; Elster, 1983, 1986; Carling, 1986; Hindess, 1984; Berger and Offe, 1982). His writings on methodological individualism have also generated a specific critical response (Warren, 1988; Levine *et al.*, 1987; Roemer, 1982). The most striking feature of Elster's preference for methodological individualism is the almost total absence of any argument for the main proposition that 'all social phenomena - their structure and their change - are in principle explicable in ways that only involve individuals – their properties, their goals, their beliefs and their actions' (1985, p. 5). Since Elster does not add to the literature discussed above, then the arguments developed against Watkins and Tucker, for example, can be deemed to hold against Elster. Marx was a severe critic of the forms of individualism confronting him in the nineteenth century, and those criticisms remain pertinent to Elster. As M. Warren puts it, Marx rejected these individualisms 'because they treat the intentional properties of individuals as metaphysically existent rather than as problematic' (1988, p. 453). Elster persistently and erroneously sees intentions in terms of individuals with properties, as the methodological individualist and rational-choice theorist is prone to do. The result is that 'an *a priori* conception of agency serves an axiomatic role in the explanation of actors' (ibid., p. 459).

The issue of agency is germane to the account of the individual in at least two ways. First, Marx eschews any fixed notion of agency. Indeed, his approach identifies the means logically to develop a critique of the agency currently 'enjoyed', to understand the internal and external limitations and strictures on agency and to see how agency might be extended in particular as well as general ways. Second, in political thought the concept agency concerns the causal status of individuals in the change process. In rejecting the structuralist, collectivist, or holist account of agency and the consequently minimal causal role for individuals in explanation or historical change, Elster prefers to see individual agents choosing and willing in the context of the choices and actions of other agents. For him, 'beliefs and desires arise in an agent by the force of external circumstances mediated by internal psychic mechanisms' (1986, p. 28: 1982, pp. 463–4). The status and derivation of preferences and beliefs is crucial here and the viability of methodological individualism as an explanation comes under serious challenge. As P. Wetherly argues:

> 'beliefs and preferences' cannot be taken as the starting point in explanation but themselves have to be explained, and the 'external circumstances' which shape preferences must encompass collective entities or 'social structure'. This entails that collective entities are not reducible but are in a fundamental sense prior to individual preference and actions. (1988, p. 432)

Wetherly concludes that a methodological individualist explanation cannot therefore exist. As Susan James points out, however, a strict dichotomy between holism and individualism can do violence to the possibility of explaining the limits and possibilities of agency

(1984, p. 178). In this vein, Warren agrees that the methodological individualism of individuals with properties is a deeply flawed enterprise, but finds some value in an approach which attends to an individualism *of actions*, and argues that some of Marx's thought should be understood from this perspective (1988, pp. 451–3, 476). In so doing, Marx is once again located between the extremes of holism and individualism, and between structuralism and Kantian conceptions of agency.

> In contrast to both Elster and the structuralists, Marx's position involved seeing attributes of subjectivity – including capacities for rational action – as possibilities developed through social intercourse. For Marx, the polarity of social determination and free individual agency is a product of a specific kind of society, as are other polarities of self and society. (ibid., p. 464)

Thus there are a number of things to be taken into account in respect of individualism. First, the history of individualism reveals inadequacies in the way the concept has come to be understood and counterposed against other approaches (humanism, material-ism, collectivism, Christianity, idealism). Second, the theoretical underpinnings of individualism (1) establish the regularities and consistencies in the ideas that characterize individualist thought, and (2) place those ideas in the contexts that differentiate one form of individualism from another. On this basis, it is possible to see that methodological and ethical modes of individualism are the most relevant to the discussion of Marx, in terms of assumptions, claims and conclusions that are common, con-tested, or open to interpretation. Of central importance have been discussions about autonomy and the role of history and society in the understanding of the individual. As E. M. Wood argues:

> If individualism as a social doctrine involves a commitment to the moral primacy of the individual in society and the right of the individual to freedom and self-realization, a host of additional assumptions must be made about man and his relationship to society before 'individualism', individual free-dom, and self-realization can be made by definition to exclude 'socialism' and 'collectivism'. (1972, pp. 6–7)

Individualist thought, in other words, creates demands and practical expectations for a social existence which it seems unable to deliver. This disjunction means that there are two possibil-ities that can be entertained separately: (1) that individualism has claims about what is a desirable social existence for the individual; (2) that individualism has claims about the proper order of society. Therefore, rejecting the individualist theory of society does not necessarily mean that claims about the importance of the individual are automatically ruled out. Second, it is important to note that Marx's images of individual existence in society are not necessarily at odds with a series of beliefs and claims germane to individualist thought. This is not to say that Marx's thought ultimately is reducible to a set of moral claims or is at base a rights theory couched in an historical materialist guise. Rather, it is to demonstrate that Marxist thought, in its structure and interest, has potentially more importance for an explanation of the individual in society than theories which purport explicitly to provide such explanations.

Human nature, autonomy and history

Marx can be labelled as an anti-humanist and an anti-individualist, but these readings do violence to the nature of his social and political theory on the one hand, and the scope of the theoretical premisses on the other. That is, his thought cannot be made to remove the problem of the individual in society - whatever the form of society. Furthermore, individualist thought - whether abstract, methodological, or ethical - is inadequate to the task of analysing the individual in society. Both the structural determinist and liberal-individualist views of Marx, therefore, misrepresent his thought and misconceive the question of the individual in society, each in their particular ways. As the discussion so far demonstrates, a defence of Marx, or a statement of a certain version of Marxism, is not all that is involved. This leads to the conclusion that it is Marx's thought which must be used to develop an account of the individual. Such a use, however, raises the problem of the role of ideas in the analysis of social change and the individual.

The development of Marx's thought, and political and economic history, both show that his legacy is double-edged. Although Marx advanced dramatically the recognition of the importance of the economic base of society and the manner in which it ought to be studied and understood, it would be mistaken to infer that this was the path to be trod by all who wish to understand and change society. What was for Marx a long-term preoccupation has tended to become a methodological imperative for Marxists. Further, the location, direction and nature of historical changes serve up no neat fit between theory and reality, between predictive comprehensibility and actual events and trends, bringing into sharper focus the issue of the related but not always simply reflexive or derivative role of the superstructure.

Against Althusser, the existence and relevance of ideas when they are not theoretical practice are not ruled out or regarded only as philosophical phantasmagoria. To do so would be to ignore a part of reality, or to decide in advance what can properly, 'correctly', be thought. As Edgley points out:

> ideas, beliefs and assertions exist in reality ... the traditional epistemological distinction between ideas and their real object should not mislead us into supposing that ideas themselves are not real, do not exist as at least a part of reality. (1983, p. 295)

Nor, on the other hand, should ideas be given a status that is conditional upon the existence of a pre-existing ideological framework. This kind of reductionist structuralism too easily stops at description, when what is needed is accompanying explanations. Further, the notion of ideology is pushed too far, beyond the scope of its original formulation by Marx, and away from the possibility that the ideas that individuals experience as personally valid are socially and historically important. This is to propose a wider and more open conception of ideology as a reading of just one part of social reality. Support for this view is to be found in D. R. Gandy's clarification of the original scope of ideology in Marxian thought:

> For Marx and Engels it is *idea-ology* – a system of ideas. Thus ideology involves theories, doctrines, principles, systems of thought. Ideologists work with concepts, hypotheses, and theories that seem true or false. Myths, images, visions, and feelings are not ideology: they are not systems of thought. Nor are interests, preferences, and attitudes a field of ideology, they are neither true nor false – they simply exist. (1979, pp. 139–40)

Thus ideas and other aspects of real existence do not always fit into models of explanation easily, and do not always have to be given a positive or negative role in the transformation of society. Even a very powerful theory of ideology cannot succeed in encompassing and grounding all ideas in a determinist framework. Description of the existence of some ideas as false consciousness similarly fails to explain every aspect of individual and social behaviour. Nevertheless, the assumption that people and groups *do* have ideas with important implications beyond the individual self requires a theoretical and practical response. It is here that an anthropological humanism finds its theoretical justification and a great deal of raw material for analysis. In other words, being forced constantly to deal with the datum of actual, living individuals demands a theory of the individual personality in society, and the choice of theoretical framework can lead to a rejection of some aspects of the 'evidence' thrown up by material reality.

To acknowledge that ideas as ideas have no intrinsic or universal causative force is not to exclude the understanding that ideas are and will be held, and will affect behaviour. Structuralist and deterministic accounts can contribute to an understanding of the way in which particular ideas and sets of ideas are connected to the political and social configuration associated with a certain mode of production. However, this is not the same as explaining the importance of some ideas themselves, nor does it amount to a complete description of society and the nature of social change.

It is these kinds of absences in deterministic accounts which suggest a useful distinction between autonomy and determinism. That which falls outside the field of ideology, as Gandy described it, is devoid not of meaning and significance but of the connecting links with a theory which seeks to explain the world with references to historical forces of a determining nature. Therefore, myths, images, visions, feelings, interests, preferences and attitudes appear to be unrelated to a mode of theorizing which is fundamentally economic determinist. They are given *autonomy* in the sense that they are allotted no significant place in the theory. On this reading, autonomous means irrelevant or theoretically uninteresting. However, it is just these kinds of autonomous factors which will be of interest in the analysis of the individual in successive modes of production relations.

The problem can be stated in terms of the theory of knowledge as it relates to our understanding of the human raw material and the way that is evidenced in social life. This is not simply to assume that there *is* an *a priori* human nature, but to acknowledge that the symbiotic relationship Marx saw between base and superstructure calls for much more than an understanding of

29

the mode of production of material life. As J. Loewenstein points out:

> It is interesting to note that in the French edition of the *Critique of Political Economy* Marx insisted that the word *bedingte*, literally 'conditions' or 'determines', which defines the relationship between the base and superstructure, be translated as *domine* rather than *determine* or *condition*. (In the new Penguin translation of the preface the sentence reads: 'The mode of production of material life *conditions* the general process of social, political and intellectual life'.) The word *domine* is not a literal translation of *bedingte* but an interpretation: it allows a degree of autonomy to the superstructure. (1980, p. 68)

The crucial distinction is not between determinism and autonomy, but between Althusser's notion of determination in the last instance by the economy and the claim that social, political and intellectual life is autonomous, to a certain degree, *from* economic determination. This is not to suggest that the status and foundation of that 'autonomy from' need only be asserted and proceeded with, or that only ethical or idealist tools of analysis remain available. Rather, it calls for the development of categories that describe and explain the nature of the structures and processes that also relate to aspects of real, individual existence not determined by economic conditions. The most obvious examples of these facets of life are sexual and racial relations. Here the generation of conflict, the belief in superiority over equals and the illegitimate exercise of power cannot satisfactorily be reduced to explanations relying solely upon existing Marxist categories and forms of thought (Hearn, 1987; Delphy, 1984; O'Brien, 1983; Parkin, 1979; Hamilton, 1978).

It is in this respect that an anthropological humanism finds its definition and its role. Such a humanism is not predicated on the belief in a certain kind of human nature, nor does it insist that certain features of human behaviour are just or can only be the expression of aspects of human nature. Instead, it is the need to be able to understand and explain society at all levels and in all respects which calls forth such an approach, with three key tasks. First, there is a need to account for the impact of the mode of production. Second, since it is accepted that the 'autonomy of the superstructure' is quite often not absolute but a matter of *degree*, the extent of that autonomy has to be ascertained. Third, it is also vital to at least sketch out the mediating links between what are after all *kinds* of conditioning influences.

The precise nature and meaning of autonomy must remain indeterminate, at least for the time being. Nevertheless, there are some things which can be asserted now. First, and against the liberal view, autonomy can have no absolute status, even though it may endure as a social value in some societies. Second, autonomy can be used to describe a relationship between aspects of a society, and in respect of individuals and groups within society. This implies that autonomy is still a social value, not an idea or principle which is to be rejected in the conduct of historical materialist method because ideas fail to represent concrete reality. Instead, autonomy has to be seen as a social value of a different kind, in the sense that the value has to be established, assigned, recognized and acted upon. In terms of the individual and theories of individualism, this is a problem for Marxian analysis, because autonomy presupposes a Kantian separateness and unique value to every individual.

The construction and conditioning of the individual in society, it is suggested, has to be seen as an interactive process between fundamental human nature and the material conditions of existence. Both human nature and the conditions of existence are the vital variables. They are transhistorical notions, share the qualities of universality, and are both dependent upon each other. This view takes into account the deep-rooted historicity of Marx's thought, but does not translate it into an unqualified relativism. That is, form and content change historically and can, of course, be relativized. This Marx does when he compares historical epochs, and, even more significantly, claims to detect progress between and within those epochs. But to do so, it must be the case that the concepts which surround or define and explain such historical change have a *non*-relativist character. They are of a different order to the realities which are relativized. They are, therefore, trans-historical and universal, until our understanding of those terms is changed, by something that may relativize key concepts like human nature and existence itself.

Social nature, the outcome of fundamental human nature as it expresses itself under specific circumstances, is then akin to a photograph of the interactive process between the two variables – human nature and the material conditions of existence. It will contain information about each variable and represent their force and impact. However, the formative and conditioning influences differ in kind and are not accessible in the same way. The material conditions of existence present themselves as objective reality, as arrangements, limits and possibilities which can be explicated in a detailed way and are subject to alteration, removal, or creation.

Fundamental human nature, on the other hand, is much less amenable to such clear and ordered analysis. Since we cannot know, in empirically verifiable form, the actual content of human nature, much less quickly grasp the significance of what we come to know, it is necessary to work with ideas about human nature, with propositions that make possible the generation of explanations.

Summary

With respect to the individual, Marx's thought produces a number of crucial distinctions. First, it facilitates distinctions between and judgements of kinds of individualism, to draw out the strengths and weaknesses of their theory and interests. Second, it is clear that Marx's contempt for the abstract individual is not to be equated with his views on the living human individual in particular circumstances. Marx is able to recognize, sometimes sympathize with, and certainly make abstractions about just this latter individual. In this context, Marx's contribution is most noteworthy, given the overwhelming tendency of anti-individualist or collectivist thought to downgrade the importance of the individual altogether, since there is support for the view that Marxian thought can encompass an account of the individual. As M. Fritzhand points out, much collectivist thought 'approaches individualism ahistorically and condemns it wholesale, whereas [humanist] Marxism conceives of it in its historical development and distinguishes between its negative and positive aspects' (1980, p. 23).

This is reinforced in the third of the major distinctions, where the individual is always placed within a social framework which is historically understood. For Marx, the individual had come to be in capitalist society and would therefore be historically unique, unlike any previous kind of individual. In other words, his thought enables us to see individuals in both a concrete and historical sense. Fourth, this understanding of the individual in history and society is accompanied by the idea that the individual is an important historical being. The individual of capitalism is 'better', more advanced, more autonomous than the individual of any previous epoch in the same way that the capitalist mode of production is superior.

This is not to commit oneself to the primacy of the individual. Rather, Marx brings to the surface the view that the extent and nature of a human's individualness are closely connected to historical development. As later chapters show, the potential to be an individual is related to the mode of production and the historical stage of development. This means that Marx transcends individualism by laying the foundation for an understanding of *individuality*. Individuality in Marx's thought relates to the extent to which the potential inherent in a person's human nature is realized in becoming a free creative individual in society. As K. Kosik suggests, 'individuality is neither an addition nor an unexplainable irrational remainder to which the individual is reduced after substracting the social relations, historical contexts, and so on' (1967, p. 189).

This is another way of suggesting that human individuals will ultimately be autonomous with regard to the material base of society, because it will be in their control. Implicitly, descriptions of and prescriptions for human behaviour are not to be located solely in terms of historical forces based on an understanding of objective social conditions. Instead, attention will be focused in Chapter 2 on the historical forces that result from the impact of society, historically defined and understood, on human nature. This means that, in Chapters 3, 4 and 5, historical epochs will be conceived and presented as the transition process from one form of production *and* an associated form of individuality to another, as each develops and then breaks down, such that the necessary features of an account of the individual in social explanation generally and Marx's thought specifically are highlighted.

The next chapter will give an interpretation of Marx's social ontology and his view of human nature that will form the basis for that account of the individual in history and society. From that point, it will be possible to examine Marx's writings with respect to various forms of social organization, in order to embellish the concept of human nature as a theoretical concept – a concept which can contribute to a theory of social change. Of particular interest will be the extent to which a Marxian concept of human nature is able to incorporate a concept of the person, under real conditions of existence, and how that might lead to a Marxian theory of the individual.

Notes

1 The 'recurring nightmare' for the individualist thinker is that individuals are *not* independent of society, just as the Marxist's nightmare is that the want for property so widely exhibited in all kinds of society proves actually to be an inherent social need

(and, for some, one which therefore constitutes a valid social and political claim); see Gouldner, 1980, p. 192.

2   The existence of a 'nature' is not of itself a precondition of its predominance or survival. Indeed, it may bring about the degeneration and destruction of the species. Moreover, a 'fixed' nature may be, and has been, used to support both radical and conservative views of society; see Forbes and Smith, 1983.

3   See Rawls, 1973, pp. 30–1 and Tucker, 1980, pp. 32, 65. Tucker's analysis leads him to equate Marx's historical materialism with methodological individualist reasoning and 'safely' concludes that he is an individualist, while Marx is labelled as a humanist individualist on the grounds that he adopted the values of ethical individualism. While Tucker's enterprise is of considerable interest, his arguments too swiftly dismiss both Marx and Marxism.

4   The quotation also provides some grounds for Lukes's view, 1973b, pp. 101, 103, 104, that Nietzsche was at once an ethical individualist, an extreme moral sceptic and an incipient existentialist. These three elements are clearly evident in Nietzsche's thought, but, when placed in the context of historical development, they lose their contradictory nature altogether. Of importance, therefore, is the residual theme of the question of the individual in society, an interest which Marx, in his own way, had unexpectedly in common with Nietzsche.

5   This passage is taken by Warren, 1988, pp. 456–7, as evidence that Marx was at one level a *materialist* methodological individualist *of events*; it 'played a crucial role in dismissing explanations that deduce empirical events from essential, metaphysical realities'. It is this level which Jon Elster, 1986, pp. 66–7, is correct to identify as 'trivially true'.

2 The individual and Marx's theory of change

Following the examination of various accounts of the individual in society, this chapter turns to an analysis of Marx's theory of change. It is argued that conventional interpretations overstate Marx's antagonism to the concept of the individual, and that his theory of change would gain strength if this aspect were developed. This would at the same time undercut the grounds for a crucial objection to the inclusion of the individual in Marxian theory. Three further purposes are served. First, the distinction between individualism and individuality is developed, and the theoretical and practical importance of the concept of individuality is described. Second, the means of discussing human nature within and between historical epochs is outlined. Third, the theoretical model which provides the basis for the examination of the individual under successive modes of production is set out and justified. In doing so, Marx's thought is assessed with reference generally to history, to human nature, to the individual and to the interconnections that exist between these three, and specifically to the view that Marx saw historical progress in developmental terms.

Sources of social change

The first stage of the argument is that Marxian analysis can legitimately contemplate the role of the individual in explanations of social change, even if this requires a particular reading or modification of economic determinism. There are two facets to this. One is the problem of seeking an account of social change by reference to economic factors as if these are primary or original in their importance. Second is the more fundamental difficulty of having any kind of determinist explanation which insists strongly upon the importance of objective and discoverable causal laws. This

35

means that there has at least to be the possibility of explanatory levels which are not rigidly economic determinist. If this is not so, then individuality is a vacant concept, given form and content only by the operation of strictly determined economic categories and structures. If, however, economics is not primary, and if objective causal laws about human action do not *originate* the possibility of individuality, then determinism needs to be reassessed, perhaps even renamed as conditionism.

In his letter to Bloch, Engels argued firmly that Marx's thought should never be equated with a vulgar economic determinism:

> According to the materialist conception of history, the *ultimately* determining element in history is the production and reproduction of real life. More than this neither Marx nor I have ever asserted. Hence if somebody twists this into saying that the economic element is the *only* determining one, he transforms that proposition into a meaningless, abstract, senseless phrase. (Marx and Engels, 1968, p. 682)

Thus Engels counselled against a narrow reductionism which would make the study of society and history one-dimensional. In so doing, he made implicit a space for the operation of non-economic factors. Clearly, a number of ambiguities remain. Engels signals a preference for multi-causality, not non-causality, but to what extent does determinism remain the fundamental explanatory concept? That is, it remains unclear whether everything can be reduced to a determining element for an explanation and have an identifiable and specifiable cause. Does this rule out factors which seem non-attributable to any known cause now, or will remain so in the future? Furthermore, the statement that economics is the ultimately determining element, but not the only one, begs questions of an hierarchy of causality and relations of dominance between 'determining' elements.

Although argument continues over the reciprocal influence of the superstructure and the role of ideology, the underlying issue or conflict concerns the mode of political, social and historical explanation that is deemed appropriate for the study of society and the foundation of political action. Determinism may be seen in a variety of ways. It may be a descriptive term, denoting a characteristic of production and reproduction, but which characteristic is not reflected in every other facet of reality. In this case, determinism indicates the discovery of that which 'shapes' society, gives it its form and general character, but which does not define it precisely or consistently. There is further ambiguity with respect to what

Engels actually had in mind. The phrase 'ultimately determining element in history' has two possible applications, one referring to the primacy of economics, the other to a proper history. Engels may be taken to mean that economics *is* history, or that economics *determines* history. The former describes economics, and history collapses into a series of economic propositions, while the latter explains the predominant influence in a much more complex pattern of historical change.

The shift between these alternatives pervades Marxian thought, without ever being completely settled. In the *Preface to a Contribution to the Critique of Political Economy*, one of the clearest statements of his approach, Marx himself moves from conditionality (an interaction of forces) on this point to causality (one law operating in a precise way) in successive sentences:

> The mode of production of material life *conditions* the social, political and intellectual life process in general. It is not the consciousness of man that *determines* their being, but, on the contrary, their social being that *determines* their consciousness. ([1859] 1968, p. 181)

Thus Marx was not prepared to claim that the economic base determined the nature of the life process, yet he stated that consciousness was determined by that life process. For the second proposition to hold true in an economic determinate sense, there would have to be no latitude, no provisionality, in the most basic connection between the economic base (structurally identified) and the general life process (the *need* for an economic base). This idea is just not present in this work, or any other. Engels, in his letter to Borgius ([1894] 1970, p. 694), again refrained from putting forward such a definitive proposition: he claimed that the economic structure is 'that which ultimately conditions historical development', but added this qualification:

> Political, juridical, philosophical, religious, literary, artistic, etc., development is based on economic development. But all these react upon one another and also upon the economic base. It is not that the economic situation is *cause*, solely active, while everything else is only passive effect. There is, rather, interaction on the basis of economic necessity, which ultimately always asserts itself. (ibid.)

This is obviously not a deterministic account, given the existence of an interactive process. For the mode of production of material life to determine life process, consciousness and social superstructure, the economic situation would have to be necessary *and sufficient* to explain historical development. However, this does not make any clearer what the additional explanatory moves might be, and Marx's statement that social being determines consciousness seems to point us in the wrong direction. Superficially, Marx is making a remark about the impact of economic conditions. However, those conditions are *not* invested with the power of determination. Rather, the epistemological *focus* on those conditions is appropriate, since it is this that forms the 'keynote ... and alone leads to understanding' (ibid.).

It is useful to concentrate on 'social being' and the way that it '*determines*' what Marx terms 'consciousness'. Such a claim might well be accepted, on condition that it strictly was not equivalent to economic determinism of the life process. As argued earlier, the life process involves the interaction of fundamental human nature and material conditions of existence. The resultant is the social being, a product of two forces, and under the total dominion of neither. This formulation is consistent with the claim that social being determines consciousness. It rules out economic determinism as the sole factor, because we have introduced the possibility at least of determinants intrinsic to something else.

Social being, on this reading, *must* determine consciousness in so far as its content is concerned. That content will be conditioned by economic factors, but the possibility of consciousness exists by virtue of one's humanity. Marx's claim, then, that people 'make their history themselves, only they do so in a given environment', can make particular sense (ibid.). Apart from the generality of social existence under any given mode of production, over which the individual has no control, this indicates that the individual being may have a degree of autonomy, that a range of responses and actions is possible and that meaningful choices may be made.

Further to this view, it can be noted that Marx did look forward to the forces of society ultimately being under *human* control. For this to be possible, autonomous human agency is logically entailed. This account of society, history and human nature draws upon and legitimizes two kinds of explanatory and descriptive mechanisms – determinism and autonomy – which are usually held to be mutually contradictory, and in the process exposes a very real tension in the Marxian account of historical development.

This tension has not been resolved in any systematic way in Marxist literature over the last one hundred years. Marx's lead has emphasized the discovery and development of historical laws of economic tendencies, gaineed through an analysis of the objective conditions of existence. This has been a necessary labour, to actualize and validate the Marxian method in the course of presenting a telling account of the nature of capitalist society. On the other hand, the focus on the deterministic elements of his theory results in, at best, a downgrading of the notion and role of an active and purposive consciousness and, all too often, a complete denial of its significance. In practice, this means that the Marxist theory of change is simplified, certainly, but at the cost of providing a convincing understanding and account of historical processes of change, except retrospectively. As V. Kiernan argues:

> Clearly one of the factors of human change is man himself, whom Marxists are often arraigned for taking far too little notice of. They deny the charge, but it is true that they have thought most commonly of mankind in the mass ... Their bent has been towards rationalising behaviour overmuch. Neither man nor his history is in any strict sense rational, though they may both come by degrees to be rationally comprehended. But this requires more knowledge of the puzzling individual, or elite group, as an indispensable part-cause of historical change. (1983, p. 85)

Kiernan makes an important distinction between intentionality and result with respect to Marxist thought. The intention has been in terms of values of justice and equality, which accords with a concern for individuals and the collectivity alike. However, the result of thinking 'most commonly of mankind in the mass' is to subject individual experience and the possibility of individuality to grand processes. Simply to choose between the determinist and autonomist accounts of human social change is not a rational way to proceed, and they represent, by their nature, two different kinds of exercise. They are, in Gouldner's words, the 'two marxisms' (1980). After a century of Marxian labours – theoretical and practical – the 'puzzling individual', and two main or competing approaches to that individual, remain.

To what extent can these be seen as aspects of the same enterprise, or are they mutually exclusive? The differences in the theories of change to which they give rise are most significant. The deterministic view, that history is and will be fashioned by the continual development of economic processes, assigns an insignificant role to human agency, but has no satisfactory answer to the problem of explaining how determinism could ever give way to human self-realization and equality. These imply autonomy and agency.

To produce an account of these things within a Marxian framework, historical materialist method has to be disengaged from conclusions which insist upon the primacy of economic forces. Rather, the method has to provide ontological clarity but allow epistemological diversity. This view stresses the importance of practical analysis, not the sanctity of the theory itself. It was just this kind of wide applicability of the Marxian mode of social and political analysis which most impressed Lenin, for example. As Kiernan points out:

> Lenin correctly ascribed to Marx not invention of the 'materialist conception of history' but 'consistent continuation and extension of materialism into the domain of social phenomena'. (1983, p. 75)

This perception is interesting in several respects. First, not only the understanding of history, but history itself, becomes increasingly coterminous with the existence and nature of material forces. Second, Lenin's suggestion that social phenomena are *amenable to* materialist (i.e. rational) explanation is in marked contrast to the view that all such phenomena spring from, are *determined by*, material forces. This formulation, then, is a useful corrective to the tendency to pursue Marx's empirical method of research as if it had no connection with a particular, and sometimes dogmatic, theory of history. For Loewenstein, even Marx was prey to the dangers inherent in an uncritical pursuit of the research method:

> It was precisely his empirical investigations that led him astray and tempted him to go too far. He was influenced by studies showing the overwhelming dominance of material interests in politics and by Hegel's *monocausal* explanation of history. Consequently, the material basis of production is for Marx not merely an important factor determining the course of history, but the *only* factor. (1980, p. 75)

In effect, monocausality becomes a problem in Marx's thought because material forces become paramount, so running directly counter to the significance of Hegel's explanation of history, which celebrates human agency. As far as Loewenstein is concerned, there is a weakness in the way that Marx confused some of his conclusions with the act of investigation itself, leading him to equate the preponderance of one factor in his specific economic studies with the singularity of that factor in a general explanation.

However, it would be wrong to claim that the historical materialist method is, thereby, responsible. Implicit in Loewenstein's criticism is the validity of the theory, coupled with sociological and psychological claims concerning Marx's application of that theory. The theory is, as M. Markovic claims: 'the result of a critical study of historical possibilities. It is a model, the symbolic expression of an idealized structure – not an empirical description' (1974a, p. 67). These methodological considerations, coupled with the difficulty of explaining how a strict determinist interpretation of Marxian method could ever be compatible with full human emancipation and self-realization and equality, lead to the conclusion that non-economically defined characteristics of social existence and social change need to be examined, albeit still using Marx's model.

Human nature and history

Having already encountered the problem of the relevance of human nature to Marx's analysis in Chapter 1, here his views on the relationship between history and human nature come under specific scrutiny. Marx had both a concept and a theory of human nature, and the early writings are important to each of these, in different ways. Marx did provide an explicit account of the content of human nature in the 'Economic and Philosophical Manuscripts' ([1844] 1975), but this account only partially fulfils the requirement of a developed theory of human nature. Thus it is still necessary to provide evidence for the claim that Marx did indeed conclude that wo/men have a nature which makes possible human social development. That is, human nature is a formative influence on the types of societies we can know about, as well as the societies we might wish to see emerge. There are, then, limitations on as much as there are possibilities for social organization inherent in the nature of humans.

The account of history must be able to deal with empirical reality at its broadest level of generalization or idealization, and it must also relate to a theory of social change – the 'transformation of social orders' (Marx, [1852] 1973, p. 15). The account of human nature must provide the theoretical framework for any discussion of the individual, in order to describe how it is possible to be an individual, and explain how s/he relates to the processes of change. Moreover, both accounts imply each other's existence – human nature is historical, just as history is human – yet the account of history itself cannot amount to a full explanation of social transformation. This is because an historical account can often result in what Gellner terms 'the once-only, European-parochial, perpetual-progress way of interpreting the transition', which appears to flow from Marx's historical work (1964, p. 139). It is necessary to distinguish between the legacy of Marx, and the much more conditional understanding of Marx and Engels themselves. As Gandy remarks:

> Marx and Engels did not see history as straight-line progress through world class systems; their conception of history was multilinear. Some lines of development led into agelong stagnation. Others progressed rapidly, then ran into a dead-end. Some stalled and collapsed, or went into reverse, returning to an earlier stage. One line spiralled up through higher and higher levels into capitalism, but this took place in one corner of the globe. This corner soon took the world into capitalism. (1979, p. 139)

This shows how distanced Marx was from Enlightenment perfectibilism in favour of a sophisticated evolutionism. The core assumption here is not the idea of perpetual-progress, but the constancy of change alone. Although there is still a core idea of progress of some kind central to the belief in constancy, the nature and form of progress is not specified. The accounts of history and of human nature take up the issue of change, and the link between these two facets of Marx's thought establishes the importance of the individual in critiques of society and transition processes.

There is no doubt that, in the early writings, Marx employed the notion of human essence to criticize both emerging capitalist society and liberal or bourgeois theories which relied on an abstract human nature. However, Marx also introduced another level of understanding concerning human nature, which focuses on social *life* rather than social organization. Social organization may describe objective reality, may identify the power and relevance of structures, but social life concerns the way that humans actually are in society. This aspect of Marx's thought is generally taken to be an insight into the way he believed structures to operate. For this reason, his insistence that social life fundamentally shapes human nature, and our understanding or consciousness of that nature, remains one of Marx's more compelling and influential notions. Moreover, it can be argued that this is central to both the 'essentialist' and 'deterministic' elements of his thought. The difference between social organization and social life is crucial here. Social life, while it may indeed conform to or reflect structural exigencies, nevertheless involves a recognition of human existence *as it is experienced*.

The so-called 'essentialist' elements of Marx's thought may fruitfully be regarded as addressing social life, the dimension of human experience where both the social organization and human nature can be taken as given. On the other hand, the so-called 'determinist' elements deal with the social organization taken as given by the essentialist position. The two elements together offer ways of analysing the range of possibilities inherent in both social life and social organization. Explanations relating to social organization need not be in direct or epistemological conflict with a focus on the micro-level or experiential dimension. They may complement each other, rather than being seen as a contradiction which weakens the force of Marx's social and political analysis.

Marx's early writings can thus be seen to present descriptions of human behaviour which gave insight into the manner in which an 'essence' is located in, and finds consistency with, determinate social forces. This meant that he began to construct what can be described as a human psychology. These assumptions underpin the attack on capitalist society and other exploitative modes, just as they are consonant with the operation of material forces in history and the eventual shape of Marx's vision of society. In this important sense the psychological assumptions are not exclusively linked to the ontology of *either* the essentialist or determinist interpretations of human nature. To argue that Marx referred to, agreed with, or relied upon such assumptions is not to charge him with Hegelian idealism or some form of bourgeois individualism. Rather, it is to reject the claim that Marx somehow ignored the importance of the individual in society and was unable to reconcile historical materialism with the needs and aspirations of people.

There were a number of ways that Marx conducted his analysis of human history. A principal requirement, however, was the need to respond to the prevailing ideology, at all times to be attuned to the sweep of ideas amongst the intellectual community. In other words, Marx had long-term goals which had to be mediated through a variety of short-term realities, e.g. the need for scientific socialist theory (long hours in the British Museum), and practical political work (long hours in meetings). In ideological terms, of course, Marx had to deal with the existing agenda in order to establish his own. As Chapter 1 shows, that pre-existing agenda promulgated abstract notions of human nature. For Marx, these notions were unconnected to the concrete social environment. As such, the individualistic claims so closely associated with these assumptions had to be attacked and rejected, not to deny the existence and importance of the individual in society, but to establish the proper grounds for a consideration of real individuals.

Central to this claim is Marx's acknowledgement of the universality of human beings. In the early works he aligned the notion of an essence with a form of naturalism that could be understood in psychological terms.

> *Man* is directly a *natural being*. As a natural being and as a living natural being he is on the one hand equipped with *natural powers*, with *vital* powers, he is an *active* natural being; these powers exist in him as dispositions and capacities, as *drives*. On the other hand, as a natural, corporeal, sensuous, objective being he is a *suffering*, conditioned and limited being, like animals and plants. ([1844] 1975, p. 389)

Naturalness, however, is not the bedrock of his explanation. Nor is essence. If they were, then Marx would be guilty of abstractly and ahistorically theorizing. Instead, he located the natural datum of existence in the realm of actual living experience. 'Living' in this sense refers to the interplay between nature and culture, involving action and reaction as the basis of objective existence. Thus individual human life is dialectically explained in terms that are equivalent to the critique of society. Each person has powers with which to affect the environment, or to act upon it. Further, those powers are not passive capacities, but drives which will *always* prompt action. Yet this naturalism has its obverse feature; inescapably, to act on either the social or the natural world is not to control and shape it, but to meet limitation and constraint, 'to be subjected to the actions of another' (ibid., p. 390).

Two things are important here. First, there is a narrow sense in which each person has agency, in that action can be undertaken which has an impact on others. This is not, however, the agency of the completely autonomous individual, but agency within specific parameters of natural capacities and objective conditions.[1] Second, Marx also differentiates between animal and human nature by pointing out that suffering, while it is *experienced* by all living things, is only *felt* by humans. Thus a tree stunted by harsh environmental conditions suffers in a similar but not equivalent fashion to the undernourished child working in the coal mine from age 6. Both 'suffer', in that they fail to flourish. Suffering itself, then, has no moral quotient, since it is a condition of life with varying intensity. However, since humans can be aware of both their suffering and their powers to affect the environment, they not only act upon the world, but will act to *change* that world. They will use their powers to vary the level or kind of suffering.

> Man as an objective sensuous being is therefore a *suffering* being, and because he feels his suffering, he is a passionate being. Passion is man's essential power vigorously striving to attain its object. But man is not only a natural being; he is a *human* natural being; i.e., he is a being for himself and hence a *species-being*, as which he must confirm and realize himself both in his being and his knowing. (ibid., pp. 390–1)[2]

Thus Marx proceeded from a rich conception of human nature and human existence, and did not employ a mere abstract essence as is sometimes suggested. It was possible to conceive of a set of general characteristics that universally defined humankind as a separate species with particular needs and powers. At base, such feelings, needs, faculties and capacities have *always* to be expressed and satisfied, in that they 'exist under all conditions and can be changed only in their form and direction they take' (Markovic, [1845] 1974b, p. 86). This is another way of saying that 'life involves before anything else eating, drinking, a habitation, clothing and many other things' (Marx, [1857–8] 1973, p. 48). Such statements are non–controversial, and can be used to advance our understanding only when it is made clear what 'many other things' might entail. Utopian thinkers, and some Marxist humanists, for example, wish to add to the list what are in essence *social* predispositions while still regarding them as a part of human nature (Fromm, 1976; Goodwin, 1978). On both logical and evidential grounds, a Marxian account precludes this move, since it is ahistorical to assume that the qualities perceived within a given epoch and under a specific mode of production are universal attributes. The question is not what life brings to humans, but, at this level, what humans bring to life that is so different from other animals.

Sometimes Marx refers to love and creativity, as if these are fundamental, yet these too are social constructs, whose meanings are varied even within a given society. The basic difference, which is put in 'scientific' terms even in the early works, is that humans are *objective* and *sensuous* – creatures with abilities to feel and to know. This means that in the activities of self-preservation and procreation both objectivity and sensuousness are employed instinctively. However, Marx is also claiming that the character of these two faculties is that, although genetically endowed, they do not entail instinctive behaviours. Rather, these qualities make humans into beings who can be aware of the rationality implied by objectivity as an 'inherent part' of human nature (Marx, [1844] 1975, p. 38), and who can be conscious of the emotionality that relates to suffering. In this way Marx undercuts the dualism usually postulated between rationality and emotionality. We are not divided, torn, schismatic beings by nature, condemned to suffer conflict as a constitutional reality, as Hegel would have it.

In society, however, Marx is firmly the champion of rationality, even if it is a recently discovered and still poorly used tool of human development. It is in society, therefore, that the separation of suffering and understanding is to be found. When looking at the effects of any exploitative society, Marx does not question the rectitude of the sensuous beings who are suffering, but looks for the reasons, the rational causes of these emotional effects. This demonstrates his confidence in human nature, in respect of both objectivity and sensuousness. They are, quite clearly, fundamental qualities, or abilities, which are not subject to change under this or that society. They are, on the other hand, the kinds of qualities which can take different forms both within particular societies and groups of societies, and between successive societies. In none of his writings, however, does Marx withdraw from the assumption implicit in the early writings that human nature has substantive content.

With this in mind, it has to be added that such content ascribes abilities, qualities, or faculties to human nature, not specific instincts with clear demarcations and links with observed behaviour. If Marx was a determinist, he was not a *biological* determinist, not clearing away philosophical idealism in order for it to be replaced by the denial of the importance of social forces by another route. In any event, the view that human nature has content argues against the view of Marx as a determinist, and suggests that he be better understood as a 'potentialist'. This means that it is possible to specify characteristics of human nature, as Marx sometimes does, without being tied to a strict ontogeny of their expression or realization. Nor is a moral claim entailed, that qualities and capacities 'ought' to be realized. More importantly, it leaves open the issue of the *phylogeny* of those characteristics, wherein the impact of social development upon human nature, and the converse effect that human nature may have on society, can be known.

This view of human nature is quite compatible with that of the later Marx, where the emphasis shifts to a scientific use of the principles of historical materialism, as set out in the *German*

Ideology ([1845–6] 1970) and expanded in the *Grundrisse* ([1857–8] 1973). In these works especially, the 'mature' Marx was pitting his method against prevailing intellectual practice, demonstrating how his approach was able to incorporate and overcome all previous systems of thought: 'it must not be forgotten that ... modern bourgeois society ... is always what is given, in the head as well as in reality' ([1857–8] 1973, p. 106). With this in mind, such an enterprise yields useful results, in terms of the accusations often levelled against Marx concerning the role and status of the individual, both in his theory and in a possible communist society.

The first stage in this presentation is to define the limits of the term human nature. The typology is based on a major distinction between what is essential to and for human existence and what is conditional. Conditional can mean that which is contingent upon human existence (however deep that contingency may be) refers to what is avoidable, or, at the extreme, to what is plainly unnecessary. Marx's claims concerning human 'essence' are either non-controversial (humans must have food, shelter, etc.), or they refer to dispositions and capacities. Should we wish to corroborate these claims, to establish their scientific validity or credibility, the prognosis is not a happy one, because most of Marx's claims are obvious and the remainder do not lend themselves to clinching proofs or clear confutations.

On the other hand, it is possible to continue thinking about human nature at this level of abstraction, in order to purge the understanding of such a basic human nature of relativism or culture-specific ideas, and to prevent the transmission of *a priori* ideas in the opposite direction, such that they diminish the strength of the claims that are made at the social–scientific level. Practically, this is to deny that human 'essence' can have a prescriptive role in political theory, except in the sense that certain options are ruled out. As Berry argues, 'nature, because it imposes constraints against which it is pointless to jibe, has authoritative status [and] humans are, of course, constrained naturally in many ways (as featherless bipeds they cannot fly)' (1983, p. 54). Nor can human 'essence' have any necessarily normative status, even if the naturalistic fallacy is avoided, since the description of human nature offered by Marx, with the interesting items designated as capacities, places the dimensions of their realization firmly in the realm of the social and political, unless those realms are seen as moral in themselves. Judgements must be made about how a capacity or faculty is to be recognized when it is expressed, and decisions have

47

to be reached about how to assess, at both individual and social levels, the value or quality of that expression. Furthermore, capacities and abilities will have different premiums at different times and places and within different organizations and circumstances.

Thinking about human nature

These, then, are some of the ways that the most basic ideas about human nature are limited. Nevertheless, they remain vital. The construction of such ideas, and their use, can fruitfully be considered as belonging together, so that they are kept conceptually distinct from ideas or claims that refer to wo/men conceived generically, or ideas and claims that refer to the individual in society. This set of ideas and claims relating to fundamental human nature, given its place in the structure of Marx's theory, will be referred to as his *conception of human nature*. In contrast to this *conception* – the broad outline of human nature – there is the account of that which Marx attributed to human nature on a different, but no less important, level, namely, that of a specific society.

On any list of passages that have led to continued theoretical controversy and dispute, Marx's Sixth Thesis on Feuerbach ([1845] 1968, p. 29) must come very near the top.[3] The statements that 'the human essence is no abstraction inherent in each single individual', followed by the claim that 'it is the ensemble of the social relations' carries a crucial epistemological message, but has produced widely divergent interpretations (ibid.). Nevertheless, the underlying intent could not be more clear: the emphasis, in any social and political explanation, must be on the objective conditions of existence in which wo/men are to be found. It is the production of this material life, the provision of the basic necessities for human existence, that also constitutes and produces *history* (Marx, [1845–6] 1970, p. 48; Geras, 1983). In other words, the conception of human nature concerns the question 'what is human nature?', whereas, the further question, 'what is human nature like?' demands a qualitatively different kind of answer.

This second order question calls for distinctions to be made when presenting views on human nature, since according to Marx it is necessary to take account of 'human nature as modified in each historical epoch' (Markovic, 1974b, p. 86). This suggests that there is a basic *conception* of human nature, but that human nature manifests itself and is affected by the environment in which it finds expression. 'Human nature as modified in each historical epoch' will be labelled the *notion* of human nature. That is, the actualized *conception* of human nature within a particular historical stage is a *notion* of human nature, and they are distinguishable on a descriptive as well as analytical level.

Thus two clear perspectives emerge. Any examination of human nature can contribute to the debate on the general *conception* of human nature, by attempting to delineate those things which are fundamental to existence, as needs or drives or instincts – in short, the constitutional elements to being a human animal. Second, there are those formulations of specific *notions* of human nature within definite historical circumstances – a social description of fundamental nature, or an account of social nature, with the attendant assumption of society in each case.

This distinction between conceptions and notions of human nature will be adhered to throughout the analysis that follows, and gives rise to a number of observations. First, any theory which employs a view of human nature, either implicitly or explicitly, does incorporate such a distinction. It is therefore possible to assess the adequacy of a theory, not only in terms of the view of human nature employed or adopted, but also with respect to the way in which the model is used to support or sustain key elements of the central arguments. Second, the differences between substantive and logical errors in a model of human nature will be highlighted, making it easier to judge what can be salvaged and discarded in a theory. Third, it is usually the *notions* of human nature which allow the most scope for interpretation and disagreement, since the relevant datum is not, for example, an Rousseauian hypothetical state of nature, but an actual society. As will be seen, this means that notions of human nature do not refer to the *genus* society, but to existing and different societies, or societies in various historical times, whether this is in the past, present, or future.

Such observations, while they have general application in political theory, have particular importance when applied to Marx's views on human nature and to interpretations of his attitude to the idea of human nature. First, the argument continues over whether Marx's theory *needs* a theory of human nature.[4] A 'soft' Marxist will concentrate less on the structure of political economy than on what can be described as expressions of communality and individuality within society, and endorse the view that it has theoretical, political and ideological significance. What has to be established in the second instance is that there is a link between Marx's attitude to human nature and a Marxian consideration of the individual. This problem lies well within the arguments between the various schools of Marxism in terms of the claims that they have to make concerning (1) Marx's real meaning, and (2) the function, if any, of a theory of human nature in a radical social theory of Marxist dimension. Opposing strands dominate Marxist political and social theory with respect to determinism and autonomy, and they are replicated in the debate over Marx and human nature.

A telling critique of these extremes is provided by Lucien Sève in *Man in Marxist Theory and the Psychology of Personality* (1978, pp. 161–7). He argues that idealism bedevils one approach, since it leans too heavily on the idea that human nature is unidimensional, with a hard core – an 'essence' – against which the impact of social and economic conditions can be counterposed and assessed. But Sève argues, much as Marx did in the *German Ideology*, that human essence is an abstract in which 'man is seen as the subject of history for whom social relations are phenomena, an exterior manifestation' (1975, p. 24). The problem is that, whenever one attempts to take into account 'real living human individuals', the slide into idealism is very difficult to avoid: 'that logical monstrosity, the abstract "general individual" is the skeleton in the cupboard of the psychology of personality' (ibid., p. 12).

Concentrating on the value that Marx placed on human nature as a theoretical tool does not amount to a proof of any kind that Marx *had* a theory of human nature, merely that he made a number of statements and constructed certain of his arguments as if he might have. Yet Marx did employ a theory of human nature, even though the grounds for such a theory have had to be teased out of his thought.

This claim rests on the distinctions that can be made between types of statements about human beings, and the differing roles that types of statements have in Marx's theory as a whole. Thus it is clear that, in the early works and in his writings on post-capitalist society, the sense of a truly human existence as an aim and justification for the social critique is very strong. Moreover, as a wide range of Marxists have shown, one can establish that such a concern remains implicit in the later and specifically economic works. Marx's position vis-à-vis human nature, while only sketched in the early works, nevertheless shadows the development of his thought, not in the way that a half-baked idea will persist until properly discarded, but in the sense that it is a necessary feature of the development, justification and application of the theory as a whole.

Such a claim is by no means as grand as it might at first appear, since the test of that claim is fairly straightforward. If human nature, when it is treated as a conception (the nature of nature) and then as a notion (the humanness of nature), is not consistent with Marx's historical materialist method, then Marx had no theory of human nature and did not need to employ any of the idealizations or abstractions that human nature implies. Stated briefly, materialism means for Marx the activity of production and reproduction of the means of subsistence, while history is 'the active life-process' (i.e. production activity and organization) of people 'not in any fantastic isolation and rigidity, but in their actual, empirically perceptible process of development under definite conditions' ([1845–6] 1970, pp. 45–6). When the force of this kind of definition is turned on to the idea of human nature, it is usually assumed that Marx was ruling out the need for any abstractions about human nature. In this vein, there is Marx's attack on 'independent individuals' and 'eighteenth-century ideas' of the 'Robinsonades great and small', and the statement that 'the human being is in the most literal sense a *zoon politikon*, not merely a gregarious animal, but an animal which can individuate itself only in the midst of society' (ibid., pp. 83–4). However, as Geras points out:

> It is not uncommon, of course, to treat this very insistence upon man's sociality, in historicist fashion, as repelling any assumption of human uniformity. But this is the simplest of logical errors. Whatever degree of historical variation the thought may imply, it is itself a *generalization about human nature*. (1983, p. 81)

There are, in fact, *two* generalizations being made by Marx. First, Marx was stating that, like some animals but unlike others, humans are gregarious. Humans are herd-like creatures – the impulse, the practice, is to congregate rather than separate. Second, however, humans have an extra capacity which is not the property of any other animal, as far as we know, and certainly not to anywhere near the same extent. That is, within our gregarious and herd-like social structure, we have the capacity consciously to become individual humans rather than just another herd animal (Marx, [1857–8] 1973, pp. 484–90). Certainly, a society of human animals is necessary for such individuation, but it is not sufficient. Marx intimates how assumptions about human nature must be made if his claims about society and the way to examine it are to make sense. If humans did not have the capacity of individuality (as a uniform universality), *then there is no society which could provide it.*

51

As Chapter 5 on the individual under communism shows, this has important ramifications for the kinds of social structures that would characterize any future society. Just as there are dangers of assuming too much, Marx's theory of change needs very close analysis too for a non-Stalinist understanding of his statement that 'for the success of the cause itself, the alteration of men on a mass scale is necessary' ([1845–6] 1973, pp. 93–4).

However, the historicist and materialist question remains; how did this capacity arise, and what form or forms does it take? Furthermore, can such questions be asked of Marx's view of human nature? In constructing answers to these questions, Marx's *conception* of human nature takes shape as much less *a priori* than, for example, some of the utopian thinkers, with their long lists of natural faculties. Also, the second order *notions* of human nature have a similar relation to historical materialist method, in both a descriptive and critical sense. The first thing to realize is that the examination of society will not produce one, coherent image of human nature that has widespread application to all other societies and times and can claim universality. An examination of the very earliest social forms will not produce an easily recognizable 'human nature', yet there will be capacities and faculties which are transhistorical, or which have seen further development.

Just which society is under scrutiny, and its stage of historical development, must be established before any conclusions about the model of human nature can be made. Also, and in the same way that the abstract 'general individual' has to be avoided, so too does the tendency to construct what Marx referred to as the 'so-called general development of the human mind' ([1859] 1968, p. 181). Depending on the 'definite stage of development of the productive forces' (ibid.), there are going to be a number of images of human nature, with each having a claim to validity within its context. These *notions* of human nature are, however, connected to (1) the underlying *conception* of human nature employed by Marx, and (2) the other *notions* of human nature which are derived from an analysis, in historical materialist fashion, of specific production totalities.

Depending on the time-span adopted, the relationship between conception and notion of human nature is an interactive one. That is, features located in the conception of human nature might well find explicit expression in the notion of human nature. In the same way and over long evolutionary time, the society-specific facets of a notion of human nature might attain the status of *fundamental* characteristics of human nature, and so come to belong in the description of the conception of human nature. In other words, the limit to the plasticity assumed by Marx and ascribed to human beings and human nature has deep significance for his theory of change and actual historical causation alike. In terms of the debate between determinism and autonomy, it could still be maintained that, in the last instance, everything was determined by the economy, or however one wished to describe the motive forces in materialistic terms. However, the crudity of this understanding, and its limited usefulness, are sufficient argument against it. On the other hand, the principle might be accepted and a reinterpretation of autonomy attempted. Autonomy, unlike Berlin's approach to liberty, would then be described in social rather than idealist terms as a matter of positivity or negativity. Positive autonomy would be the situation where both the choices, and the need to choose, are very loosely or even indefinably constrained, whereas negative autonomy would consist in situations where the choices and the necessity of making choices are closely structured. It is not questioned that individuals have the right or ability to choose between alternatives. Nor is it assumed that choices are always either free or unfree, or that positive autonomy is superior to negative autonomy, or vice versa. And human nature, like social structure, has to be included in the equations of constraint. To these kinds of ends, it is necessary to conceive, as Engels insists, of 'the real science of men and of their historical development' (Marx and Engels, 1968, p. 607).

Social change and individuality

The means of proceeding with such a task derives, once again, from historical materialist method, and Marx is quite clear on this point. For example, when he castigates the view of human nature of Smith and Ricardo, he notes that they have made the mistake of assuming that their ideas about the individual have the authority of the 'natural'. As a result, they see the eighteenth-century individuals

> not as a historic result but as history's point of departure. As the Natural Individual appropriate to their notion of human nature, not arising historically, but posited by nature. This illusion has been common to each new epoch to this day. (Marx, [1857–8] 1973, p. 83)

In these few sentences, several important things are established. First, Marx demonstrates that the perception of the individual in society should be informed by the realization that individuals express an historical process – they are a result of past development and the operation of social forces, not the baseline from which to comprehend history. Second, Marx makes the distinction between an underlying conception of human nature (although he calls it a notion here, it equates to the definition of a 'conception') and the so-called 'Natural Individual' to be found in a particular set of economic and social circumstances (i.e. the 'notion' of human nature). Third, Marx does *not* reject the argument of Smith and Ricardo because they have a view of human nature, but because they have failed to employ that view legitimately. Specifically, they used their idea of human nature to establish what people must be like in a given society, instead of looking at the society to see what they *might* be like, to see how that social form affected or actualized or thwarted their original nature.

This bears directly on the appropriate approach to Marx and the individual. Implicitly, the correct way to proceed, the method that is consistent with the strong historical materialist flavour of this section of the *Grundrisse*, is to see how history and human nature together result in the 'individual' as a possibility and a reality in a given society. When this process is repeated for each 'epoch', there is a series of 'historic results' and it is the relations between them that are of particular interest. That is, Marx's conception of human nature is something to which he held firm and it constitutes a solid base in the premises of his theory as a whole. On the other hand, the more difficult area of *notions* of human nature is one in which he made a substantially different kind of contribution. Since his focus was on the economic aspects of relations of production, there is less said about the nature of individual development and existence, and more about the nature of social organization (that which appears given for an individual's social life).

None the less, it is within the structure of Marx's thought concerning the basic model of human society as material production that the pattern of the theoretical approach is to be found. The first requirement is an apprehension of the developmental nature of the three major modes of production to which Marx ascribes certain important qualities. The interpretation relevant here is that provided by C. Gould, in *Marx's Social Ontology* (1978). Her argument is not particularly controversial and is well supported by other writers in this field, such as Gandy (1979) and Kiernan (1983). Gould takes very seriously the first premise set out by Marx in the *German Ideology* that we are to deal with 'real historical men' – by claiming that 'for Marx the fundamental entities that compose society are individuals in social relations' and that 'these individuals become fully social and fully able to realize human possibilities in the course of a historical development' (1978, p. 1).

To establish this, Gould argues that the dialectic 'fundamentally characterizes the development of practical activity and social relations', such that Marx 'sees the Hegelian form of the dialectic as the logic of historical development' – a logic that connects the stages of pre-capitalist formations, capitalism and communal society (ibid., pp. 4, 5). Gould bases her arguments on the *Grundrisse*, but as Kiernan points out, Marx and Engels had already hinted at this schema in the *German Ideology*:

> They were feeling their way towards a very broad threefold demarcation: an epoch of 'primitive communism', or 'clan society'; a second, relatively brief but dynamic, of class division; then a synthesis of these two, socialism or classless society on a high technological level. (1983, p. 61)

Moreover, the idea that human history was to be understood in these developmental terms is also given expression elsewhere. 'In the theoretical schema of the *Communist Manifesto* he provided a universal formula for human progress: tribalism – slavery – feudalism – capitalism – communism. Like Hegel he was a spectator of all time and existence' (Gandy, 1979, p. 5). And, for all these commentators, Marx was a thinker who, having seen the disparate parts of history, wanted to integrate the elements into an all-embracing wholeness, free of contradictions. Later chapters will assess the weaknesses of both Marx's scheme and his ambitions to predict the end of pre-history – communism is made to carry too great a burden, for example. Furthermore, Gellner's cautionary remark, that 'to place something – for instance a social order – in a developmental series, is *not* to explain it', can be assessed (1964, p. 15).

To return to Gould's schema, the three historical stages have corresponding forms of social relations:

(1) personal dependence
(2) personal independence based on objective dependence
(3) free social individuality.

To this is added the further claim that:

the social relations in the three stages may be characterized as

(1) Community.
(2) Individuality and external sociality.
(3) Communal individuality. (1978, pp. 4–5)

What is immediately striking about this view of Marx's overall thought is the neatness, the clear and logical progression from the earlier stages through to the ultimate, communal society, and the way that only the achievements of the preceding stages seem to survive. Thus pre-capitalist societies offer us the basic model of community, establishing Marx's beliefs that community is no new and revolutionary notion, that it is not, as is so often averred, 'against human nature'. It would appear that communal living has almost the status of the natural, so long-standing is its existence, so recent its transformation into the 'individuality and external sociality' of capitalism. Yet that same capitalism brings dramatic and novel possibilities – glimpses of human social equality and the birth of the individual self, which might yet attain full realization. However, Marx's third historical stage is not so much a vision as a suggestion, the seemingly logical culmination of the historical processes he subjected to critical scrutiny. It is here that Marx has to rely on the strength of the dialectic and his historical materialist analysis, on their ability to grasp the reality of each totality of production relations, and to represent accurately the way that the production and reproduction of material life condition social life.

The three historical stages, although they appear distinct, should not be seen as mutually exclusive entities in all particulars. Paraphrasing Marx, Gandy puts it this way:

> Each of the different social formations is defined by *the mode of production dominant in it*. For in each formation there is also 'passive survival of antiquated modes of production'. Every economic base contains 'remnants of earlier stages of economic development which have actually been transmitted and survived – often only through tradition or by the force of inertia'. Economic evolution 'takes place only very slowly: the various stages and interests are never completely overcome, but only subordinated to the prevailing interest and trail along besides for centuries afterwards'. Societies are historical museums: they contain remnants of economic forms humanity has passed through 'with their inevitable train of social and political anachronism'. (1979, p. 151)

This admixture – dominant conditioning of features of human social existence coupled with other economic and social remnants – has important implications. It is certain on the one hand that the historical stages can properly be distinguished and that the social relations can be accurately described. On the other hand, the blend of forces and the slow development of reproductive processes mean that an *explanation* of historical change is also possible, so answering Gellner's criticism concerning development and change:

> From my standpoint, says Marx, 'the evolution of the economic social formation is viewed as a process of natural history'. A formation embraces both the past and the future: dying modes of production; the dominant, defining mode; and seeds of coming modes. Historical epochs, like geological ages, have no hard and fast lines between them. (ibid.)

There are, then, qualifications that have to be taken into account if Gould's schema of a Hegelian progression of social formations from pre-capitalist modes through capitalism to communal society is to be utilized. First, these stages, while conceptually distinct, are by no means pure forms. Second, the processes, mechanisms and intricacies of change from the first to the second and then the second to the third stage will not be identical. In a developmental series, where the move from feudalism to capitalism is progress, but where the move from capitalism to communal society is progress *but also the end of pre-history*, additional, different and much more significant changes occur. Marx, however, appears to have failed satisfactorily to reveal the nature of all these changes, or the reasons for them. For him, individuality is subject to grand processes, and his concern is that those processes prevent the emergence of a genuine individuality. The undeveloped aspect of this thought is that, in some respects, the *experience* of individuality does occur, and Marx was unable to acknowledge it.

In effect, Marx delivered much less than can be reasonably expected of his methodological approach, as it has been presented here. If his historical materialism means that historical explanations must be given in terms of people and their needs in concrete situations, then he is demanding not only that these explanations be in terms of the facts of nature, but of *human nature* in its concrete aspects of development.

Nevertheless, Marx did not rule out the legitimacy of such an exploration, and even if there is no clear-cut or unproblematic developmental pattern to be discerned from the examination of the three historical epochs, there is still the useful exercise of a comparative analysis of human social existence between those stages. To underpin this view of his ontology, Marx believed 'that individuals freely create and change their nature through their activity' (Gould, 1978, p. xiv).

> Where Aristotle conceived of the essence of a given thing as a fixed nature, Marx holds that individuals create their nature in their activity and therefore it is neither fixed nor presupposed. This eventuates in a conception of a changing and developing essence. He calls this creative activity labor. (ibid., p. 34)

There are two claims here with which to take issue. While accepting the principle that human nature cannot be fixed or unchanging, it seems that Gould remains with the fixed versus malleable nature dichotomy, as if that were indeed a real argument. To argue against fixity of nature by asserting but not specifying its malleability is to obscure the issue or to leap directly from the idealist presentation of human nature to the scientism of Althusser, where human nature is a mystifying term for a much more significant reality, like labour itself. Gould appears to be reiterating a singular interpretation of the Sixth Thesis on Feuerbach, where it is social relations which appear to constitute actual as well as realized human nature. If this is true, it is difficult to see how the idea of human nature can have any explanatory strength, or even academic interest, since it could have no motive force or defining characteristic in a social explanation.

Second, Gould makes the very strong claim that such a nature is created and changed *'freely'* by *'individuals'*. Hence she assumes, but does not establish, the plasticity of human nature, and also argues that this creative process arises from labouring individuals. Even if such an individual is, for Marx, 'the primary ontological subject … properly speaking, a social individual', it can be seen that Gould is taking large steps across a number of explanatory divides (ibid., p. 35). Furthermore, the alternative meaning of the use of a different 'essence' is equally problematic, since it appears to preclude the formative influence of the dominant and defining mode of production.

The first of these problems can be overcome, to a large extent, by differentiating between the levels of statements about human nature. The conception of human nature, then, refers to Gould's idea of human 'essence'. Here there is a set of characteristics that are, in the short term, fixed. Regarding the *notion* of human nature, on the other hand, the potentialities and faculties and abilities of that 'fixed' human nature will be expressed with some uniformity within the particular social environment created by the dominant and defining mode of production. Although there will be a degree of uniformity, it is also the case that human nature at this level will be very closely related to the 'creative activity' of labour, but should not be restricted to just this form of definition. Ass Marx argued, each formation, and therefore the modes of labour, is a conglomeration of the past, present and future modes of production. Thus it is important to be aware of and able to distinguish between that which is replicating the past, reproducing the present, or forming the future.

In effect, this complements Gould's claim for a developing 'essence', given the historical connection between the three historical stages in terms of the changes in the forces and relations of production, and the cultural and social details that accrue and are altered and survive those transitions. 'Development', then, becomes a much more specific concept, because it relates to something concrete. First, the modes of production become more advanced – they entail greater possibilities both materially and socially. Second, the individuals who are to fill and sustain the roles implied by the advancement of the modes of production must themselves reflect this heightening of sophistication and complexity. This is the phylogenetic and the ontogenetic perspective on development – the focus is on the way that the *species* develops, with consideration given to the development of *individuals* within a specific mode.

The two levels of human nature thus give rise to two ways of thinking about development, and care must be taken not to confuse a flowering of individuality in one society with the growth of individuality as an historical phenomenon. Although the two are related, the mediating links between them are by no means direct or simple, just as adaptive behaviour in an animal's life does not automatically result in adaptation of the species. The development of the conception of human nature is an idea that requires the lonng historical view of social organization, while the development of human nature within a given society calls for a narrow and sharp focus on social structure and social life. Marx's dialectical method does allow such a broad as well as specific view of society and human nature, and therefore makes it possible to see how the developments within a mode of production can contribute to development across a series of modes of production. For this to hold, changes must occur in the capabilities of human beings as well as constancies in what is reproduced, such that progress means the building upon and embellishing of that which already existed, instead of just change in what it means to be human.

Such insights will illuminate the transition processes which rest upon developments within society, and which are essential if the species humanity is to continue to progress. Moreover, they will reaffirm the links between materialist social forces and the mechanisms of change, without falling into the trap of assuming that on *physicalist* grounds material forces can be taken into account. As Edgely points out, not only what is thought, but the *way* that thought is conducted has material import:

> The historical materialist conception of thought implies material social change as a crucial determinant of differential cognitive access. Continuity in the social transmission of ideas makes plausible the concept of historical change as having the potential for cognitive progress, later generations benefitting cognitively from what has gone before. (1983, pp. 288–9)

This idea of intergenerational cognitive progress suggests that it is indeed worthwhile examining Marx's thought for evidence of the ways in which he did take into account non-economic determinants of behaviour, and the extent to which the personal and cultural components of social change are acknowledged, or can find their place in an account of 'Marxian individualism' (Forbes, 1989; Carver, 1987).

Summary

To achieve this, it is necessary to accept, for the time being, that Marx had a conception of human nature, and that such a conception did not provide *the* justification for his analysis of social change, even though it is supportive of that analysis. Thus, while Marx believed that, for the imaginable future, human animals would remain fundamentally the same, this does not mean that he could successfully delineate anything but outlines of future societies. His reluctance to describe communist society is the clearest proof of this, as is his awareness that the future always represented choices for humanity, whether they were consciously taken or not. A close analysis of his *conception* of human nature, then, will reveal nothing of great significance for his theory of change, apart from the vital feature of human potentiality.

It is possible to focus on Marx's *notions* of human nature, as they can be observed in his writings on the various historical stages. In this way, Marx's vision of the social life of 'real, living individuals' can be drawn out. On the basis of the earlier discussion of individualism, it will then be seen to what extent pre-capitalist societies displayed and incorporated what is now termed individualism. In other words, descriptions of social beings and distinctions between what was necessary and what contingent (if contributory) in a particular social order will be of particular interest. Further, indications of the continuities in the succession of social formations will be assessed for their 'naturalness', or their necessity for the development of humanity.

When dealing with capitalist society, on the other hand, Marx's notion of human nature will be more articulated. Instead of just one notion of human nature – capitalist human nature – there will be distinctions between the kinds of people produced by early, middle and advanced capitalist social formations. This is necessary because (1) Marx's perception of the timing of the transition to communal society was either optimistic in the extreme or revealed a considerable flaw in his reasoning and understanding of historical conditions and probabilities, and (2) in any event, the continued development (and not merely survival) of capitalism has produced the kinds of individuals and social groupings he may or may not have anticipated. Capitalism has also to be treated differently because, unlike feudalism or the ancient and Asiatic modes of production, the capitalist social formation is unique, coming, as it is supposed to, at the end of pre-history and heralding at least the possibility of a communal society of freedom, equality and creativity. Therefore, the processes and mechanisms whereby individuals can undergo the quite massive changes in ability and attitude necessary to bring about and sustain such a radically different kind of society – the first non-exploitative yet still technological social formation – must exhibit a degree of complexity of a special order.

Finally, the notion of human nature which relates to the stage of communism is of especial interest, partly because Marx has so little specific to say. Yet this image of individuals in society is a crucial one. As Eisenberg argues, 'the behaviour of men is not independent of the theories of human behaviour that men adopt' (1972, p. 123). That is, 'what we choose to believe about the nature of man has social consequences', and Marx has left us in no doubt of the viability of communism and his approval of it (ibid., p. 124). It will be intriguing, then, to see how closely Marx's notion of human nature under communism accords with his general *conception* of human nature, to assess the extent to which, not history, but the actions of individuals under capitalism might serve ultimately to unify conception and notion. The starkness of the contrast between the individualism of capitalism and the individuality of communal society, combined with the historical connection of these two social formations and expressions of human nature, will be the principal focus here. As Marx maintained:

> Men do not build themselves a new world out of the fruits of the earth as vulgar superstition believes but out of the historical accomplishments of their declining civilization. (Markovic, 1974b, p. 262)

The next three chapters, then, seek to explore Marx's understanding of the historical accomplishments of the major historical stages as they relate to individuality specifically and human nature generally.

Notes

1 An objective being 'does not descend from its "pure activity" to the creation of objects; on the contrary, its objective product simply confirms its objective activity, its activity of an objective, natural being' (Marx, [1844] 1975, p. 389).

2 Writing some forty years later, Nietzsche ([1888] 1968) was to express this naturalism as the will to power; the drive to survive and be effective was connected to suffering as a condition of life.

3 Other principal contenders are Marx's passages dealing with the base/superstructure distinction ([1859] 1968, pp. 180–4), and 'the revolutionary dictatorship of the proletariat' ([1875] 1968, p. 327).

4 Geras distinguishes between human nature and the nature of man. Geras' interesting discussion on the Sixth Thesis on Feuerbach shows how easy it is to confuse a constant 'human nature' with the 'nature of man' in a 'broader, more inclusive sense' (1983, p. 37). While being in general agreement, the term 'nature of man' does have its semantic drawbacks, not least from a feminist point of view. Moreover, retaining the term 'human nature' but referring to either conception or notion is a deliberate reminder of the interconnections between the two expressions of human nature, and the way in which the focus has to shift between humans as a species in relation to the natural world and other species, and humans in a world that is not natural.

3   Pre-capitalist societies and the absence of individualism

In turning to the existence of individuals in pre-capitalist societies, this chapter demonstrates a number of related things. First, form and content are given to the proposition that each epoch provides a broadly typical expression of human nature consonant with the ensemble of social relations. Second, this superficially relativist position may show that human nature, at fundamental and substantive levels, remains integrally connected to human nature under other forms of social organisation. Third, the description of pre-capitalist individuals employs historical materialist method, and illuminates the role of economic factors in the construction of social explanations. A further outcome will be insights into the processes of change assumed by Marx to be at play in the development of successively more sophisticated modes of production.

Marx, like Rousseau before him, could only hypothesize about the origins of society. A description of people in 'original' society would amount to an extrapolation of the description of the earliest societies that preceded capitalism, in so far as the basic premises and generalizations relevant to *any* society are stated. Thus:

> As individuals express their life, so they are. What they are, therefore, coincides with their production, both with *what* they produce and with *how* they produce. The nature of individuals thus depends on the material conditions determining their production. (Marx, [1845–6] 1970, p. 42)

Certainly, this is a rich enough claim, one that has encouraged a massive literature. Nevertheless, it is very interesting to observe that Marx appears to remain neutral about the relative significance of the human possibilities of individuals and the material nature of individual lives. Production does not *decide*, but *coincides with* what individuals are.

The human's *original* appearance as a clan or herd being indicates

63

a human existence which is structured by the nature of the human animal. That existence is limited not by that nature, but by the determinate social and economic forces. Those forces define, at this stage, what a human *is*, but imply that which has yet to be achieved. This may be true at any point in human history. For Marx, the difference between performance and potential is great, and a matter for concern, whenever social arrangements contrive to prevent so many from even *attempting* to live according to their abilities.

The nature of individuals in a specific society, in other words, has been described as a notion of human nature. That notion of human nature is clearly in a dependency relationship with economic and social forces, which do not determine the individual's nature, but interact with a fundamental and universal human nature. This is of particular interest in the pre-capitalist situation, because here the mode of production is so different, so technologically minimal, and so overshadowed by the exigencies of an omnipotent nature. It might be concluded, then, that fundamental human nature would be less overlaid, less warped by the relations of production but also less developed than under more advanced modes of production.

However, there are many instances where Marx makes claims of a much more mechanistic kind. These appear to establish once more the primacy of economic forces. For example:

> the fact that pre-bourgeois history, and each of its phases, also has its own *economy* and an *economic foundation* for its movement, is at bottom only the tautology that human life has since time immemorial rested on production, and, in one way or another, on *social* production, whose relations we call, precisely, economic relations. (Marx, [1857–8] 1973, p. 489)

In other words, Marx insists upon the intrinsicality of the economic analysis, whatever the form of words he may have employed to describe any part of history. Furthermore, those relations are logically, historically and materially connected to capitalist economic relations. There is a direct line of development, through a series of stages, from original property to capitalist property (ibid.). This forward extension of the argument, across very long historical time, raises the question of its extension back through time. Did Marx imply an infinite regress? By no means. Immediately following the above quotation, Marx places a logical limit to extending backwards the derivation and formation of economic relations, by stating that '*the original conditions of production ... cannot themselves* originally *be products* – results of production' (ibid.). If they are not the results of production, then there must be another, *fundamental* element in the explanation of the development of economic relations. This concerns the lives of individuals with which these economic relations are associated.

The *developmental* aspect of this historical process reveals the nature of the connections between historical epochs. Marx believed that his analysis of history and capitalism showed him to be at a turning point, midway between 'natural' as distinct from 'human' history (i.e. he was between feudalism and communism). By placing himself and all other human subjects in such a position, Marx seems to have sidestepped a confrontation with his early emphasis on a human essence and the implied spectre of idealism as an underpinning explanatory approach. Development through history allows Marx to be critical of a specific society, but interested in the progress which it indicates has taken place in terms of the sophistication of human social organization. The 'first social forms' may have exhibited only a minimal impact on 'human productive capacity', but even here the principle is established that the expansion of human capacities and needs can give rise to new social relations, which in turn permit the development of further capacities and needs (ibid., p. 158). Crucially, however, all societies to date have tended to underemploy existing human capacities, and fail to meet needs.

Second, the 'historical' links are dialectical in the sense that the significance of the first stage of society for the nature of modern society is not accidental. The relationship between historically adjacent forms of society is a conditioning one, making it possible to posit a future *by the act of* analysing the present.[1] There is a *process* in operation here, and there is 'progress' of a particular kind. The type of process involved is the outcome of the twin driving forces of the developing material productive forces and the expansion of human capacities and needs. The interdependency of these two forces, close and fundamental as it is, does not warrant their compression into a single category. This would be to equate materialism with determinism and permit the generation of a single historical path of change, confusing an historical result (modern society) with predetermined historical inevitability. The process is one of constant interaction, which does not imply or require contradictions to focus on, resolve, or even produce that process itself. What is required, therefore, is an account of pre-capitalist society which includes an analysis of elements particular to that period, but which can also be seen as factors in the general development of humankind.

At the same time, it is possible also to consider progress as a constant feature of the history of humanity, as long as such progress is not invested with any moral valuation. That is to say, the idea that the expansion of needs and capacities is progressive should not exclude the possibility that the *loss* of a capacity, and, perhaps, the diminution of a need or needs, can be as progressive as the *creation* of capacities and needs. An example of a positive loss might be the decreasing need for spiritual explanations of everyday events, presupposing a gain in ability to comprehend the world in a more complex fashion, and a reduction in unreal fears.

This means that Marx's pronouncements on both the past *and* the future are mere peripheries to the real object - the comprehension of contemporary society – and are to be analysed for their content and judged according to their contribution toward 'the practical process of the development of men' ([1845–6] 1970, p. 48). This may explain why Marx did not construct a conventional history of feudalism, but limited himself to brief and expository excursions into the past. His account has an uneven and incomplete appearance, with emphasis placed in a fashion that is unique among other accounts of this period. That is to say, neither mainstream nor avowedly Marxist historiography endorses the view of feudalism that Marx provided. On the other hand, this admirably demonstrates that Marx was concerned with those aspects of feudal society that shed most light on the tendencies in modern society, and the way that change in socieeety is to be understood and brought about:

> our method indicates the points where historical investigation must enter in, or where bourgeois economy as a merely historical form of the production process points beyond itself to earlier historical modes of production ... Just as, on one side the pre-bourgeois phases appear as *merely historical*, i.e. suspended presuppositions, so do the contemporary conditions of production likewise appear as engaged in *suspending themselves* and hence in positing the *historic presuppositions* for a new state of society. ([1857–8] 1973, p. 460)

In practice, this model of analysis is better observed by more recent writers, since Marx adopted for the earliest societies a simplistic kind of naturalism, very akin to Rousseau's leap of humankind into the 'new-born state of society', ostensibly 'the very best man could experience' (1973, pp. 82–3). In echoing Rousseau, Marx saw the breakdown of this natural cultural unity as the first step toward capitalist relations of wage labour and capital. That is, the original conditions of production are said to be 'natural presuppositions', *'natural conditions of the producer's existence'* (Marx, [1857–8] 1973, p. 489). Those conditions presuppose subjective and objective connections to others and nature, and take the form of clan membership (ibid.).

Leaving aside the numerous objections to this view of original economic society,[2] Marx has succeeded only in labelling these original preconditions as natural. In other words, he has sought the origin *only* of the dominant influence of economic relations as they are to be understood socially and materially. This does not of itself establish that no other forces pre-exist economic relations, or that economic relations henceforth override any other influences. Marx succeeded in placing human nature – the '(bodily) being is a natural presupposition' – within a specific framework once more, but he did not thereby *describe* that human nature ([1857–8] 1973, p. 490). Moreover, Marx leaves unstated the crucial way that the nature of humankind must have had a defining impact on individual lives, establishing the legitimacy of the argument that human individuals have always had capacities and potentialities which enable them to rise to and then exist within and change various modes of production.

For these reasons, a particular focus on pre-capitalist societies may serve to illuminate interesting features or patterns in the history of the precursors of capitalism.

> The economic structure of capitalist society has grown out of the economic structure of feudal society. The dissolution of the latter set free the elements of the former. (Marx, [1867] 1976, p. 875)

In the light of Marx's many descriptions of the alienated and crippled individuals of capitalist society who enjoy freedom in only a limited, political sense, the status of the individual in feudal society must be significant, given the dialectical link between the two forms of society. And, as Marx pointed out in the *Grundrisse*, the dissolution of feudal society by no means precludes the possibility that feudal characteristics could and would be carried over to the new form of society.

Since, furthermore, bourgeois society is only a form resulting from the development of antagonistic elements, some restrictions belonging to earlier forms of society are frequently to be found in it, though in a crippled state or as a travesty of their former self, as for example communal property. ([1857–8] 1973, p. 356)

Furthermore, Marx castigated the apologists of feudalism for failing to appreciate both the result of an historical movement, and the very process of that movement:

the feudalists forget that they exploited under circumstances and conditions that were quite different, and that are now antiquated. In showing that, under their rule, the modern proletariat never existed, they forget that the modern bourgeoisie is the necessary offspring of their own form of society. ([1847] 1968, p. 54)

Thus Marx himself provided sound reasons for turning the full weight of his historical method on to a consideration of the individual in pre-capitalist society. Such an individual is an expression of human nature under given conditions, thereby making possible later comparisons with another expression of human nature within another productive mode. From this may be drawn a variety of conclusions pertaining to that which is fixed or mutable, and those aspects of nature which relate to change processes. This will establish the extent to which capitalist society reflects earlier developments as much as it carries with it restrictions of the past.

Feudalism and the individual

Beginning, then, with the premisses that Marx laid down in *German Ideology*, the life of real wo/men is built up through the 'moments' which relate to fundamental needs and to practical social consequences of those needs. Hence the 'production of material life itself' – the means to survive physically – creates new needs, which, in combination with early social relationships, provide the substratum upon which any consideration of the 'actual life process' must be based (Marx, [1845–6] 1970, p. 47). From these premisses, Marx concluded that:

The production of life, both of one's own in labour and of fresh life in procreation, now appears as a double relationship:

on the one hand as a natural, on the other as a social, relationship ... the multitude of productive forces accessible to man determines the nature of society, hence, that the 'history of humanity' must always be studied in relation to the history of industry and exchange ... Thus it is quite obvious from the start that there exists a materialistic connection of men with one another, which is determined by their needs and their mode of production, and which is as old as men themselves. (ibid., p. 50)

Marx here maintains the distinction between that which is natural and that which is social, even though both of these aspects of life are intertwined. Labour and procreation, as natural needs, bring about but do not require *a priori*, social relationships, and this duality of the natural and the social demands an explanation of both of these facets, as well as requiring an examination of the manner in which they coexist and manifest themselves.

In effect, this is the central problem for Marx's work – to deal with elements of difference without prejudicing or ignoring particular aspects. The suggestion that Marx's conception of human nature constitutes the 'natural', while the notion of human nature (how individuality expresses itself) is the 'social', provides a theoretical means of handling the important distinctions that are usually characterized as the nature/nurture duality. They are related but separable aspects of the same general assumptions about the nature of human existence, such that neither the 'natural' nor the 'social' has a greater or more fundamental significance than the other. At the same time, Marx recognized that some societies, and certainly some ideologies, did assume a primacy of the natural, or misconceived the relationship between nature and society, to the detriment of living human individuals. For him, this was not a problem to be tackled by argument alone. The ultimate *practical* solution lay with the material conditions of existence under true communism.

This communism, as fully developed naturalism, equals humanism, and as fully developed humanism equals naturalism; it is the genuine resolution of the conflict between man and nature, and between man and man, the true resolution of the conflict between existence and being, between freedom and necessity, between individual and species. ([1844] 1975, p. 348)

Of itself, however, such a solution fails to provide the details of some of the categories employed. Only hints as to the content of individuality and sociality are given, since Marx's principal objective is to throw into sharp relief the necessity of examining the 'materialist connection of men with one another'. Thus the second point to be made is that the emphasis on material conditions should not obscure Marx's reliance on his concept of 'humanity', albeit with a *particular* 'history'. In other words, while the material conditions of existence are crucial in that they have determinately produced our society and our history, materialistic connections are themselves *determined* by human needs – needs which *can be, and are, natural* needs. Even as those needs change and develop, so, nevertheless, they become natural in a part of a growing human nature.

In the discussion of the individual in feudal society, then, the following points are important. First, Marx examined history with the clear but limited intention of discovering those tendencies which were instrumental for the development of the capitalist mode of production. Second, the methodological approach adopted by Marx was directed toward highlighting in very broad outline the material conditions of existence, resulting in less emphasis on the status of individuals in human terms. This means that Marx's theory of society and historical details will have to be blended, interpreted and augmented by more recent scholarship in such a way as to draw out the connections between feudalism and individualism. Finally, attention will be focused upon those aspects of feudal individualism which are antagonistic to feudal society, the better to indicate their importance, positively or negatively, for 'progress' toward modern forms of individualism.

These complexities with respect to wo/man and society, not entirely conveyed by an examination of the economic structure, are taken into account in Marc Bloch's study, *Feudal Society* (1962). For him:

> The framework of institutions which governs a society can in the last resort be understood only through a knowledge of the whole human environment. For though the artificial conception of man's activities which prompts us to carve up the creature of flesh and blood into the phantoms *homo economicus, philosophicus, juridicus* is doubtless necessary, it is only tolerable if we refuse to be deceived by it ... A society, like a mind, is woven of perpetual interaction. For other researches, differently

oriented, the analysis of the economy or the mental climate are culminating points; for the historian of the social structure they are a starting point. (ibid., Vol. I, p. 59)

Thus the 'whole human environment' is much more than the combination of a variety of viewpoints of wo/men, according to their particular activity at a given moment. Also, Bloch's reference to the 'mental climate' indicates that one important means of grasping the intricacy of that human environment, and allowing for its 'perpetual interaction', consists in a full acknowledgement of the thoughts *and* feelings of individuals. At the same time, Bloch applies to feudalism the historical method Marx found so essential to the explanation of the emergence of capitalist society.

European feudalism should therefore be seen as the outcome of the violent dissolution of older societies. It would in fact be unintelligible without the great upheaval of the Germanic invasions which, by forcibly uniting the two societies originally at very different stages of development, disrupted both of them and brought to the surface a great many modes of thought and social practices of an extremely primitive character. It finally developed in the atmosphere of the last barbarian raids. It involved a far-reaching restriction of social intercourse, a circulation of money too sluggish to admit of salaried officialdom, and a mentality attached to things tangible and local. When these conditions began to change, feudalism began to wane. (ibid., Vol. II, p. 443)

An epoch of history, therefore, carried within it the basis of both its development and decline, characterized in social relations and modes of thought. Bloch suggests, too, that feudal society was quite primitive even by pre-feudal standards. This raises several interesting issues. First, it should be noted that Bloch did not question the robustness of either of the two societies, even though they were at different developmental stages. Therefore, the 'primitive' thought and practices to which he alludes can be regarded as relating to fundamental aspects of human social organization *and* to individuals. That is to say, the restricted social intercourse and a sense of the world as manageable in only a limited scope are peculiarly tribal when placed in the context of the absence of a money economy and broad social networks. Although, as a form of productive activity, feudal society was by no means tribal, the modes of thought and social practices were a reversion to those found in ancient society.

Marx himself provided an illuminating account of the human development consistent with primitive society, an account that is couched, nevertheless, in terms whose principal function is to describe capitalist society.

> Those ancient social organisms of production are, compared with bourgeois society, extremely simple and transparent. But they are founded either on the immature development of man individually, who has not yet severed the umbilical cord that unites him with his fellow men in a primitive tribal community, or upon direct relations of subjection. They can arise and exist only when the development of the productive power of labour has not risen beyond a low stage, and when, therefore, the social relations within the sphere of material life, between man and man, and between man and Nature, are correspondingly narrow. ([1867] 1976, pp. 441–2)

As he stated it, in primitive modes of production, *individual* wo/man is as yet underdeveloped. In other words, the development of the productive power of labour is responsible for the individuals becoming aware of themselves as beings apart, beings in relation to others, to nature, and to the relations of production in which they move, on a much more sophisticated level. This implies that bourgeois individualism signifies a development toward maturity, that it, too, is a necessary outgrowth of earlier forms, and one which indicates further stages of development. This is to suggest that humans, generically, develop toward individuality, and that Marx went so far as to pinpoint a crucial stage of that growth – the breaking of the post-foetal bond that binds immature individuals to the tribe.

In the *Grundrisse*, Marx made very clear that this interpretation is entirely justified, and there is the implied notion of a *strong and basic*, although undifferentiated, human nature, the constant upon which material forces establish human development and give rise to the social individual.

> But human beings become individuals only through the process of history. He appears originally as a *species-being [Gattungswesen]*, *clan being, herd animal* – although in no way whatever as a *zoon politikon* in the political sense. ([1857–8] 1973, p. 496)

Originally, human nature is both unrealized and underdeveloped. Nevertheless, human nature does give form to human existence. If Bloch's interpretation of feudalism is correct, then feudal wo/man displayed this dualism, simultaneously a primitive species-being and socially developed individual (if only in a partial way). Marx's account of human social relations should reveal an acknowledgement that the European middle ages presented images of wo/man that reflect considerable social development, the full expression of which is unfulfilled or fragmented by feudal society. On the other hand, some of the social elements of feudal life contained the seeds of capitalist social relations. Indeed, in Volume I of *Capital*, Marx counterposed the idealist image of the abstract individual with the historical background provided by the European middle ages:

> Here, instead of the independent man, we find everyone dependent, serfs and lords, vassals and suzerains, laymen and clergy. Personal dependence here characterized the social relations of production just as much as it does the other spheres of life organized on the basis of that production. But for the very reason that personal dependence forms the groundwork of society, there is no necessity for labour and its products to assume a fantastic form different from their reality. They take the shape, in the transactions of society, of services in kind and payments in kind. Here the particular and natural form of labour, and not, as in a society based on the production of commodities, its general and abstract form, is the immediate form of social labour. ([1867] 1976, p. 170)

The personal dependence here emphasized by Marx is a good example of the tensions within feudal society with respect to the development of individuality. The equivalence of the natural form of labour and the form of social labour, while primitive, are nevertheless *immediate* and not abstracted. Therefore they do not exhibit the alienating effects of the transformation under capitalism of real life activity into abstract labour and social relations into relations between commodities. On the other hand, dependence itself bespeaks a low level of social organization, one in which wo/men are not permitted to establish truly human associations, but must bind themselves to others socially as much as economically. This, in human terms, is feudalism's limitation – 'definite self-sufficient development of one-sided abilities', of an *economic* variety – a limitation that had specific political ramifications for feudal society (Marx, [1857–8] 1973, p. 497).

As Marian Sawer points out in *Marxism and the Question of the Asiatic Mode of Production*, 'it has frequently been observed that for Marx industrialisation was synonymous with capitalism, and hence, he tended to view history in terms of the preconditions of capitalism – ie, increasing individuation' (1977, pp. 218–19).

It is necessary, however, to examine not only the economic and material changes that enhanced individuation, but the structural process of that developing potentiality termed here individuality, as a necessary complement. The intertwining of the sociopolitical and the economic, and the centrality of Marx's premisses concerning historical change, are apparent in Bloch's view of the personal dependence inherent in feudal relations.

> Vassal homage was a genuine contract and a bilateral one. If the lord failed to fulfil his engagements he lost his rights. Transferred, as was inevitable, to the political sphere ... this idea was to have a far-reaching influence, all the more so because on this ground it was reinforced by the very ancient notions which held the king responsible in a mystical way for the welfare of his subjects and deserving of punishment in the event of public calamity ... It was above all the circles of the vassals which translated these ideas into practice, under the influence of the institutions which had formed their mentality. In this sense, there was a fruitful principle underlying many revolts which on a superficial view might appear as mere random uprisings ... [The] famous 'right of resistance' ... resounded in the thirteenth and fourteenth centuries from one end of the Western world to the other, in a multitude of texts. Though most of these documents were inspired by reactionary tendencies among the nobility, or by the egoism of the bourgeoisie, they were of great significance for the future. (1962, Vol. II, pp. 451–2)

It should first be observed that Bloch assigns a particularly important role to the mass, the vassals (and to a lesser extent the serfs), in that belief and custom incorporated obligations on the part of the landowner, which came increasingly to be enforced (by virtue of the bilaterality of the contract) in favour of the less privileged majority. As Bloch concludes, 'oppressive as it may have been to the poor, it is bequeathed to our Western civilisation as something with which we still desire to live' (ibid.). In other words, feudal institutions contained the contradictions that were to contrive to change perceptions of self and one's place in the world. It is, it can be argued, one of the principal features of modern individualism that here began to be formed – the belief that certain rights pertain to groups of individuals, or simply individuals, and that some *higher authority* is *responsible* for vouchsafing those rights. The idea that a contract must be made persists, and the individual, although sure of this need, remains uncertain with whom the contract is to be made, and of the means of its enforcement.

In terms of general ethical development, however, it is essential to focus on the fundamental changes taking place in towns, and examine their implications. If the relations between persons within the system of landownership had significant effect, the emerging forms of property ownership in the towns were crucial for the development of individuation.

> This feudal system of landownership had its counterpart in the towns in the shape of corporative property, the feudal organisation of trades. Here property consisted chiefly in the labour of each individual person. The need for association against the organized robber barons, the need for communal covered markets in an age when the industrialist was at the same time a merchant, the growing competition of the escaped serfs swarming into the rising towns, the feudal structure of the whole country: these combined to bring about the guilds. (Marx, [1845–9] 1970, pp. 45–6)

Here property as individual labour is increasingly offset by the growth of the markets, in size and complexity, and the need for protection from and exploitation of the nascent labour force of the escaped serfs. Association and co-operation became the means by which the forces of change were harnessed and enhanced, and brought into direct conflict with the primitive monetary system of the feudal economy.

Effectively, it was the mental climate of feudal society which was uniquely significant, including as it did the individual's perception of his or her place in the world, as well as formal religious teaching. As Tawney points out in *Religion and the Rise of Capitalism*:

> When the sixteenth century opens, not only political but social theory is saturated with doctrines drawn from the sphere of ethics and religion, and economic phenomena are expressed in terms of personal conduct, naturally and inevitably as the nineteenth century expressed them in terms of mechanism. (Tawney, 1926, p. 7)

This cool account quite adequately describes the reversal in the role of economic analogy that was taking place, whereas Bloch's view of the religious mentality in the eleventh and twelfth centuries gives a far more focused insight.

'Ages of faith', we say glibly, to describe the religious attitude of feudal Europe. If by that phrase we mean that any conception of the world from which the supernatural was excluded was profoundly alien to the minds of that age, that in fact the picture which they formed of the destinies of man and the universe was in almost every case a projection of the pattern traced by a Westernized Christian theology, nothing could be more true. That here and there doubts might be expressed with regard to the 'fables' of Scripture is of small significance; lacking any rational basis, this crude scepticism, which was not a normal characteristic of educated people, melted in the face of danger like snow in the sun. It is even permissible to say that never was faith more completely worthy of its name. (Bloch, 1962, Vol. I, pp. 81–2)

Feudal wo/man's faith was, it seems, as strong as his or her fear. The imminence of the Last Judgement, then as now regularly predicted, was not so much disruptive of life as an ever-present spectre, a reinforcement of the prevailing faith. Moreover, the belief that 'the material world was scarcely more than a mask, behind which took place all the really important things', meant that 'the generality of mankind imagined the opposing wills of a host of beings good and bad in a state of perpetual strife; saints, angels, and especially devils' (ibid., p. 83). And Bloch (ibid., p. 87) aptly sums up: 'these features are an essential part of any accurate picture of the feudal world, and in the face of them who can fail to recognize in the fear of hell one of the great social forces of the age?'

Therefore, an economistic perspective of the material conditions of existence is inadequate if it does not take into account this substratum of medieval belief concerning people and their place in the world. The feudal individual clearly has a determinate place and a distinct character, and can barely be described as an individual even in Enlightenment terms. The attempt to write modern, capitalist individualism back into feudal productive and social relations is thus deeply flawed (Macfarlane, 1978). More recent scholarship, which focuses on real living individuals and their communities, provides considerable evidence of emotional and political sophistication in the construction of individual identity. As David Aers argues:

> The continuation of the human species, let alone the practice of what may count as vices and virtues, is inextricably bound up with the existence of particular communities, a fact as axiomatic to Aristotle as to Thomas Aquinas and much pre-enlightenment moral thought - no Robinsonades here. Human beings are necessarily born into communities they did not choose and

they grow into given social identities with which they encounter their specific circumstances. (1988, p. 2)

The transformation of the person whose perception of reality was shrouded by mysticism and took shape within a 'web of discourses and social practices ... which determined its horizons' (ibid., p. 4) into a being who could separate and comprehend portions of reality in more naturalistic fashion does not appear to have a strong connection with the developing forces of production. In other words, not all of the significant social forces can be shown to have a causal connection in the last instance with the economy. Tawney located the collision between religious ethics and the demands of mercantilism and the ever-increasing sophistication of the money economy as occurring most crucially in the sixteenth and seventeenth centuries, whereas Bloch identifies qualitative changes occurring no less than 400 years earlier, brought about by cultural influences of an 'intellectual renaissance':

> The whole tendency of the new literature was towards the rehabilitation of the individual; it encouraged the growth of a more introspective habit of mind, reinforcing in this direction the influence of the religious practice of auricular confession which, after having long been confined to the monastic world, became widespread among laymen during the twelfth century. (Bloch, 1962, p. 106; Tawney, 1926, p. 5)

The twofold significance of this statement lies, first, in the suggestion that individuality was in the process of being *reinstated*, rather than being an unique creative event. Thus wo/man's nature is here regarded as essentially individual. Second, that individuality, even in this early re-emergence, was closely associated with religion. In other words, the role of religion in this development was reflexive in that religion itself was vouchsafed a new and invigorated status in the affairs of humankind, at least for several centuries. In any case, it was these types of changes which point to a renewed process of individuation.

> In many of his characteristics the man of AD 1200 or thereabouts, in the higher ranks of society, resembled his ancestor of earlier generations: he displayed the same spirit of violence, the same abrupt changes of mood, the same preoccupation with the supernatural; this last – where it took the form of an obsession with evil spirits – being perhaps even more pronounced as a result of the dualist influences with which the Manichean heresies, then so flourishing, were infecting even the orthodox.

But in two respects he differed profoundly from his predecessor. He was better educated. He was more self-conscious. (Bloch, 1962, p. 106)

The themes which began to emerge, then, are those of particular relevance in Marx's thought centuries later. The view of human existence in pre-capitalist society put forward by Tawney and Bloch establishes and makes intelligible the original absence of modern individualism, just as much as it indicates the reasons why and the manner in which the individual began to appear and become more notable. Feudal society is pictured and analysed according to ideas of individuality, consciousness and the development of human faculties. These are related to the material connections contained in and growing out of the economic structure, but they are also related quite strongly to the relationship with nature and religious belief. The agreement with Marx's much more potted version of feudal history is due in part to the interpretive style of their historical studies. Tawney and Bloch are, after all, Marxist historians, applying a methodology through which some of Marx's assertions will filter and be reasserted to some extent. Nevertheless, it must be remarked that the growth of individualism was of even more interest to pre- and then non-Marxist thought, since it was thought to support the emergent bourgeois class. It is of importance that it was Marx who was able to subject the common categories – the individual, progress – to a more far-reaching critical analysis. As Marx wrote:

The more deeply we go back into history, the more does the individual, and hence also the producing individual, appear as *dependent*, as belonging to a greater whole. ([1857–8] 1973, p. 84)

The break out from what was largely a mystical palace involved the complex reorientation, on the part of individuals and groups, of the comprehension of the natural world. An enhanced self-consciousness, while by no means a motive force, certainly proved to be a powerful catalyst – a development within humans which was, in turn, its own facilitative agent, bringing about further development. And in discussing consciousness, Marx seems to have thought his way forward through history along the path of the very individuation of humankind.

Consciousness is at first, of course, merely consciousness concerning the immediate sensuous environment and consciousness of the limited connection with other persons and things outside the individual who is growing self-conscious. At the same time it is consciousness of nature, which first appears to men as a completely alien, all-powerful, and unassailable force, with which men's relations are purely animal and by which they are overawed like beasts; it is thus a purely animal consciousness of nature (natural religion) just because nature is as yet hardly modified historically ... On the other hand, man's consciousness of the necessity of associating with the individuals around him is the beginning of the consciousness that he is living in society at all. This beginning is as animal as social life itself at this stage. It is mere herd consciousness, and at this point man is only distinguished from sheep by the fact that with him consciousness takes the place of instinct or that his instinct is a conscious one. ([1845–6] 1970, p. 53)

Thus Marx established the logical and historical connection between human nature and development as an individual. First, humans have their own particular instincts, their own particular *nature* (human nature is not sheep nature, though they were/are both herd-like). Second, human instincts create possibilities in a way the instincts of other creatures have not. The connection made between instinct and consciousness is vital, because it enables Marx to categorize action as natural, while still being able to show that such action (even in the form of consciousness or thought) need not be fixed or limited. The mediating links are twofold, each of which involves a distinctive dichotomization within human consciousness, continually bringing about change to human nature and society. The first matches the claim made in the *Grundrisse*, that there is a split between what is subjectively and what objectively experienced. Second, humans, not only separated from external reality, characterize nature as distinct from society. Other humans are not regarded as natural, but as constituting the elements in a rudimentary form of social relationships.

These connections between original human nature and social development have relevance for the discussion of the feudal individual. In the specific sense, growing consciousness is the means by which the feudal being is able to escape some of the restrictions that the view of self and objective reality entails. The comprehension of nature, for instance, gives some mastery over that nature. Concomitantly, the mystical interpretation of the world is drawn into question, and modified, though not always accordingly, as supernatural causes lose their explanatory appeal.

But this growth in stature as a conscious being has a dual quality, as Marx indicated but failed ultimately to resolve. In

79

the early stages, 'herd-consciousness' is a recognition but not yet a redefinition of the immediate sensuous environment. Wo/men apprehend that they are no longer conterminous with nature, a phenomenon for which Marx provided two alternative explanations. Either 'consciousness takes the place of instinct' or the 'instinct is a conscious one'. Thus separation from nature results in the acquisition of human capacities. However, nature in this sense also includes other life forms. Instinct continues to be the motive force for action for animals, but, in Marx's thought, to be human is to transcend instinct. Humans still have instincts, but do not necessarily behave instinctually. This qualitative difference sets the human animal apart in three ways.

First, *homo sapiens* becomes species-being. Consciousness of instinct creates the awareness that wo/man is *of* the natural world, but no longer within it, and that this applies solely to the human species. Second, consciousness, while a generic capability, always has an individual manifestation. Therefore, each person also becomes aware of the distinction between self and other. Third, each self-conscious individual is at the same time an instinctual animal.

It is this last point which is most unclear in Marx's thought. At times he argued that animal nature had been lost altogether – i.e. wo/man was no longer determined by instinct, but by social existence. On the other hand, Marx also referred to *drives*, perhaps a potentialist interpretation of instincts, as important basic elements which defined the way that humans reacted upon and to their social existence. Ultimately, Marx failed satisfactorily to establish that wo/man had ceased to function entirely in any animal sense. If 'human nature' was not evacuated of content, nor was there a sufficient explanation of the way in which the remnants of an 'essence' would be fully integrated into the sociological interpretation of the human condition.

Nevertheless, Marx did demonstrate that the complexities of human consciousness did not amount to an all-embracing problem, the resolution of which would suffice as an account of wo/man and society. Rather, there is a duality and reflexivity in the relationships between individual, nature and productive circumstances.

> History does not end by being resolved into 'self-consciousness' as 'spirit of the spirit', but that in it at each stage there is found a material result: a sum of productive forces, an historically created relation of individuals to nature and to

one another, which is handed down to each generation from its predecessors; a mass of productive forces, capital funds and conditions, which, on the one hand, is indeed modified by the new generation, but also, on the other, prescribes for it its conditions of life and gives it a definite development, a special character. It shows that circumstances make men just as much as men make circumstances. (Marx and Engels [1845-6] 1970, p. 59)

Those changes in circumstances in feudal history are crucial, keeping in mind always that wo/men and circumstances remain in this dialectical relationship.

Feudalism and change

Tawney's focus on the predominance of religious ethics in economic and social belief reveals a doctrine that is incapable of being sustained.

The weakness of an attitude which met the onset of insurgent economic interests with a generalized appeal to traditional morality and an idealisation of the past was only too obvious. (1926, p. 150)

There were several changes taking place in the human mind and in material affairs to which the Church was unable to respond. Nor could it easily accommodate itself to such changes and incorporate them. The relationships of people to nature and religion were undergoing a profound shift of emphasis. As nature became more tractable, so did the means by which it was understood and exploited become more sophisticated. The rapid growth of commercial civilization threw into sharp relief the inappropriateness of an ethical system designed in accordance with an agricultural subsistence economy. Personal contact, trust based on local knowledge and shared interests, common futures and aspirations ceased to be capable of defining the norms of economic interaction. Religion did not so much lose ground as it continued to occupy a position that was increasingly irrelevant to human social needs. Into its place grew the state, which took account of the Church, but saw its own task as the resolution of the demands created by the changing economic structure. The Church was, in effect, overruled on the crucial question of usury, thus vouchsafing the development of new doctrines upon new philosophical principles.

> The assertion of economic liberty as a natural right comes at the close of a period in which, while a religious phraseology was retained and a religious interpretation of social institutions was often sincerely held, the supernatural sanction had been increasingly merged in doctrines based on reasons of state and public expediency. (ibid., p. 175)

Thus the individual emerges from 'a greater whole', in this instance from the overarching morality of the corporate Church. That it was replaced in large part by the state was nevertheless an advancement in terms of individuation, primarily because the state rested upon the use of human reason and drew its conclusions in the light of material factors rather than religious belief. Tawney went on to argue that it was the process of reorganizing the understanding of society that brought about, or at least assisted in, the creation of new institutions of fundamental importance:

> An organized money-market has many advantages. But it is not a school of social ethics or of political responsibility. Finance, being essentially impersonal, a matter of opportunities, securities and risks, acted among other causes as a solvent of the sentiment, fostered both by the teaching of the Church and the decencies of social intercourse among neighbours, which regarded keen bargaining as 'sharp practice' ... Problems of currency and credit lend themselves more readily than most economic questions to discussion in terms of mechanical causation. It was in the long debate provoked by the rise in prices and the condition of the exchanges that the psychological assumptions, which were afterwards to be treated by economists as of self-evident and universal validity, were first hammered out. (ibid., p. 177)

In other words, an organized money-market could not exist without a series of assumptions about wo/man and the objective world. In this case, wo/men made the circumstances which were to have such a profound effect on feudal economic relations and the consequent development toward capitalism. Moreover, individual wo/man was beginning to structure the environment in a more purposeful way, even if in reaction to false demands arising from the role that money had acquired. In doing so, wo/man claimed unto themself new powers and a new primacy.

The process by which natural justice, imperfectly embodied in positive law, was replaced as the source of authority by positive law which might or might not be the expression of natural justice, had its analogy in the rejection by social theory of the whole conception of an objective standard of economic equity. The law of nature had been invoked by medieval writers as a moral restraint upon economic self-interest. By the seventeenth century, a significant revolution had taken place. 'Nature' had come to connote, not divine ordinance, but human appetites, and natural rights were invoked by the individualism of the age as a reason why self-interest should be given free play. (ibid., pp. 179–80)

Clearly, individuality had by this time reached the stage where the ability to distinguish self from nature entailed the ability dramatically to redefine nature. Alienation from nature was followed by the production of an account of nature that served self-understanding and self-realization. Knowledge of nature was, conveniently, equivalent to political and social understanding. This represents an attempt to become a part of nature once again. Alternatively, it could be argued that nature was made to be a part of wo/man, albeit a nature that could now be subjected to human power. In either event, the significance of nature is humanly defined, the knowledge of nature is humanly constructed. This was not merely an expedient that could justify and formalize the impact on society of the prevailing forces of production. Wo/man was in fact changing the perception of self, partly as a result of the realization of a separate existence, and this led to the new and mechanistic laws of causation being turned to an examination of the self. As wo/man was being changed, so s/he learnt that this was so. One result was a search to define both these changes and the very substance of the self. The theory of nature which was used was directly connected to the way that individuals saw themselves. Just as Copernican astronomy 'changed Man's concentric view of himself at the centre of the universe', so, R. Morgan argues, more recent 'discoveries' recast the individual as the 'ultimate' unit in society (1982, pp. 281, 292). As Marx himself noted, wo/man was being taught to be, and expanded as, an individual in the course of establishing new relationships with nature.

The appropriation of these forces is itself nothing more than the development of the individual capacities corresponding to the material instruments of production. (Marx and Engels [1845–6] 1970, p. 92)

At this point, the development of the individual, and emergence from the tribe, the herd and the feudal socialities, begins to become complicated by new forms of dependency, new myths and interpretations concerning wo/man and society. This coincided, of course, with the accelerating decline of feudalism in the face of the changing mode of production and capitalist relations of production that were already of significance. It is as well, then, to end the discussion of pre-capitalist societies and individualism with a summary of findings.

The most important facet has been the relative absence of modern or bourgeois forms of individualism in feudal society. There are, however, two crucial qualifications that must be made. First, Marx and more recent writers convey a sense of individuality as an essential constant of humanity. The feudal age is one which is characterized by low population density, minimal cross-cultural contact, primitive social relations and an agrarian subsistence economy. On a strict reading of Marx, one would expect the immersion of the person in the greater whole would mean a low level of differentiation as 'individuals', and that such individuals would be as yet insufficiently developed and therefore unable to change themselves and their natural and social environment to any great degree. The individuation of man, in so far as it occurred, constitutes for Bloch a reaffirmation of past development and a 'natural' display of wo/man's true nature. While this is not a vital revision of Marx's thought, it nevertheless prompts a closer look at the historical development of the individual that Marx presented, in order to ascertain the points at which he ascribed to a social system qualities that should more accurately be attached to the conception of fundamental human nature.

Second, the re-emergence of the individual in feudal society is based on particular changes, in terms of consciousness, comprehension and mastery of nature, and the structure of religious belief with which the world was organized and made sensible. Thus the breakdown of primitive communism, and the loss of its affiliations and solidarities, is compensated for by an alteration in the conscious ordering of the universe, bringing about changes in the nature and role of the individual within that universe, and, ultimately, creating the possibility for change under human social control.

Thus feudal society prefigured the possibilities for individual existence in the social organization which was to succeed it. There was a steady, if unspectacular, increase in the capacities and abilities of human individuals, and the generation of fresh or altered human needs. At the same time, this created the potential for greater control over the forces of nature and society that always confront the individual. In the next section, these developments will be seen as preparation for the capitalist mode of production, and attention will be focused on the particular ways in which feudal individuality expresses itself and prepares the way for capitalist individuality.

The feudal individual

In relating the structures of the feudal and capitalist economies, Marx left open the nature of the connections between the two types of society. This suggests that the economic structures, while being of great importance, are by no means the sole consideration in respect of historical change. This is to argue, along with Gandy, that 'for Marx world history is a process of individualisation' (1979, pp. 30–5).[3]

Labour is the key to living human individuals. The concrete activity of such individuals is central to the argument concerning the content and meaning of the term 'human nature' and leads directly to the productive sphere within which that labour takes place and takes shape (Geras, 1983). As Marx described it:

> Labour is, first of all, a process between men and nature, a process by which man, through his own actions, mediates, regulates and controls the metabolism between himself and nature. He confronts the materials of nature as a force of nature. He sets in motion the natural forces which belong to his own body ... Through this movement he acts upon external nature and changes it, and in this way he simultaneously changes his own nature. He develops the potentialities slumbering within nature, and subjects the play of its forces to his own sovereign power. ([1867] 1976, p. 283)

This complex interrelationship between humans, nature, the productive process and their associated forces does exhibit a specific character under feudalism. Here two aspects are to be observed. First, feudal relations are themselves linked developmentally with earlier but less refined stages, and second, the feudal stage is the most advanced form of the pre-capitalist productive modes. Marx's pronouncements on feudalism point to only a few of the conditioning elements that characterize the mode of production, the basis of which was formed by 'peasant agriculture on a small scale and production by independent artisans' (ibid., pp. 452–3). In individual and social terms, production at this level and on such a small and personal scale resulted in a society which reflected the intimacy of the productive process, the adjacency of humans and nature, and the primacy of the individual's own labour powers, as 'proprietor of the instrument', as Marx's notes indicate.

> Here labour itself still half artistic, half end–in–itself etc. Mastery. Capitalist himself still master-journeyman. Attainment of particular skill in the work also secures possession of instrument etc. etc. Inheritability then to a certain extent of the mode of work together with the organisation of work and the instrument of work. Medieval cities. Labour still as his own; definite self-sufficient development of one-sided abilities etc. ([1857–8] 1973, p. 497)

Thus, while 'serfdom is a defining characteristic of feudalism', these 'relations of personal dependence' are more than a description of the objective conditions of exploitation of vassal by lord (Gandy, 1979, p. 31). They constitute, at the same time, the expression of the developmental stage, the application of abilities and capacities. That is to say, the feudal individuals operated to the extent of their abilities, and even developed their capacities, but always within the circumscribing realm of feudal relations of production. As Marx stated with reference to communism, labour is a liberating activity in so far as obstacles are overcome ([1857–8] 1973, p. 611). This holds true for any mode of production, and means for the feudal individual a particular development of those abilities that relate to self-sufficiency. The experience of labour in feudalism has, therefore, a dual character, leading to the privatization of the individual even as the community remains a static and limiting reality. This, then, is the medieval Europe that Marx had in mind.

> No matter, then, what we may think of the parts played by the different classes of people themselves in society, the social relations between individuals in the performance of their labour appear at all events as their own mutual personal relations, and are not disguised under the shape of social relations between the products of labour. ([1867] 1976, p. 170)

This image of intimacy and relatedness is interesting in so far as it gives an insight into what Marx regarded as the positive aspects of the feudal mode of production. Specifically, the equivalence of appearance and reality with regard to labour and its product, albeit at such a 'medieval level', is to be praised even if the relations of production are exploitative. In this respect, feudal society achieved that which bourgeois society could not, and would be realized in its highest form only under communism.

Part of the reason for the particularity of labour and the associated social relations concerns the degree to which humans had attempted successfully to master nature. At the feudal stage, nature still dominated wo/man because the productive powers of labour had not yet proceeded to the point at which the dominion over land could seriously be threatened by the harnessing of real forces of nature. The gains over nature were limited, such that individual labour was still most likely to secure 'the instrument of work', fortifying the individual social position but not altogether altering it, exercising capacities but extending them only partially.

Marx augmented this idea with an interpretation that stems directly from the economic analysis of capitalism. When the exchange of these products of labour is considered, it is not the market system as the vehicle that is important, but the power of the *medium* of exchange that matters. The medium of exchange is important because it indicates the level of abstractness that characterized the social relationships between members of society.

> The less social power the medium of exchange possesses (and at this stage it is still closely bound to the nature of the direct product and the direct needs of the partners in exchange) the greater must be the power of the community which binds the individuals together, the patriarchal relations, the community of antiquity, feudalism and the guild system. (Marx, [1857–8] 1973, p. 157)

With the relative lack of power of the medium of exchange, then, feudalism constituted a crucial stage between more primitive forms of community and its nemesis, capitalism. The individual, although personally dependent, has 'internal relations that are concretely particular', in such a way as to permit 'definite self-sufficient development of one-sided abilities'. In other words, this kind of development meant that feudal individuals became cognitively more complex in the way that they responded to the material world. This created one of the conditions which led ultimately to the overthrow of the feudal mode of production (Gould, 1978, p. 4).

Such a coexistence of community and individuality prompts comparisons between feudalism and its economic and social successor, which did not escape Marx's attention. Although he did not commit the folly of suggesting that some aspects of feudalism were somehow superior, he recognized that these images of wo/man in previous stages might make it appear that feudalism was more advanced than its successor.

> In earlier stages of development the single individual seems to be developed more fully, because he has not yet worked out his relationships in their fullness, or erected them as independent social powers and relations opposite himself. ([1857–8] 1973, p. 162)

It is at this point that Marx appears to go beyond an historical examination of the development of individuality and begins to prescribe, in specific detail, the requirements for the proper developmental progression. At the very least, Marx was prepared to insist that it was the individual's responsibility and task to comprehend the true nature of relationships and reconstruct a personal version of social reality. But feudal society reflected only a partial development of the person as an individual, who

> directly and naturally reproduces himself, or in which his productive activity and his share in production are bound to a specific form of labour and product, which determine his relations to others in just that specific way. ([1857–8] 1973, p. 157)

The limitation of feudal society resides in the impossibility of achieving sufficiently radical change to will and consciousness. It was not just that human productive powers were quite over-shadowed by the forces of nature which resulted in a reliance on ownership of land for the material wealth of the society and the serfdom that this implied. Mastery over some of the physical laws of the universe was certainly to be crucial in the rapid and dramatic bourgeois revolution of manufactures, but important too was an habitual social practice which endorsed and reflected the dominance of nature over human existence. This was constricting in its manner and narrow in its scope. Geographical confinement was also a social confinement, and the common view of economic subsistence meant a lack of any broader human perspective was characteristic of social relations. Parochial problems were thought to be common to all, and, probably, of most importance. Nature dominated social relations to the extent that the feudal individual felt that relations were not social – i.e. artificial – but were natural, and therefore immutable and uncontrollable.

As Michael Evans points out, these constitute crucial charac-teristics of any pre-capitalist society: 'social life is dominated by external nature, and men in society are subjected to traditional social relations, which they regard as natural' (1975, p. 59). It must be noted that Evans sees these two facets as *related*, and both soluble under the effects of 'trade, division of labour and exchange' (ibid.). However, he does not explain that relation or the nature of the interconnections. On one level, it can be accepted that social relations were intertwined with the reality of a dominant nature, since the products of labour had immediate use of subsistence value. However, to argue that feudal individuals are not alienated from their products cannot be an explanation, especially since, for Marx, 'every serf knows that what he expends in the service of his lord is a specific quantity of his own personal labour-power' ([1867] 1976, p. 170).[4] It is that, in feudal society, wo/man is subjected to 'traditional social relations' as much as the organization of production. Viewed in this manner, it is possible to construct a response to Evans' criticism that 'Marx never sketched the internal contradictions of feudalism as a mode of production. He talks rather of the disintegrative effects of urban developments on agrarian feudalism, but gives no reasons why it should be so soluble' (Evans, 1975, p. 77).

First, it is possible that those internal contradictions are so glaring that they can be missed by the modern eye. The domination by nature of human endeavour had, for feudalism to persist, to continue at very primitive levels indefinitely. Given Marx's belief in the nature of human capacity and need, and the tendency for new needs to be developed with the satisfaction of existing needs, the possibility of a static mode of production continuing is ruled out. It is not conceivable that feudalism fully utilized the potential of humankind, even if the feudal individual is taken to be at a much lower developmental stage than that evinced by capitalism. The capacity of humans, whenever it is under-utilized or suppressed, is a contradictory or antagonistic force within any mode of production predicated on landed wealth in particular and restrictions on change in general. Any mode of production which attempted to control human abilities for the purposes of exploitation was fundamentally flawed and was the clearest indication possible of an internal contradiction, and one which, over time, could be held at bay only by the use of force. Force, however, could be effectively wielded only in the close relationships that serfdom offered, with a reliance on vassalage ultimately working against the lords' wish to maintain their influence or extend it. As F. J. West points out:

the desire for more property, for more benefices or fiefs, led men into becoming vassals for a number of lords. Whereas the original bond between lord and man was unique, its association with land led to the lord-vassal ties being duplicated or multiplied, and this multiplication of personal arrangements weakened any single one of them by the conflicting duties and obligations it set up. (West, 1975, p. 56)

In one respect, this pattern is consistent with the kinds of results one would expect from Marx's method. In economic terms, the need to find new ways of maintaining income levels amounts to a material indication that the feudal system could not survive without changes occurring. But the kinds of change that were both necessary and possible could result only in the destruction of that mode of production. On the other hand, the overriding antagonism Marx wished to stress between the bourgeoisie and the ruling feudal relations of production is seriously undermined, since it was the bourgeoisie who, as revolutionaries promoting the new mode of production, were thought to be the principal agents for change. The underlying implication is that it was from within feudalism, after all, that the changes which meant its ultimate destruction, but which were also to create ideal conditions for the unleashing of the massive productive power of the rising bourgeoisie, actually originated.

This interpretation is not entirely surprising, given Marx's account of the destruction of capitalism via the growth of consciousness and power of the proletariat. It is part of his general theory of change that class society or pre-human history is based on the working out of a set of factors that are fixed until, presumably, the dissolution of capitalism in favour of communism. It means, too, that the feudal individual has a particular character. The stolidity of feudal relations does not rule out the generation of an increasing flexibility and openness to change in feudal individual existence.

All previous forms of society – or, what is the same, of the forces of production – foundered on the development of wealth ... The feudal system, for its part, foundered on urban industry, trade, modern agriculture ... With the development of wealth – and hence also new powers and expanded intercourse on the part of individuals – the economic conditions on which the community rested were dissolved, along with the political relations of the various constituents of the community which corresponded to those conditions: religion ... the character, outlook etc of the individuals. (Marx, [1857–8] 1973, p. 540)

Marx made a direct connection between the development of wealth and the development of individuality. Development in general is comprised of a network of influences, forces and capacities, and it is the notion of 'wealth' that best displays the reciprocity involved. That is to say, wealth is not strictly an economic notion. Wealth incorporates the product of the developments that have taken place both within the mode of production and with respect to humankind as producer and social animal. The feudal mode of production called for the exercise of only a limited portion of individuals' abilities. As such, requisite human needs were fulfilled at a low level, where subsistence rather than creativity dominated. The result of such meagre demands upon human ability meant also that human potential was extended minimally, leading to only a gradual development of the forces of production through the search for new avenues for the accumulation of wealth. Thus wealth, too, is a transhistorical concept, especially when it is applied to human nature as it is exhibited in all forms of society. Marx could imagine no other explanation:

> what is wealth, if not the universality of needs, capacities, enjoyments, productive powers etc, of individuals, produced in universal exchange? What, if not the full development of human control over the forces of nature – those of his own nature as well as those of so-called 'nature'? What, if not the absolute elaboration of his creative dispositions, without any preconditions other than antecedent historical evolution which makes the totality of this evolution – ie the evolution of all human powers as such, unmeasured by any *previously established* yardstick – an end in itself? What is this, if not a situation where man does not reproduce himself in any determined form, but produces his totality? Where he does not seek to remain something formed by the past, but is in the absolute movement of becoming? ([1857–8] 1973, p. 97)

The importance of this passage should not be minimized. By emphasizing the broad significance of the term wealth, in its application to both capital accumulation and developing human capacities, Marx reiterated that the underlying theme of the movement of history concerned humans as individuals, such that the 'absolute movement of becoming' presupposes an historical notion of individuality.

That notion of individuality is not the outcome of pure speculation. It emerged, as this chapter seeks to demonstrate with specific regard to pre-capitalist modes of production, out of his analysis of the social forms associated with various modes of production. One such example is found in consideration of the mechanisms behind economic and social change. It will be recalled, first, that satisfaction of human needs inevitably produces new needs, which themselves prompt greater productive effort, and so on. Second, Marx identified the point at which the production of new needs no longer necessitated determination by the economy. Third, Marx consistently argued that it was the developing forces of production that brought about changes in the mode of production. It is the relation between the forces of production and the progress of humanity that Marx does not always keep separate, as his view of production modes demonstrates:

> The evolution of the forces of production dissolves them, and their dissolution is itself an evolution of the human forces of production. Labour is initially undertaken on a certain basis – first primitive – then historical. Later, this basis or presupposition is itself cancelled, or tends to disappear, having become too narrow for the development of the progressive human horde. (ibid.)

The pre-eminent role of the forces of production clearly incorporates an economic function within an economic substratum of society. And yet, there is also the suggestion that labour is at base an expression of human needs and capacities, not a mechanistic response springing entirely from the nature of material necessity. Moreover, even when labour takes on a more advanced and historically important form, Marx insisted that such a development is but one stage in a larger schema. That is, 'the development of the progressive human horde' is seen as the underlying reality which sets in motion the forces of production as the instigators and destroyers of various modes of production.

> In all these forces the basis of evolution is the *reproduction* of relations between individual and community *assumed as given* ... and a *definite, predetermined objective existence*, both as regards the relation to the conditions of labour and the relation between one man and his co-workers, fellow tribesmen, etc. Such evolution is therefore from the outset *limited*, but once the limits are transcended, decay and disintegration ensue. (ibid., pp. 83–4)

The fundamental human activity, therefore, is this reproduction of individual and community. This is a most revealing assumption. It establishes that such an enterprise must be a transhistorical one and indicates the dialectical nature of the mode of production. Given that all human social existence involves the reproduction of social relations, it is possible and certainly necessary to consider the 'objective existence' that serves to define the limits of that reproduction. Thus the mode of production is an account of the concrete possibilities for the display of human capacities. In other words, the material base of society, which is also the environment that allows for forces of production to be exhibited and extended, does not of itself produce the kinds of change in wo/man that Marx would wish to describe as progressive, at least in any absolute sense. A consequence of the existence of such an arena for the exercise of human productive powers – an arena which cannot advance those powers or satisfy new needs – must be the eventual disappearance of that mode of production. This does not necessarily mean that significant change does not occur within any and all stages. As Marx went on to say:

> Considerable developments are thus possible within a given sphere. Individuals may appear to be great. But free and full development of individual or society is inconceivable here, for such evolution stands in contradiction to the original relationship. (ibid.)

It should be noted that this statement supports the distinction between individuality as a transhistorical abstraction and particular historical expressions of individuality. As Marx looked back at pre-capitalist societies, then, he identified specific *forms* of individuality within their limiting historical context and regarded them as evidence. There was on the one hand evidence about the nature of individuality under a given mode of production: feudalism was characterized by a greater control over society, nature, and therefore the individual and social self, compared to earlier societies. On the other hand, there was evidence relating to the historical development of individuality and its connection to the nature of change in society. For example, the 'herd animal' is made superfluous and dissolved, and a more complex being is created, one who is capable of dealing with reality as an abstraction (ibid., p. 96). The implication is that a definite form of the individual exists in a manner pertaining to every period of history. As such, the feudal individual displays aspects of development that are of a general or transhistorical nature, alongside those aspects which relate solely to the limited mode of production designated as feudal society.

The community itself appears as the first great force of production; particular kinds of production conditions (eg stock-
breeding, agriculture), develop particular modes of production
and particular forces of production, subjective, appearing as
qualities of individuals, as well as objective [ones]. (ibid.,
p. 495)

Thus it is also the relations between individuals as members of
the community which can serve as a creative force, bringing about
changes in the mode of production. This is not a reduction to what
method is used for production (hunter-gathering, agriculture) but
how individuals associate. It is only after individuals become social
that the mode of production can begin to bring about a corresponding social change. As far as Marx was concerned, feudalism
sprang from no immanent historical process, but emerged out of
the transition from more primitive modes of production, or ones
which were based on slavery. It is characteristically European,
then, that the feudal system emerged and developed in the way
that it did. And as Hobsbawm notes, feudal development starts on
a much more extensive territory and one prepared by the Roman
conquests and the spread of agriculture concerned with these (1964,
p. 28). In practical terms, the combination of a widespread if not
very developed agriculture and a sparse population results in the
countryside being 'the locus of history' (Marx, 1964, p. 78). Specifically, this statement allows Marx to enunciate the *necessary* relation
of the individual to the material conditions of existence. He established, first, that for any given society in any historical setting,
it is the *reproduction of the individual* that is of prime significance.
Such individuals, it might be added, cannot be abstract, ahistorical
beings, but must be part of the chain of evolution and history in as
much as they can be conceived only within the context of a given
society. The feudal individual is a characterization of a concrete
existence, as well as an analytical construct to reveal the social and
historical forces intrinsic to human development.

The crucial point here is this: in all these forms, where landed
property and agriculture form the basis of the economic order
and consequently the economic object is the production of use
values, ie, the *reproduction of the individual* in certain definite
relationships to his community, of which it forms the basis,
we find the following elements:
(1) Appropriation of the natural condition of labour ... The
chief objective condition of labour itself appears not as the
product, but occurs as *nature*. On the one hand we have the living

individual, on the other the earth, as the objective condition of his reproduction.

(2)   The attitude to the land, to the earth as the property of the working individual ... What immediately mediates this attitude is the more or less naturally evolved, more or less historically evolved and modified existence of the individual as *a member of a community* – his primitive existence as part of a tribe, etc. (ibid., pp. 80–1)

Marx argued that, in particular, the twin characteristics of agriculture and landed property in the feudal mode of production led to, and were supported by, specific human and social responses. The first of these elements, concerning the objective conditions of labour, encompasses a complex set of implications. Here Marx touched upon more than the economic determinants of existence, making feudal wo/man's comprehension of nature of crucial importance. The *apparent* significance of nature to the individual is not matched by a deep understanding of that nature – a lack of comprehension which is not entirely due to the defining role of the mode of production. That is to say, mastery over nature is a developed and developing human characteristic. This development occurs within an historical epoch, but survives beyond that stage of history. It is not therefore subject to construction in conformity with a particular mode of production. This means that, while feudalism required the assumption that nature was the wellspring of human productive capacity, it was beyond the capacity of humanity to consider itself *and* nature in any other fashion. Such a realization was dependent upon further development, which could take place only under a more sophisticated mode of production.

Summary

Marx's grouping of assumptions about wo/man, society, productive forces and history enabled him to avoid ahistorical and merely positivistic accounts of human development. In the case of the feudal mode of production, the changes in the causal relationships between individuals, nature, productive activity and other similarly individualized humans have been highlighted. It was demonstrated that there was an absence of what is conventionally recognized as individualism in pre-capitalist modes of production, either as an ideology or in terms of autonomous and atomized beings. Nevertheless, the conditions for such individualization are to be found in those earlier societies. In the process, no idealist essence of human nature was called forth to identify and define the nature and basis of '*objective dependence*', nor was the 'personal independence' of the individual in modern society offered without reference to the preceding feudal phase, a life-process instrumental in producing earlier flowering of human capacities. As Marx stated:

> As soon as this active life-process is described, history ceases to be a collection of dead facts as it is with the empiricists (themselves still abstract), or an imagined activity of imagined subjects, as with the idealists. Where speculation ends – in real life – there real, positive science begins: the representation of the practical activity, of the practical process of the development of men. ([1845–6] 1970, pp. 47–8)

Although Marx's major consideration may have been the analysis and description of capitalist or bourgeois society,[5] of almost equal importance was this concomitant development and application of a dialectical and materialist conception of history with which to comprehend human existence in the widest sense. In respect of the analysis of labour, the decisive increase in the powers of individuals in society and the changes in their needs amounted to a new and developing force for social change. The historical movement of economic structures, therefore, has its counterpart in the historical development of individuality.

The individual of feudalism shows that development has taken place and that it did become possible for an individual to sever communal bonds and become an atomized being under the emerging mode of production. So with the passing of feudalism, the passing of the feudal individual, 'the *objective individual*' who relates to a given mode of production in a given community comes about (Marx, [1857–8] 1973, p. 495). However, that objective feudal individual – narrow, insular, attached to community by geography much more than affinity, and relatively overawed by nature – does not disappear, but is *dissolved* in the creation of another form of objective individual, this time under the capitalist mode of production. It is the possibilities for individuality under capitalism which are examined in the following chapter.

Notes

1 This approach is to be distinguished from an utopian vision of the future, for which fixed assumptions concerning human nature are essential; see Goodwin, 1978, p. 47.

2   The most telling deficiencies in this account are the same for Marx and Rousseau. Both accounts see as 'natural' the division of labour between women and men, when such a division can only be social. The existence of the (patriarchal) family, marriage and clans presupposes a series of social and economic relations that make Marx's claim to have stopped at the *original* conditions of production quite inadequate. See Coole, 1988; and O'Brien, 1983.

3   It is interesting to note that Gandy's examination of the entire *Marx–Engels Werke* reveals only a sketchy account of the feudal mode of production, and there seems even less to say with respect to the kind of society within which that stage of individualization might have realized itself. The account of 'the feudal mode' suffers from a lack of definition, either temporally or specifically. Thus we are told that 'for Marx and Engels serfdom is a defining characteristic of feudalism', but any real explanation of such a relationship is suspended until Gandy, 1979, pp. 37–8, discusses the *breakdown* of feudalism. Although he stresses that feudalism was regarded as 'neither a network of cultural institutions nor a special political system', the vital dimension of feudalism as a 'social formation' is entirely ignored, ibid., p. 150.

4   As McBride, 1977, p. 111, observes, 'the economic relations and categories of those times were considerably more evident to the members of society than they are in a capitalist structure'.

5   As Evans, 1975, p. 59, points out, 'in both the *Grundrisse* and *Capital*, Marx's basic concern is with the nature of modern bourgeois society. In the former, the history is largely illustrative, and resorted to in order to clarify the differences between the capitalist order and the pre-capitalist ones, and where a general view is attempted, it remains a sketch. In *Capital* the account of the formation process is greatly expanded, but it remains secondary to the main theme: the structural features of the capitalist mode of production.'

4 *Individuality in capitalist society*

The change from feudal to capitalist society is an historical achievement of great moment for Marx. Technically, an enormous increase in productive power occurs. Socially, the possibility for human freedom is at last within reach. Historically, he saw a strong probability of its realization. And politically, it establishes to his satisfaction that class conflict is the medium of social change. The transition from feudalism throws into sharp relief the differences in requirements, at an *individual* level, of capitalism. It transpires that, for Marx, capitalism develops the individual as never before, beyond the narrowness, insularity and superstition that characterized feudal society, and prepares the historical ground for the highest possible expression of individuality.

It is necessary to probe the extent to which capitalist society actually was progressive and revolutionary in these respects, since the conventional view generally emphasizes only Marx's piercing critique of the injustice, exploitation and alienation of that social formation. That conventional critique dismisses the significance of the capitalist individual; a more open account of such individuals is crucial to a better understanding of Marx's thought. This chapter will show that Marx provided a view of capitalist individuality with contrasting features. On the one hand, the development of the individual is a preparation for the true individuality of communism, but on the other such development is confronted by the inadequacy of capitalist social and productive relations. The apparent contradiction between the development and degradation of individuality within one mode of production is thus a major concern. Even a partial or unsatisfactory form of individuality can either exhibit progression from a more limited form or be a prerequisite for further change.

In fact, there are a number of images of capitalist existence to be found in Marx's works, and these images can be placed within the context of the distinction between the conception and notions of human nature so far observed in his thought. The approach to the question of human nature is predicated on the location of Marx's position historically and methodologically: that is, from the viewpoint of capitalist society, and with the intention of seeing that society transmutated into a superior form, namely, communism. Thus Marx's thought is composed of: a critique of society, containing the negative images of individuality; a vision of a future society, or society as it might be, with alternative images of individuality that are preferable (on a variety of grounds[1]) to existing expressions of social existence; and a theory of change, wherein the images of individuality are presented in such a way as to mediate, theoretically and practically, the transition from negative to positive expressions of individuality. These three perspectives within which Marx might have made his statements concerning individual social existence under capitalism indicate a pattern of human development arising out of contradictory social elements. The method of assessing these statements, and the forms of individuality under capitalism, must therefore be a dialectical one. That is, one form of individuality gives rise to another, both within a particular form of social organization, and from one society to the next.

This suggests an additional way of organizing Marx's statements. The focus on the development of individuality across the historical epochs outlined by Marx provides an enhanced perspective of our understanding of individual life in bourgeois society and a key to understanding the future. The progress of capitalist society itself can be treated in the same manner. In other words, the history of all societies will be repeated or reflected in the history of capitalist society. This can be inferred from Marx's claims: (1) that the study of bourgeois society gives rise to an understanding of previous social forms; (2) that he had unearthed the general laws of motion of history; and (3) that he saw history as the history of class conflict through successive epochs and stages. That is, Marx's critique will reflect these propositions, and capitalism can be considered in a dialectical movement from a thrusting, early capitalism, through a middle or reactionary stage, to a late or pre-transitional phase.

The implications for a consideration of the expression and realizations of human nature are important here. As an historical epoch, capitalism relates to fundamental human nature in a dual fashion. Capitalism is both consistent with fundamental human nature *and* brings about changes, by developing new capacities and needs. Second, capitalist human nature, human nature as it is expressed under specific social conditions, will be quite different from its immediately preceding form, feudal human nature. Third, capitalist human nature will not be a constant form, but will change as the society on which it is based develops and changes. This chapter, then, charts the progress of the superseded feudal individuality through the quite dramatic changes, internal to capitalism, that have to occur if the Marxian communist society is to be created, build up its radically different forms of social relations and survive.[2]

The transition from feudalism to capitalism

Feudal development was slow and measured. Gradually, changes to society arose, and the impact of those changes spread outwards in society and inwards in individuals. The forces of production, by contrast with capitalism, were developed in a painstaking fashion, and nature retained the ascendancy in the struggle to produce material existence. Although the accompanying bourgeois revolutions which swept Europe were not all swift and dramatic, they were in Holland, England and France, and it is there that the kinds of changes for and to individuals can be seen most clearly. As Gandy argues:

> These revolutions were great social earthquakes. Centuries of subterranean changes had gradually run fault lines through the economic foundations of feudalism: revolutionary convulsions tore away old political forms; and feudalism waned before rising capitalism. The classic bourgeois revolutions were nodal points in world history, transitions to a new age. (Gandy, 1979, p. 41)

And this new age heralded the quite sudden overwhelming of nature, as the forces of production reached the point where they broke through the long-standing barriers to the improvement, on a mass scale, of material existence. Having wrested control from nature, human life and society were irrevocably altered; human existence was delimited and broadened as never before. This called forth and brought about changes in the people who were both subjects and objects of that development.

Taking classic bourgeois revolutions as the model, it might be concluded that the changes in the demands made on the basic potentialities of Marx's conception of human nature would produce a notion of capitalist nature of a radically different kind – that there would be a direct and relatively uncomplicated displacement of feudal individuality by a capitalist variant. Indeed, this is much the substance of E. P. Thompson's argument in both *The Making of the English Working Class* (1968) and 'Time, work-discipline and industrial capitalism' (1967).[3] But the focus on the classical models can create the illusion that human nature is unproblematically mutable. It is as well, then, to recall that it is not only the broad and general characteristics, but specific issues also, that are important, and take full account of Marx's reminder that 'epochs in the history of society are no more separated from each other by strict and abstract lines of demarcation than are geological epochs' ([1867] 1976, p. 492). As Hassan has pointed out; 'history is a palimpsest, and culture is permeable to time past, time present, and time future' (1985, p. 121). It is no wonder, then, that the transition from feudalism to capitalism was not just slow, but often partial and contradictory. The political and social changes entailed in the transition, taken as a whole, may be said to reflect the development of the productive forces and validate the claim that, at base, capitalism supplanted feudalism in clear economic determinist fashion. On the other hand, the detail of the transition suggests that there were other kinds of change necessary. Part of the explanation for the kinds of changes that occurred, and the way that the transition had a variety of levels and areas of success, lies in the nature of the peoples that were concerned.

This is not to undermine or sidestep Marx's method. On the contrary, it endorses it to the extent that changes in human individuality had already to be occurring within the feudal social order if capitalism was ever to challenge the supremacy of feudalism. Moreover, the longevity of the feudal social formation meant that its associated human nature was very well established, not just reflecting the conditions of the mode of production, but permeating very deeply every element of the society, especially the customs, traditions, language and everyday habits and expectations. Relatively, capitalism is a young and fresh culture in those areas where it can be called new, and not simply a transmission or reorientation of past cultures. Thus, at one level it is *against* human nature (in feudal form). Despite Marx's focus on the minutiae of the development of the productive forces and the differentiations he makes between their impact, his account of the transition lacks any equivalent consideration of the ways in which the development of individuality in feudalism would act as both a restraining and facilitating influence on the speed at and directions in which change would occur. Gouldner makes much the same point: for Marx, the focus is first on the economic and then on the political as a sphere

101

shaped by the former: while the social and indeed, civil society itself thus slips away, remaining an undeveloped, residual concept (1980, p. 357).

It is not suggested that an understanding of the 'social' is not to be found within Marx's thought. However, it is necessary to pick up the threads of this 'undeveloped, residual concept', in order to provide a balance to his presentation, especially since his account of transition processes is so vital to the very meaning of his enterprise – the emancipation of humankind by means of a radical restructuring of the economic and social order.

This means that the change from feudalism to capitalism was by no means merely an economic phenomenon which had specific social ramifications. The forces of production were not the only forces that were contributing to the transformation of society, nor were those forces of production free of influences on the way that they operated and affected the social order. Although the transition was a time of considerable change with respect to the expression of human nature, it is important to consider the extent to which the feudal form of individuality, and the particular characteristics of social relations under feudalism, would have an impact on social and individual development.

Feudal relations were local in their scope and influence, and vulnerable to the way that emergent capitalist relations cut through and across such intimate relations. However, such dislocation was not simple and quickly achieved, and meant a loss of valued forms of social relations. Other, uncapitalist, features of the production process carried within them a much closer contact with each element of the production process. The greater intimacy of production and consumption, conceivable only under conditions of a small market and a narrow range of products that served demands of basic kinds, meant a close equation of labour and exchange value, involved a high proportion of socially produced goods and implied a direct relation between producer and product. Pre-capitalist production means an absence of certain kinds of alienation or estrangement associated with production for money. Specifically it meant a greater control over decision-making, especially for women, with little separation between production and consumption decisions.

In many ways, this account has similarities with the image of everyday life under communism to be seen in Chapter 5. Implicitly, Marx valued the intimacy of feudal relations, if not the associated form of social organization. But in focusing on the feudal mode of production as it gave way to capitalism, Marx ignored the effect that particular relationships had on the transition.

The interweaving of new and old took many forms, sometimes bringing about compromise between the bourgeoisie and the parts of the old nobility, at others shaping and then reshaping political structures as the bourgeois revolution waxed and waned. Whether the bourgeois revolution was, in this or that country, regarded as a gradual achievement, as in England, or was brought about quite suddenly, as in France, the transition to capitalism was nevertheless a very long process. As Gandy claims:

> In Europe as a whole the transition from feudalism to capitalism spanned centuries of historical evolution. Engels sees this as a single gigantic process: from the twelfth to the nineteenth century the revolution rose in wave after wave, each stronger than the last, until it flowed over the walls of feudal society. (1979, p. 43)

Notwithstanding the image of the wave cataclysmically overwhelming feudalism, it is the concept of historical evolution that is important here. The wave changes its constitution each time. It can finally engulf feudalism because it has taken into itself and away from feudalism the social forms and practices that once were part of the reproductive elements of that society. Feudalism, then, is in the end not so much a fortress as an empty shell, hollowed out by the twin developments of the relations of production and of individuality.

Such individuality is associated with broadened social relations and the development of rationality, contrary to the superstitious emotionality of feudalism. These things give the individual in the transition to capitalism greater autonomy. The weakening of the feudal social definitions, based on the lack of mastery over nature and the subjugation of the individual to supernatural authority via the Church, meant that the individual effectively had a greater understanding of the world, and that understanding made greater control over action possible.

In other words, developing rationality and emotionality meant that *agency* could take new and more potent forms. In the transition to capitalism Marx's evolutionary view of human development thus far emerges – 'the forming of the five senses is a labour of the entire history of the world down to the present' (O'Neill, 1973, p. 108) – and forms a part of the explanation for change in society. Under capitalism, the development of humanity undergoes significant advancement. The powers and potentialities of individuals begin to be freed from the realms of mystical explanation or sheer ignorance. The antagonism with nature within feudal existence, arising from the alienation from nature, and the subjugation of the forces of production to that nature, begins to be resolved with capitalism. Humans realize that they can control, however imperfectly, themselves and their environment. As Carver notes: 'we know incontrovertibly that Marx accepted such a concept of agency from his voluminous "political" writings where individual agency and indeterminacy are all too manifest' (1987, p. 7; Marx, [1852] 1973, pp. 143–249). Marx believed that social change could produce altogether new social forms, forms that dispensed for ever with society based on exploitation of human by human, and even of nature by humans.

History, nature and early capitalism

Of course, Marx is no apologist of capitalism, which makes even more interesting those parts of his work where he praises, most fulsomely, the development of this new yet highly exploitative society. The focus here is on *early* capitalism. Marx by no means confused his understanding of what was progressive in terms of the history of humanity, and repressive in terms of living individuals under specific circumstances. Given his dialectical approach to human nature and social reality, his attitude to early capitalism is particularly illuminating. He reveals in practice the distinction between the conception of human nature (as a universal abstraction) and the notion of human nature (relating to definite economic and social conditions). This suggests that there is a history of human nature in Marx's thought. Such a history relates to the way that fundamental human nature has been associated with a series of social formations and has given those forms particular shape and direction.

At the same time, there is another history of human nature to be found. The perspective of this history stems from the way in which human nature can be and has been expressed in a series of social formations. It concerns what people were actually like in specific circumstances. The two histories of human nature, although distinguishable in this way, are interconnected. Marx's view of historical development presupposes that change brought about at the level of social organization will ultimately produce change in our basic human nature and so will change the possibilities and create the conditions for new social forms. Consequently, Marx recognizes and applauds the revolutionary and civilizing aspects of capitalism, in its formative and dynamic stage, even in the *Communist Manifesto*, the most polemical and politicized rendering of his theoretical rejection of capitalist society. The bourgeoisie, for example, the exploiter and the enemy of the proletariat, is presented as having played 'a most important part' in his version of history ([1847] 1968, p. 37). Capitalists, in this stage, are clearly to be admired, because they are progressive, express human qualities of creativity and drive and, in the process, amplify those powers.

The success of this kind of human activity in conjunction with the developing forces of production is to be understood in a number of ways. First, there was the delimiting or cathartic effect on society. As Marx pointed out, there was 'an end to all feudal, patriarchal, idyllic relations', with significant results:

> All fixed, fast-frozen relations, with their train of ancient and venerable prejudices and opinions are swept away, all new-formed ones become antiquated before they can ossify. All that is solid melts into air, all that is holy is profaned, and man is at last compelled to face with sober senses, his real conditions of life, and his relations with his kind. (ibid.)

This view of the individual has a central importance in Marx's thought, for two reasons. In the first place, it highlights the emancipatory aspect of a conception of human nature that is not predesignated and fixed. On this basis, notions of human nature, specific expressions of individuality, convey the extent of the flexibility of expression of human nature under differing conditions. Humans are invested with the ability to break down or through the conditions of their existence and establish a new comprehension of themselves in a world of their making. Second, Marx was making another claim about the nature of capitalist society – that it was producing very favourable conditions under which individuals were freed from mystifications about themselves which served to maintain a system of exploitation. Apart from flexibility, then, human nature is, under given circumstances, composed not just of abilities and needs, but *powers*.[4] Taken together, these factors demonstrate Marx's reasons for enthusiasm for the capitalist mode of production. If there are revolutionary and progressive elements in capitalism, then his major statements concerning the transition to socialism have an historical precedent. There clearly *is* a precedent for positing another very radical transformation of society.

The second effect of the capitalist or bourgeois revolution on society was in the way that the restructuring resolved, for Marx at least, feudalism's quite varied mix of productive relations. With the sweeping away of the 'motley feudal ties', the classes and all their gradations were simplified, the system of industry and commerce was transformed into a semblance of a 'rational' order, the modern state replaced the various kinds of political institutions, and the social relations between individuals, as well as the material relations between individuals and nature, were irrevocably altered ([1847] 1968, p. 40). This simplification of classes is more than a mere identification of a sociohistorical phenomenon. On this claim rests the organization of Marx's critical social theory. The reduction of the antagonistic forces to those of capital and labour, bourgeoisie and proletariat, is crucial for both the critique of society and the theory of change. These categories are not simply opposites. Labour and the proletariat represent both the negation and transcendence of capital and bourgeoisie, the summation of history and the potentiality of the future. Given the significance of these claims, the complexity of Marx's description of the emergence of these forms warrants further attention.

First, the connection between feudalism and capitalism indicates that there are certain aspects of human social organization that Marx believed to be constant, at least within the transition from one mode of production to another. History, therefore, was not merely the 'activity of man pursuing his aims', where the 'aims', since they lack any serious definitive boundaries, could be as free-flowing and indeterminate as, say, the whims of fashion ([1844] 1975, pp. 379f). Nor is history simply the result of the intertwining of nature and humanity, 'a process between man and nature' ([1867] 1976, p. 643). It is also the revelation of the constancies implied by these two forces. For example, both feudal and capitalist modes of production required the exploitation of labour, even though only the latter required the wage-labourer.

> The starting point of the development that gave rise to the wage-labourer as well as to the capitalist was the servitude of the labourer. The advance consisted in a change in the form of this servitude, in the transformation of feudal exploitation into capitalist exploitation. (ibid., p. 875)

Exploitation as both aim and structure persisted and required only a new and more satisfactory form, given the relevant condition of the productive forces. What is interesting about this shift from one mode to another and the retention of a basic productive relation of servitude is that Marx claimed that it was only under capitalism that such exploitation would lead to class conflict. The rising class under feudalism, namely the bourgeoisie, did not suffer the basic form of feudal exploitation, but brought about revolution. Yet under capitalism, the proletariat would arise precisely because of capitalist exploitation.

The human pursuit of aims, then, must be placed in the context of productive forces and emerging class orientations, such that individual and social development is active and reactive, and capitalism has a clear role to play in the generation of new and progressive social forms. For Marx, the exploitation of surplus labour is one of them.

> It is one of the civilising aspects of capital that it reinforces this surplus labour in a manner and under conditions which are more advantageous to the development of the productive forces, social relations, and the creation of the elements for a new and higher form than under the preceding forms of slavery, serfdom, etc. ([1873] 1959, p. 496)

Capitalist relations of production are constructive in the way that labour activity is organized. Marx apprehended the potential of these new conditions, both for the amount and kinds of work that may be done, and the positive effects this can have on the capacities of individuals. At the same time, capitalism is destructive of other forms which set limits to productive potential, and are even more oppressive for the individuals concerned. The key difference between capitalist and pre-capitalist modes of production is presented as an exclusively materialist one. The bourgeoisie was 'the first to show what man's activity could bring about' ([1847] 1968, p. 38). That is, production under capitalism saw a massive extension of the boundaries of the possible – the material results of the potentialities in human social labour when applied with the sophistication of the new productive processes of natural raw materials.

> The bourgeoisie during its scarce rule of one hundred years has created more massive and colossal productive force than have all preceding generations together. Subjection of nature's forces to man, machinery, application of chemistry to industry and agriculture, steam navigation, railways, electric telegraphs, clearing of whole continents for cultivation, canalization of rivers, whole populations conjured out of the ground – what earlier century had even a presentiment that such productive forces slumbered in the lap of social labour. (ibid., p. 40)

Thus Marx suggests that some powers of humanity were indeed nascent, that they 'slumbered' until the development of capitalism made their expression a concrete reality. In other words, pre-capitalism was not just inadequate to the capacities of individuals, but was a denial of human powers and human potentiality – a potentiality which existed regardless of the conditions at any one stage of human history. Hence, simply to focus on a social forma-tion will not necessarily provide an unproblematic representation of human nature. The empirical placement of human individuals within a social milieu does not automatically lead to a complete understanding of human nature.

The reflexive aspect of Marx's historical materialist method is at issue here. Humanity and nature, as O'Neill remarks, are 'involved in a cultural matrix in which the natural history of man is interwoven with the humanization of natural history' (1969, p. xviii). History, then, is not just made by living human individuals, but also confronts them in the present. History is the context that confines and shapes living human individuals, but it does not, cannot, define what it is to be human. To focus only on *social* labour, from which can be derived the definition of humanness, does not resolve the dilemma, unless it is argued that *living* human individuals as a descriptive term is interchangeable with *labouring* human individuals. Another way of proceeding might be to posit labour as the creative use of human powers. But here, too, form and content are not sufficiently distinguished, leading full circle to the initial premise of living human individuals in a given socioeconomic set of circumstances at a historically defined point.

This is by no means a weakness in Marx's thought, although it is certainly an inadequately explored issue. There are, nevertheless, plenty of indications that he felt that human development was proceeding along particular lines, and toward a specific kind of end.

> In the present epoch, the domination of material conditions over individuals, and the suppression of individuality by chance, has assumed its sharpest and most universal form, thereby setting individuals a very definite task. It has set them the task of replacing the domination of circumstances and of chance over individuals by the domination of individuals over chance and circumstances. ([1845–6] 1970, p. 117)

Put another way, Marx is referring to the development of a most extensive autonomy as a principal feature in the historical prog-ress of humankind. Moreover, autonomy from the domination of material conditions has become a possibility only under the revolutionary and universalizing impact of capitalism. This is not the autonomy of Kant, who posits an agent in contrast to the material and social world. Rather, this is an autonomy of being in a more complete and individuated sense. In *Capital*, for instance, Marx sets out in some detail the way that capitalist private property brings about a general pattern of human development. First of all, the change from the fusion of 'the isolated, independent working individual with the conditions of his labour' to 'formally free labour', is a 'metamorphosis' which 'decomposed the old society throughout its depth and breadth' ([1867] 1976, p. 928). Furthermore, this clearing away of the old is accompanied by much that is new and far-reaching in its effects:

> other developments take place on an ever-increasing scale, such as the growth of the co-operative form of the labour process, the conscious technical application of science, the planned exploitation of the soil, the transformation of the means of labour into forms in which they can be used in common, the economizing of all means of production by their use as the means of production of combined, socialized labour, the entanglement of all peoples in the net of the world market, and, with this, the growth of the international character of the capitalist regime. (ibid., p. 929)

These are the general claims that Marx was making in respect of the capitalist mode of production. The most important thing to note is that capitalism is unique in that it is a *universal* mode of production. It is not just dominant, outweighing the impact of all other modes and forcing those modes to adapt and become derivative or perish. More than this, it alone has been capable of transcending boundaries within and between societies. Certainly, this is destruction, for Marx, but it is also a great clearing away of tradition, involving a refreshing disregard for the ostensible limits to the possible, and demonstrating the potential of human social organization. This is in the context, moreover, of 'the development of social production and of the free individuality of the worker himself' (ibid., p. 929).

The capitalist mode of production satisfies the condition of universality in the discussion of human nature in that the universalizing character of capitalism gives the analysis world-historical relevance. This means that human nature under capitalism has dual application: as an historically specific expression of human nature; and as an exemplar of historical development of human nature. Earlier modes of production, earlier social formations, then, achieve progress only within the confines of their specific and parochial social history. By contrast, capitalism affects not just this and that section of the world's population here and there, sometimes sooner and sometimes later, but, in Marx's understanding, comes to reflect the history of humanity as a whole.

This universality means that the analysis of human nature and of individuality under capitalism also has a universal relevance. Marx's critique of capitalism can be said to satisfy the criterion of universality not only in respect of the conception of human nature. His views on individual capitalist existence have world-historical significance in the same way. That is, individuality is a human potential, which takes particular forms in the process of its expression and self-development.

There is also a second kind of claim that Marx makes. Having argued that capitalism affects the whole of humankind, he pinpointed one of the most important aspects of development – control over nature. Crucially, nature is made subject to human powers and organization. It is not that nature has changed. Rather, the change has been one that can be described only in *human* terms, involving a conscious application of technical knowledge for definite ends. Consider the way that Cohen presents the relationship between humans and nature as one of scarcity:

> Human need, whatever may be its historically various content, is rarely well catered for by unassisted nature. Some mammals get what they need easily, while for others life is an endless struggle for sustenance. Men would, apart from special cases, be among the unlucky ones, except that they, uniquely, can continually refashion their environments to suit themselves ... Mammals with less intelligence are unable to effect cumulative improvements in their habitats with each generation building on the achievements of its predecessor. (1978, pp. 152–3)

Such a relationship has many facets. The constant factor must be the way that humankind will remain in this superficially unfortunate position of having to struggle (i.e. work) regardless of the achievements that previous generations have bequeathed. On the other hand, the relationship is a variable one, wherein humankind is fortunate in being able to perceive, construct and exploit the difference between one's environment and nature itself. Within that variability, each mode of production can be assessed in terms of the degree that the 'natural' is brought into the realm of the constructible environment. The impact of capitalism, when viewed from this perspective, is dramatic and unique. *All* of nature, Marx was claiming, is capable of being made subject to human powers, either in thought or action.

This does not mean that human social organization can exploit and harness all natural forces and resources. The practical ability to achieve total control is secondary to the change in the *approach* to nature. Nature is seen as an object for manipulation, to be used and made to serve the interests of humans made powerful. With the fall of a once-dominant and unchallengeable nature, Marx is implying, so fall other apparently 'natural' features of social organization. They become merely transitory phenomena rather than deified or reified 'necessities'. The power that was presumed to reside in nature and traditional social forms does not dissipate or disappear, since the property of such power was, in the first place, built into a perception of nature and tradition by humankind itself. The source and substance of that power, being derived from human self-understanding, were necessarily limited. But the limits were not set by nature, but are described by the limits to the realization of human capacities. Thus the 'power' of nature was in fact the nascent power of humankind. Once nature became an object for humankind, Marx is demonstrating how the powers of humanity actually develop. They develop in this sense of capacities which reside in human nature coming to fruition, whereby such capacities are felt and understood and so form part of the abilities and techniques which can be employed consciously in the shaping of the environment.

As such, control over nature is 'progressive', but only in one sense. Certainly, capitalism brought about the practical expression and universalization of the ability to see nature instrumentally – in other words, make it subject to human powers of comprehension and manipulation. However, humans in society have always 'assisted' nature, thereby demonstrating the long-standing capacity to do so. Therefore, control over nature must rank as a capacity inherent in our conception of human nature, meaning that the contribution of capitalism is not a change in basic human nature, but a shift from one nature to another. The 'new' relationship to nature, then, is the decisive differentiation between the feudal individual and the capitalist individual. Only the latter has the ability to understand that nature can be placed in a subordinate relationship to human rationality and activity.

This is the kind of change in humans that is not likely to be reversed. As Cohen has pointed out, historical precedents clearly establish that a more primitive mode of production very rarely replaces an advanced one. Such an occurrence would be the only thing that could change the expressed capacity of humans with respect to the control and understanding of nature, to reduce it to a relationship of mystification or ignorance once again. Thus it can be accepted that the development brought about by capitalism will change its form certainly, but will retain its content. Consequently, it makes sense to talk about human nature on two levels. Cohen accepts the proposition that human nature does change, 'but it is also true that there are permanent attributes of human nature, in some equally important, perhaps the same, sense' (ibid., p. 151).

It is change in the human relationship to nature under capitalism which explains why Marx could speak of this mode of production in such glowing terms. By contrast with the local nature of progress under feudalism, control over nature made dramatic new openings in the possibilities of production, since it allowed the capacities of human creativity and expressiveness a whole new range of resources and freedoms for exploration. Freedom, in this context, derives its meaning and force from the imperative to realize human capacities. Implicit in Marx's developmental conception of human nature is the belief that capacities ought to be expressed and not constrained. This is an end in itself. Also, opportunities for realization are the necessary conditions for the continued expansion of needs and capacities, as a *means* to the continued development of humankind as a whole. Furthermore, small changes in the relationship with nature encouraged experimentation and innovation, an inquiring rather than accepting attitude to objective reality (which itself had only just become 'objective'). When this is coupled with the freedom from feudal social relations, and the freedoms and restraints of the new and still emerging social relations under capitalism, a nodal point in Marx's thought is reached, the pivot around which his historical analysis, encompassing his attitude to the development of individuality, turns. This is, quite simply, capitalism itself.

The placement of Marx's critique

Bourgeois society is the most developed and the most complex historic organization of production. The categories which express its relations, the comprehension of its structure, thereby also allows insights into the structure and the relations of production of all the vanished forms of social formations out of whose ruins and elements it built itself up, whose partly still unconquered remnants are carried along within it, whose mere nuances have developed explicit significance within it, etc. ([1857–8] 1973, p. 107)

This has specific ramifications for the analysis of the new individual. It means, first, that Marx's attitude to human individuality is a function of his approach to the study of capitalism. Second, this passage incorporates a recognition of the way that previous social formations and their social relations are connected to the present mode of production, even to the extent that residual forms and practices are carried on and become a part of the new and dominant mode of production. Marx presents this latter point not as a matter of internal contradiction within capitalism, but as an unproblematic historical reality. Marx's attitude is sometimes over-deterministic, however, and such remnants do not simply remain because they have yet to be properly conquered. Equally, the notion that the 'mere nuances' of an earlier stage will have come fully to fruition implies too mechanistic an account of change and social renewal and reformation.

Nevertheless, the optimism and simplicity of Marx's account do not detract from the significance of these kinds of claims or the observation that they are reliant upon a critique brought into existence as one of the achievements of bourgeois society. It must be noted that Marx makes explicit reference to the *society* that spawned these insights, not just the economic structure, thereby giving notice that where development and complexity were found in a society, then these same elements ought to characterize every account of that society. As Marx points out, with respect to economic categories:

It would be inexpedient and wrong therefore to present the economic categories in the order in which they played the dominant role in history. On the contrary their order of succession is determined by their mutual relation in modern bourgeois society and this is quite the reverse of what appears to be natural to them or in accordance with the sequence of historical development. The point at issue is not the role that various economic relations have played in the succession of various social formations appearing in the course of history ... but their position within modern bourgeois society. ([1857–8] 1973, p. 147)

This interest in the 'organic connection' is a methodological point which must also be reflected in the treatment of human nature within historical epochs. The qualities and abilities of human nature, then, will have some connection with one or more modes of production, but their place in an 'order' is not significant. At issue is the way that those qualities combine to produce capitalist nature, and how that nature might figure in the transition to socialism.

Thus Marx's critique of the capitalist individual is one that is historically located in a special way. It is not simply the perception that Marx had of life under capitalism, at a particular time and in specific circumstances. Marx was, after all, much more than a gifted social commentator. His view of capitalist individuality had to express the general validity of historical materialist method and highlight the dialectical realities that both indicated and precipitated change. As such, the structure of Marx's thought gives rise to the expectation that there should be found in his writings a range of descriptions of capitalist individuality, depending on the particular intent of the argument. Moreover, such descriptions will reflect a duality of purpose, or, more accurately, the comprehension that a knowledge of the present reshapes and demystifies perceptions of the past and makes possible new visions of the future. According to Carver, this vision includes the proposition that society and socially constructed individuals 'could be built anew':

> [Marx] discusses this possibility in terms of a revolutionary politics that depends on conscious, individual agents, not on some holistic agency that is metaphysical or teleological. Marx's language concerning 'class' and 'history' has been read in a way that is contradictory to any individualism, whereas it makes more sense to read it as presupposing ... individualism. (1987, p. 14)

Marx's thought has been roughly divided into three functional units: the critique of society; the vision of a future society; and the theory of change. Each of these incorporates an image of humankind and together they represent the capitalist notion of human nature. As with the feudal notion of human nature, this structure to Marx's thought means that human nature and human existence under capitalism will exhibit marked differences. His references to humans are likely to be at one time laudatory of their potentiality, but at another time critical of the way that humans are so easily crushed, mutilated and prevented from realizing that potential. Such differences have the status of dialectical contradictions within Marx's *notion* of human nature, while his conception of human nature expresses the general beliefs about the historical progress of society toward the possibility of a society of freedom based on new individuals and true equality.

In Marx's critique of society humans are presented as they are under the historical and cultural conditions pertinent to early capitalism and up to the late nineteenth century. There are two qualifications that underlie this view. First, this is clearly *not* a universalistic account, even though it relies on its logical connection with the universalizing effect of capitalism. The description provided relates quite specifically to the ensemble of social relations. Thus in itself, the description is quite limited and remains bound by its historical time. Marxian method, therefore, requires a reproduction of accounts of existence under capitalism, or indeed any social formation, to take account of the shifting economic and social factors that constitute the ensemble of social relations, and the connection with the universal categories dealing with both society and human nature. That is, Marx is not simply 'updated', but his method is used to produce the best contemporary critiques.

The second qualification underlying the critique of society is the principle that such a critique will focus on the dominant features of the form of society, dominant in so far as they generate the limits of a particular kind of human being in society. This means that the presentation of the individual will be a partial one, since it does not concentrate so much on unrealized potential, but on the inadequacy of what the society requires and allows. For this reason, the account of alienation need not be considered an all-encompassing view of existence under capitalism. It need not be used to explain every social relation. In this sense, alienation *from* something (essence, as some would argue) is not so important as the claim that capitalism *can* alienate, that it will do so in its 'normal' operation. Thus his view of capitalist existence emerges from, and remains the servant of, the critique of society.

These two features of the critique of society mean: that the understanding of the individual under capitalism is enhanced only to the extent that the very same economic and social conditions exist; and that capitalism is able to make humans, more than they can learn what they are or might be. Marx's critique, then, provides the means to grasp the impact of society, and gives a great deal of insight into the powers of capitalism, but less insight into the powers of humans *qua* humans.

The vision of society supplies obverse images. Here Marx was suitably cautious, and was careful not to commit the errors he and Engels identified in utopian socialist accounts of future society. The limitation was, of course, that no post-capitalist

115

social formation yet existed. There were examples of alternatives to capitalist productive relations, but Marx was aware that the dominant mode of production would for some time remain capitalist. Nevertheless, the critique of society and the expressions of social existence it entailed constitute a requirement for alternative images, and Marx did not shy from this requirement. It should not be imagined, however, that the claims that Marx made about human existence in a post-capitalist society related only to the structure of that new society. Rather, the vision of society dealt with here is *strictly in the terms of capitalism*, for the reasons stated at the beginning of this section. This is to concentrate on those features of capitalist individuality which led Marx to expect that *any* kind of new society is possible, let alone one as specifically structured as communism. A Marxian account of society will always incorporate alternative images, that this is indeed a part of social reality. Therefore, a society might well be judged both for the existence and range of its alternative visions.

Under capitalism, the visions of society available are much more objectively based. They lie within the context of advanced forces and relations of production. Since capitalism has to a large extent superseded mystifications pertaining to nature and hence the place of humans in the world, its visions and images are similarly less in terms of supernatural or mystical alternatives. Nevertheless, this breaking down of mystifications also entails new mystifications, a new view of that which is 'natural'. Specifically, Marx referred to the way that a particular kind of socioeconomic relation came to be seen as 'natural': 'the state, private property, etc, change human beings into abstractions, or are the products of the abstract man, instead of being the reality of individuals, of concrete human beings' ([1845] 1956, p. 255). The 'progress' of capitalism always has a complex context, however, and also contains the elements necessary to confront these more 'objective' versions of the 'natural', and to find them 'objectively' inadequate. An example of this point occurs in Marx's discussion on the manner in which the circulation of money confronts individuals.

> As much, then, as the whole of this movement appears as social progress, and as much as the individual moments of this movement arise from the conscious will and particular purposes of individuals, so much does the totality of the process appear as an objective interrelation, which arises spontaneously from nature ... Their own collisions with one another

produce an *alien* power standing above them, produce their material interaction as a process and power independent of them. ([1857–8] 1973, pp. 196–7)

Capitalism relies upon individuals with will and purpose, but transforms their contribution into a power over them and presents itself as natural. This outcome is universal. It does not stem from structure or process.

> The social relation of individuals to one another as a power over the individuals which has become autonomous, whether conceived as a natural force, or as chance or in whatever other form, is a necessary result of the fact the point of departure is not the free social individual. (ibid., p. 197)

Such a claim has a number of interesting features. First, it indicates that a certain type of individual is perceived by Marx as being crucial to the understanding of social relations. Second, he postulated the 'free social individual' before the communist society which is supposed to make such an existence possible. Third, individuals may be mystified by nature or by chance, but they become subject to an economic and social system which actively seeks to overcome nature and fate. Given that this is the way the social relations appear to individuals, they become disposed to question those very interpretations which accompany their powerlessness and subjection to process. Self-understanding and self-perception on the part of the individual begin to take new forms according to their situation in the world–capitalist system.[5] At the same time, Marx included an indication of how an individual should be conceived, of how an individual might be under differing circumstances, but in respect of *every* analysis of society. Capitalism thus has intrinsic to it the basis for the critique of capitalism, and the vision of freedom and wealth which must bring individuals to apprehend the future in terms that transcend the contradictions of capitalism and realize true freedom and wealth.

In all, the vision of society takes a different tack from the starting point of the critique of society, by concerning itself, at the same time, with what can be expected *of* humans, and *for* humans. Hence the focus is entirely on humans as they are now, and it is this that forms the basis of the inquiry into the possibilities for the rational reordering of social forces.

The critique of society and the vision of society are key elements of Marx's thought, and they complement each other.

The critique is a clinical look at people as they can be expected to be only under specific historical and cultural circumstances – limited and fragmented, with a lack of freedom as a consequence of conditions of inequality. The vision of society concentrates on these same limitations also, but from the point of view of the implied alternatives and possibilities. It is, for the most part, an optimistic but not necessarily utopian reading of the potentiality inherent in any given situation, person, or mode of production. Each of these facets of Marx's thought reflects the totality of his enterprise ([1844] 1975, p. 351). That is, each one can stand on its own, representing reality via a particular abstraction. In the process, the insights that are provided into human nature at the level of conception and notion combine to provide a multi-dimensional view of what it is to be human.

Nevertheless, since the point is not just to describe the world, both critique and vision and the contributions they make remain dependent in turn upon a further perspective. This is provided by Marx's theory of change. Marx's understanding of history is predicated on the persistence of change; it was change that he attempted to make comprehensible, in order to make possible the next major advance for humankind. Capitalism had overcome nature, but chance still dominated change. Thus the control of change, requiring praxis – the combination of understanding and action – was next on the agenda for the development of the species.

However, the soundness of Marx's treatment of change at the general theoretical level is not matched by the provision of convincing detail at the level of historical particularity. The theory of change relies upon a clear knowledge of the possibilities of change in humans. Additionally, an account of the habits and ways of thinking which impede or advance change is required. That is, the scope of human change and the details of significant change need to be mapped out. Without such information, the limits to change cannot be drawn and taken account of, and the means of bringing about change may be rendered useless simply because the time-scales individuals or classes employ or imply are unrealistic. Marx's statements thus have to be carefully sorted out, and it is here that this tripartite division into critique, vision and theory of change serves its most important function. For example, it is mistaken to assume that Marx's more visionary statements are evidence of the ability or propensity to make the necessary changes to realize that vision. Similarly, an indictment of a system of exploitation does not establish the means for its replacement. Thus the most significant statements that Marx made about human nature under capitalism will relate to the place of the individual in the process of change. How does individuality relate to historical change at the general level, and to what extent is the individual a change agent in the particular transition from capitalism to communism? Marx's thoughts on change in humans make a contribution to his conception of human nature – i.e. that which he regards as in a limited sense 'fixed' – and to his notion of human nature, namely, features of special interest to those implementing radical social change or analysing developments in current society.

Under all forms of social organization to date, the relations of production, the real conditions of existence can operate to deny 'true' individuality. Within capitalism, this is but another way of describing the alienation of labour, or, more precisely, the debilitating impact of the limiting existence offered by capitalist society, permitting only unsatisfactory roles and a partial and unfulfilling utilization of human capacities. There is nothing unfamiliar or unremarkable about such an argument, but it is important to realize that this argument, and the image of humanity that underlies it, stems not from Marx's critique of society, but relates to his vision of a future social formation.

In other words, the conditions – civil and political – of social existence conformed to an image of humanity that negated true individuality. For capitalist society, then, humans are made into abstract, objectified entities. This is a special achievement of capitalism, and its most explicit manifestation was in the activity of labour. Labour was disassociated from the human agency that, for Marx, was a fundamental part of the labour process (Street, 1983, p. 131). This is in marked contrast to labour in feudal society, where work is in much closer relation to the worker's own individual *needs*, where those needs form the object of the labour (Marx, [1845] 1956, p. 30). Feudal society and economic relationships were exploitative, but the mode of production did not require this separation of need and labour in the same way that capitalism does. As Gould sees it, capitalism 'presupposes the dissolution of the immediate unity characteristic of pre-capitalist community, both the unity of the producer with the community and with the soil' (1978, p. 13).

For capitalism, these minor virtues of the feudal mode were also fetters to the development of the productive forces. It was necessary for capitalism not just to ignore needs which are human, but actively to destroy the equivalence of individual needs and human needs. In so doing, capitalism, in Marx's critique, distorts and distends

119

the reality of the human individual by separating aspects of the self that would go to make up a 'concrete human being'. The restructuring of social relationships has this dual character. First, Marx noted that the principal mechanism of establishing human social reality is transformed into an obstacle for all individuals.

> Never, in any earlier period, have the productive forces taken on a form so indifferent to the intercourse of individuals as individuals, because their intercourse itself was formerly a restricted one. On the other hand, standing over against these productive forces, we have the majority of the individuals from whom these forces have been wrested away, and who, robbed thus of all real life-content, have become abstract individuals, but who are, however, only by this fact put into a position to enter into relations with one another *as individuals*. The only connection which still links them with the productive forces and with their own existence – labour – has lost all semblance of self-activity and only sustains their life by stunting it. ([1845–6] 1970, p. 92)

Individuals here have powers and forces, which are restricted and wrested away. Individuals *as individuals* are, in this dialectical account, stunted and made abstract, and *thereby* prepared for (capitalist) social interaction. Second, and this is less obvious and deals with the lack of a fully articulated theory of individual change in Marx's thought, an abstraction of what it is to be an individual in society is created and imposed upon capitalist individuals. But this is not in the mind: it resides in the social relationships within which individuals are forced to exist. Moreover, it relates to something definite within humans and so draws strength from its partial relevance. It is in this sense that the images of human nature and individuality created and fostered by capitalist social relations express the dialectical nature of human progress: the more that capitalism approximates to the needs of humans and employs their latent abilities, the harder it becomes simultaneously to allow only a partial expression of those abilities.

Development: human nature and capitalism

The task is to examine individuals 'not in any fantastic isolation and rigidity, but in their actual, empirically perceptible process of development under definite conditions' ([1845–6] 1970, pp.

47–8), understood as a developing capitalist society. The link between the abstraction, human nature and the empirical reality of an individual life under concrete circumstances is not short or taut, reflecting easily and automatically the practical promptings entailed in the abstractions of human nature and society.

> As individuals express their life, so they are. What they are, therefore, coincides with their production, both with *what* they produce and with *how* they produce. The nature of individuals thus depends on the material conditions determining their production. (Marx, [1845–6] 1970, p. 42)

Marx, in the way that he presented this fundamental methodological argument, was setting out the limits not of determinism, but of human potential. This is a view supported by O'Neill:

> The evolution of human nature proceeds in terms of the interaction between man and nature and the technology and social relations of production which mediate that process. In this sense the potentiality of human nature may be regarded as a function of the means of production. (1969, p. xix)

For individuals to be determined narrowly by the mode of production, it would have had to exist prior to the individuals who produced, just as the method of production would logically have to precede individuals *qua* individuals. Now in one sense this can be accepted: the mode of production, and the entire superstructure, exists for the new-born child and really does precede it. Yet Marx could not take this argument seriously, since it entails a static abstraction of the kind employed in consent or contract theory. For him, how that reality came to be remains a part of what it is. Therefore, the mode of production is now, as it ever was, rooted in the activity of individuals within a wide range of interactions, without which it has no existence.

> Thus it is quite obvious from the start that there exists a material connection of men with one another, which is *determined* by their *needs* and their *mode of production*, and which is as old as men themselves. This connection is ever taking on new forms, and thus presents a 'history' independent of the existence of any political or religious nonsense which in addition may hold men together. (Marx, [1845–6] 1970, p. 42: italics added)

This means that Marx's conception of human nature stands above, or is distinct from, the environmental variation of specific societies in their particular stages. Moreover, it is Marx's conception of human nature which prescribes the quality of potentiality. The ability to alter and develop is not something which is reliant on or reducible to a specific set of concrete circumstances. Only the form that alteration and development takes is dependent upon those circumstances. The different notions of human nature, then, can be understood as functions of production, leading to new forms of development.

Production

> The fact is, therefore, that definite individuals who are productively active in a definite way enter into these definite social and political relations. The empirical observation must in each separate instance bring out empirically, and without any mystification or speculation, the connection of the social and political structure with production. (Marx, [1845–6] 1970, p. 46)

Production is thus the basis of the consideration of the development of both capitalism and human nature. But this should not be taken to mean that production is the *source* of reality, rather than the methodology with which to view the world. The insistence, on Marx's part, that empirical observations must be undertaken both broadly and constantly is an indication that the kinds of change and detail that Marx was dealing with could be used to establish the veracity of his general schema. Nor did he make the task seem a simple one of differentiating between what was real and important, and what was superficial or misunderstood. For example, Marx was aware that a naive empiricism could overlook the subtlety of some changes and compress all events into explanations that were predicated on the determination of the productive system.

> It is necessary to distinguish these definitions which apply to production in general, in order not to overlook the essential differences existing despite the unity that follows from the very fact that the subject, mankind, and the object, nature, are the same. (ibid., p. 126)

Marx is here referring to humankind, what has been termed the conception of human nature. This is the bedrock of his explanation, the abstraction of the living individuals as a subject in history. The existence of humankind as a subject is crucial, because it requires that the subject has content, a content which may not be immediately identifiable, or converted into a list of properties and characteristics. Nevertheless, that content is assumed to exist. The 'general uniformity' to which Marx refers is the existence of production through history, the exploitation of nature by humankind, as object and subject.

Yet within that general uniformity, the pattern of production and the 'connection of the social and political structure with production' shows that a definite shift has occurred in the basic data of production. With the greater sophistication and complexity of the production process comes a more variegated and intricate set of social relationships. Consequently, individuals are required to operate in a more complex and flexible manner. Their relationship to themselves, others and the material world alters significantly, bringing forth a range of different activities and orientations.

> Hence exploration of all nature in order to discover new, useful qualities in things; universal exchange of the products of all alien climates and lands; new (artificial) preparation of natural objects, by which they are given new use values. The exploration of the earth in all directions, to discover new things of use as well as new useful qualities of the old; such as new qualities of them as raw materials etc.; the development, hence, of the natural sciences to their highest point. (Marx, [1857–8] 1973, p. 409)

That is, the subject, humankind, is not an historical constant, but is capable of changing and developing by being culturally expanded and becoming more universal, whereas the object, nature, has remained, at the most general level, the same. Certainly, nature has been modified, checked, or extended, but it cannot regenerate the changes imposed upon it as a matter of course in the way that human subjects can.

This is not a simple change. As humankind does battle with nature, it becomes more cognitively complex and overcomes, but that complexity brings new ignorance, a similar kind of helplessness to control and understand the array of natural forces and possibilities. Thus while a tree still grows as it always did, this manifestation of nature has been transformed in human terms from an exhibit of the grace of God to an equally spectacular example of photosynthesis and cell structure, and this change is merely a most recent one. Accordingly, nature too, is a particular

123

object only at the level of abstraction. Through capitalist productive activity:

> For the first time, nature becomes purely an object for humankind, purely a matter of utility; ceases to be recognized as a power in itself; and the theoretical discovery of its autonomous laws appears merely as a ruse so as to subjugate it to human needs. (ibid., p. 410)

As soon as a discourse of a particular production process or mode is constructed, then the definition of nature becomes one that is a part of the social and political structure, just as the conception of human nature can only be approached via a notion of human nature (Philp, 1985, pp. 69–70). The identification of the subject – humankind – and its content, therefore, comes through: the interaction of humankind and nature, and here Marx suggests an empirical approach; the understanding of nature itself; and humankind.

Given that these all change, but the general uniformity of subject and object do not, it becomes possible to see the contrasts between different epochs and so to decide what belongs in Marx's conception of human nature and what is more properly to do with a notion of human nature. In particular, the development of humankind is the outcome of this interaction between humanity and nature, identifiable as a propensity and a quality of human nature, one which can therefore have a role in the making of history by the forces of its existence and the drive of its potentiality and capacity:

> the direct production process ... is then both discipline, as regards the human being in the process of becoming; and, at the same time, practice, experimental science, materially creative and objectifying science, as regards the human being who has become, in whose hand exists the accumulated knowledge of society. (Marx, [1857–8] 1973, p. 712)

Production takes place in the context of the basic *power* of humans to modify nature and their social existence. In so doing, they modify themselves, becoming not what they essentially are, but what is possible given the development of the forces of production achieved in previous epochs, and under more primitive modes. Humankind, both becoming and stretching the limits of what it is possible to become, makes clear advances over nature and alters the interaction between nature and society. Both the reality and the understanding which follows it reflect a growing independence from definitions and practices which placed nature in an enhanced position. No longer is it a nature 'which first appears to men as a completely alien, all-powerful and unassailable force, with which men's relations are purely animal and by which they are overawed like beasts' (Marx, [1845–6] 1970, p. 44). The fruit of this form of change can be referred to as *the progress of individuality*, wherein living human beings become individual in so far as their social existence – their practical, sensuous life activity – is more and more under their control, and where their decisions and reactions approximate successively to reality. Marx referred to this as 'the universal appropriation of nature as well as of the social bond itself by the members of society' ([1857–8] 1973, p. 409). This move toward control over the material and social world represents a stage development of society, 'in comparison to which all earlier ones appear as mere *local developments* of humanity' (ibid., pp. 409–10).

Marx's focus on production, especially at the birth of capitalism and its dramatic success over other social formations, is perspicacious, but that does not mean that *all* facets of human social existence can be explained within its framework. The argument concerning the development of individuality makes clear that the most marked shift in human potentiality occurred with this relatively sudden overtaking of the natural world, reducing it to a series of laws which can be transmitted and apprehended, and used for practical purposes of control as well as the creation of greater knowledge. Humans 'grew' proportionately. They became empowered, relative to feudal individuals, by the ruling assumptions concerning the nature of the world and its amenability to new forms of control and change. Associated with capitalist production was

> the discovery, creation and satisfaction of new needs arising from society itself; the cultivation of all the qualities of the social human being, production of the same in a form as rich as possible in needs, because rich in qualities and relations – production of this being as the most total and universal social product, for, in order to take gratification in a many-sided way, he must be capable of many pleasures, hence cultured to a high degree – is likewise a condition of production founded on capital. (ibid.)

The generation of new needs is a product of *society*, not production alone. Similarly, a high level of culture is not confined to productive activity, and will affect the relationship and attitudes of the individual to production as much as it enables him or her engage in it.

Simultaneously, the *consumption* process reflects this kind of change. For Marx, the capitalist certainly wants to change workers as consumers at the deepest level, at the level of their needs:

> he therefore seeks for means to spur them on to consumption, to give his wares new charms, to inspire them with new needs with constant chatter etc. It is precisely this side of the relation of capital which is an essentially civilizing moment, and on which the historical justification, but also the contemporary power of capital rests. (ibid., p. 287)

Notwithstanding its capitalist character and form (and therefore the brutality of its exploitation), Marx clearly saw the general development of humanity occurring, creating the possibility for a specifiable and identifiable role for human agents who are universally rich in needs and culture.

Social relations

However, there is still the problem of the relationship between that emergent individuality and the production process under which it develops. Capitalism may need such individuals, but they may come not to need capitalism. For Marx, some aspects of the development of the forces of production have negative effects on individuality, and the expression of it, in the next stage. And if Marx looked forward to the self-determination of the communist stage, as he does in the *German Ideology*, then it is to be expected that his aim was to neutralize the impact of the production process on the living human individual in favour of some quality or other that he felt had greater importance ([1845–6] 1970, p. 54). But this would be a society which is, in Dawe's words, 'the creation of its members; the product of their construction of meaning, and of the action and relationships through which they attempt to impose that meaning on their historical situations' (1970, pp. 207–8). Such an image of the autonomous individual is at odds with Marx's other statements, which see 'action as the derivative of system', but both views exist: there is a 'conflict in the Marxian dialectic between the notion of socially creative man and the essentially Hobbesian view of nineteenth century capitalist man' (ibid.).

Where there is a dialectic, there must be conflict, and this is the idea that will be pursued. Certainly, those discrepant views are to be found. Yet they are not contradictory in a logical sense. The contradiction comes from the nature of the development of capitalism itself. As such, 'every limit appears as a barrier to be overcome', and limits are understood, among other things, as national barriers, prejudices, and 'old ways of life in general' (Marx, [1857–8] 1973, pp. 408, 410).

> But from the fact that capital posits every such limit as a barrier and hence gets *ideally* beyond it, it does not by any means follow that it has *really* overcome it ... The universality towards which it irresistibly strives encounters barriers in its own nature, which will, at a certain stage of its development, allow it to be recognized as being itself the greatest barrier to this tendency, and hence will drive towards its own suspension. (ibid.)

Social relations emerged from feudalism, but they did not then cease to develop. Given that change is a constant in Marx's view of society, the images of human existence that capitalist society produces will also change, and earlier practical expressions of human nature will clash with later ones, especially in the light of the fundamental flaws in the mode of production. The Hobbesian view of nineteenth-century capitalist individuals is to be found in Marx's critique of society precisely because this is the kind of individual that capitalism created. However, humans are not simply determined by the sociological and economic structures that are extant. A treatment of the individual in capitalism, then, has to reflect the levels at which Marx's thought operates. This is because Marx's historical framework does not assume that what society does create must be the only thing it can create. As Golubović argues, the historical framework

> merely represents a sum of socio-cultural conditions which provided the basis of the corresponding degree of individual development, that will more or less determine (meaning to limit and frustrate) and shape, in one way or another, the basic character structure; while biology and culture appear as the ready-made entities which more strictly determine the formation of personality structures (either as inherited dispositions or through the patterned 'social characters'), as against the historical alternatives which present a variety of alternatives. (1983, p. 11)

In the terms in use here, the conception of human nature relates to the character structure, and the notion of human nature to personality structure. This is not an absolute equivalence, however. For example, the biological constancies of humans belong in the conception of human nature, too, but the variations relating to particular skills and differentiable dispositions that are directly inherited do not. What, then, is the relevant 'degree of individual development' in the historical conditions that were early capitalism? The early writings of Marx, where he was much more concerned with the human social changes that capitalism wrought and severely criticized the received wisdom of the nature of that social existence, provide some answers.

Capitalism, individualism and individuality

For Marx, capitalism was to be viewed from a variety of directions, but within the same historical materialist framework, which, in Geras' opinion, *rests squarely upon the idea of a human nature* (1983, p. 108). Thus to examine these aspects of Marx's thought where he concentrated on the individual is not to invalidate Marx's scientific socialism, to trivialize it with bourgeois concerns, or worse, divert a critical methodology to reactionary purposes. Rather, this is to focus on human nature as a fundamental tool and assumption, and provide concrete knowledge of that nature. Because the focus is on something that is not abstract, a comparative perspective has to be adopted. This involves analysing the way in which capitalist individuality is expressed as a difference, as a *development* from pre-capitalist individuality, and examining the relationship of individuality to *individualism*. This may augment class analysis, for example, which is generally taken to be the best critical and descriptive view of property-based societies, and extend the understanding of the change processes so basic to Marx's view of history, and vital for any vision of a communist future.

As Golubović points out, it is erroneous to suggest that Marx's understanding of the individual should be interpreted exclusively in terms of

> the priority and dominance of social factors over individual ones, as if these two components were independent from one another. One should be warned once again that the dialectics of Marx's thinking implies both a difference (that is, non-identity of social and individual) and unity which is manifest on both sides. (1983, pp. 11–12)

It is this question of priority and dominance that is most at issue in respect of Marx's view of the individual. Under feudal relations, the individual began to emerge as an historical entity with the ability to be differentiated from nature and society, even though remaining entirely dependent on them for survival and definition. As Wood argues, the dialectical model suggests that the development of the individual and society is linked, in whatever form is appropriate, given the status of the focus of production:

> the dialectical approach, unlike the metaphysical, emphasizes the dynamic unity, the reciprocity, of individual and society, the ways in which individuality and society are mutually re-enforcing rather than antagonistic. It also conceives of individuality and sociality as evolving through a dialectical interaction in which the nature of self-consciousness and the sense of community develop and mutually change each other in a dynamic process. (1972, p. 10)

In the specific case of capitalism, in the transition from a mode of production dominated by nature to one which attempts its technical transcendence, individuality (that propensity to understand and control as a conscious choice) increases dramatically. And with that change, whose midwife was the forces of production, the new relations of production reveal more of the capacities of human nature. If individuality develops in history, then it must mean that control over nature and human history develops, at least as a potentiality. It means that the particularity of individual human existence confirms and realizes being and knowing. However, in capitalist society specifically, that particularity is most likely to take a non-fulfilling form. The emergence of the particular individual can be both a critical statement about the social formation, *vide* the emergence of a deformed individuality, while still revealing that Marx could see what true individuality could or would be like under different conditions. Marx's criticism of bourgeois understanding of the self and egoism reflects awareness of this confusion over the results of historical development and the way that such development came to be a part of the present.

> Man is equated with self. But the self is only *abstractly* conceived man, man produced by abstraction. Man *is* self ... The self abstracted and fixed for itself is man as *abstract egoist*, egoism raised to its pure abstraction in thought. ([1844] 1975, p. 387)

Marx was arguing against turning a practical understanding of individuals into an abstract theorization of their faculties as they were evinced and developed in society. This does not reject the notion of self, but is an attack on the assumption that selfhood is separate to social existence. He was not the enemy of egoism and consciousness of selfhood, as if these were only the trappings of false consciousness, a self-indulgent bourgeois perception. Rather, he was focusing on the dominant and idealist interpretations that made such concepts seem acceptable or accurate. Marx criticized Hegel, for example, for failing to understand that the primary reality was material existence of real human individuality, not their *ideas* about their existence.

> Hegel makes man *the man of self-consciousness* instead of making self-consciousness the *self-consciousness of man*, of real man, living in a real objective world and determined by that world ... everything which *betrays the limitations of general self-consciousness* – all sensuousness, reality, individuality of men and of their world – necessarily rates for him as a limit. ([1845] 1956, p. 254)

For Marx, of course, the reverse applies, and it should be noted that individuality is among the features of social and historical reality which are fundamental. Attention must also be paid to Marx's explicit reference to the real objective world 'determining' the life of the individual. Here Marx is referring at a high level of abstraction to the way that the conditions of existence are the key to a grasp of the possibilities for human conduct and understanding. This is not the same as the claim that those conditions can provide the *detail* of human conduct and understanding, that they do indeed determine the actuality of the possibilities at a given stage of development of the forces of production. Marx can assert with confidence that a glance at the historical level of development will provide a fair indication of the kind and quality of the self-consciousness that will accompany that stage. But when he does that, in the next sentence of the above passage, his observations are in very particular terms which describe the world not as a series of manipulating forces on humanity, nor as a collection of structures which strictly determine the life of the individual. Instead, he refers to 'sensuousness, reality, individuality of men and of their world'. These first two, sensuousness and reality, can be seen as alternative descriptions of his materialist method. 'Sensuousness' for Marx is the means by which the concrete world impinges on humans, just as it is the practical means through which humans fashion their existence and build a consciousness of themselves and the world. 'Reality', then, is the construct of the sensuous being, either in the material sense of producing and reproducing the means of existence, or in the social sense that the human builds up a consciousness of the interactions between the material elements of that existence.

Marx's reference to 'individuality' shows that it is not just the objective world that counts. Individuality also relates to the degree of autonomy that is to be found in any social organization. This autonomy, in respect of Hegel's argument, refers to the 'limitations of general self-consciousness', such that Marx wished to deny that all individuals were allied by the level of their consciousness with the rest of society. But in this rejection of the Absolute Idea also lies the correct way to perceive individuals and their self-consciousness. At the level of theory, individuality is to be seen as a result of long history, the outcome of the progressive development of the forces of production. As such, individuality is a materialist conception, since it has developed entirely in the context of the labour of humans under successive modes of production and incorporates the progressive shift to more complex relations of production, which implies the extension and articulation of the faculties of humans.

Thus it is also possible, indeed necessary, for Marx to talk of the individuality 'of their world'. This is a reference to the character of the specific form of social organization in which wo/men find themselves – the social, political and cultural environment that conditions self-consciousness. By implication, then, it is important not only to analyse the extent to which particular wo/men are individualized under a given set of conditions, but also to recognize that such expressions of individuality are within the context of the possibilities set by the nature of the economic and social formation. Wo/men, then, achieve a certain level of individuality, whatever their lives, and this must be known and judged. Further, a society can be assessed for the limits it sets to individuality. Of interest is the extent to which humans are able to act in accordance with their abilities and capacities to reach a self-understanding of their position in society, and control their individual lives. That is, a society can be seen as a set of parameters to self-consciousness and individuality, wherein 'all sensuousness, reality, individuality of men and of their world' are necessary to elucidate the actual nature of the 'real objective world'. The world that 'determines' self-consciousness, therefore, is one which always includes a particular measure of autonomy. There can never be a totally closed society, or even one near to that.

131

This model reveals how Marx viewed capitalist society from the perspective of potentiality and actuality of individuality. For him, the 'civil society of the present is the principle of *individualism* carried to its logical conclusion. Individual existence is the ultimate goal; activity, work, content, etc., are *only* means' ([1844] 1975, p. 147). This passage gives the key to the differentiation between the individuality to which Marx refers, and its liberal counterpart, individualism. Capitalist individualism constitutes a notion of human nature appropriate to a capitalist social order riven by contradiction. It provides an ideologically coherent model for social existence, but is not a theory of society. Where the principle of individualism is put into practice in society, Marx is claiming, there individuals are allowed to express their individuality only within the narrow confines of that principle. The norms for behaviour and self-understanding are consistent with an existence which validates a total separateness and an associated competitiveness with all others, thereby depriving sensuousness and reality of their full potential for human meaning. Individuality, by implication, relates to free expression of a creative and flexible range of faculties and capacities within human nature, in a social environment so constructed that individuals, in their work and content, could be self-defining as well as other-legitimating.

The norms of capitalist individualism place severe limitations on the individual and relate to two theoretical points. First, it is assumed that the world can be understood and structured on the basis of the individual as the prime source of reality. Marx rejects this form of individualism because essential human activities come to be seen as instrumental rather than fundamental facets of life. It has its counterpart, in this respect, in methodological individualism. Second, there is the further assumption that individual existence is given a status on its own, such that the real content of individuals, which is to be derived from an understanding of their human potential and the possibility for its realization in society, is treated as a secondary phenomenon. For Marx, the nature and form of human activity is of the first importance. It is true that sometimes these things will be means, that sometimes it makes sense to think of them as means, but this must be done only in the context of an explanation that does not employ an abstract notion of agency. Individualism does just that, since it assumes that individuals can choose to exist and utilize their potentialities through the medium of activity and work. Marx, on the other hand, argues that individuals derive agency from those human efforts themselves, that it is through them that choice and agency become possibilities.

Marx's attack on capitalist society is an appraisal of the ability of that society to extend the parameters of individuality, in the broad historical sense – i.e. in the context of societies that have been superseded. Moreover, it is also an appraisal of the actual form of the civil society, in order to assess the extent to which individuals can express their potentiality. 'The modern age, civilization ... isolates the objective essence of man, treating it as something purely *external* and material. It does not treat the content of man as his true reality' (ibid.). Civilization, then, is 'modern', but these connotations of progress are soured by the manner in which the clear development from less sophisticated and advanced social formations is negated by the treatment of the 'content of man'. Again, the two senses of human nature that are being employed here can be distinguished. Marx is not referring to the conception of human nature, since that is not an 'objective' essence. The notion of human nature, however, is in terms of the actual social existence in civil society. And it is the nature of capitalism, Marx claims, to deny the equivalence of the 'objective essence' of human individuals and the material conditions of existence.

The consequence of this is the misperception of the relationship between the individual and the material world. Civil society is regarded as something with its own status and content, within which the human individual exists and which he or she must accept as valid reality. Adherence to principles such as individualism, in this event, do have an impact on the nature of society – individual members of society have to adjust themselves to the institutions and the way that they are made to operate, without any regard to their actual and felt needs. Thus a set of individualist principles, while they could not alter the material foundations of the particular society and make it into, for example, a communal one, may have a significant bearing on the way that individual development *within* a social formation will take place. It may also mean that people in the same society may be at different stages of 'development'. That Marx thought this possible is clear from his statements about the superiority of the proletariat when acting as a class-for-itself.

For Marx, the massive potentiality of the productive forces under capitalism, their power swiftly to overcome an inferior mode of production and their ability to tame nature, are all accompanied by the exploitation of the potentialities, the powers and the abilities of the living individuals who represent the outcomes of that development, and who both embody and actualize those forces.

> Thus, just as production founded on capital creates universal industriousness on one side ... so does it create on the other side a system of general exploitation of the natural and human qualities, a system of general utility, utilising science itself just as much as all the physical and mental qualities, while there appears nothing *higher in itself*, nothing legitimate for itself, outside this circle of social production and exchange. (Marx, [1857–8] 1973, p. 409)

Thus Marx's focus is on both form and content at any one time. Equally important is the way that he validates the existence of sources of value and judgement outside the realm of economics. Moreover, in a rare kind of remark, Marx referred to the mental qualities of individuals which a developing mode of production appreciates (if in a strictly utilitarian way).

His treatment of any feature of capitalist society as an abstraction means that it represents the totality of the social whole, the interconnections and the historical developments to that point of individual and society. This enables Marx to see clearly the contradictory character of capitalist society and locate the appropriate structural feature – private property ownership – for analysis. 'The greater and the more articulated the social power is within the relationship of private property, the more *egoistic* and social man becomes, the more he becomes alienated from his own nature' ([1844] 1975, p. 276). At the same time as Marx pinpointed the structural relationship which underpinned exploitative social relations, however, he was able to recognize that the development secured under the emergent capitalist mode of production was denied its full or rounded expression in the social relations of civil society. The most advanced mode of production in history, then, was accompanied by a corresponding extension of the *possibility* of human autonomy, but in no way did the experience of living individuals *actually* reflect these new possibilities. Marx still 'preferred' capitalism, because its developments over the power of nature were real enough. But he could as easily see that the costs to individuals were high, and that individuals could not hope to realize their potential. Instead, they would be forced to express themselves within the limiting and debilitating frameworks that ignored the objective connections between themselves and the production and reproduction of social life. That is, a civil society which was in accordance with principles of individualism rather than the reality of human nature and the production of material life was bound to allow only a partial and skewed expression of human faculties. Hence the basic human activities, to be found in all social formations, are dissociated from their real function, such that those once-human qualities involved in the production of life – human nature – are ever distanced from the actual (alienated) social existence, to the point where they appear to be unrelated.

Individualism, for Marx, was equated with the distinction between the self and others that is implicit in an exchange economy, where interactions reflect the transmission of the *result* of human activity. Recognition of others could no longer be a recognition of oneself, as it was under earlier social formations, where the link between producer and product, between use-value and exchange value corresponded more closely. And where there is no recognition of others, there is no recognition of what it is to be truly human. It is no surprise to find that Marx described the egoist as 'an individual separated from the community, withdrawn into himself, wholly preoccupied with his private interest and acting in accordance with his private caprice' ([1844] 1975, p. 26). This direct result of the exchange society and the division of labour on which it was based was, however, a process which is contradictory. Despite the increasing sophistication of society and the advancement of humanity, there was nevertheless 'a diminution of the *capacity of each man* taken *individually*' (Marx, [1844] 1975, p. 373).

This is the nub of Marx's critique of capitalist society. The revolutionary nature of the capitalist mode of production in respect of all other modes of production is offset by the impact on the individuals in that society. The improving potential of the capitalist revolution is subverted to the detriment of the individual. 'Instead of the individual function being the function of society, the individual function is made into a society for itself' (ibid., p. 148). At one level, there is an account of human nature to provide a part of the explanation of the emergence of capitalism in its primitive and more developed forms. This leads to real insights into the ideology and behaviour of contemporary individuals, on the basis of the form and content of the opportunities they have to express their individuality and develop their self-consciousness. Yet on another level, that awareness of the role of human nature in the formation of the social life of individuals provides evidence that society should be radically restructured. Specifically, the civil and political institutions and practices should be superseded not merely suspended. Individuals could then display the potential for individuality that corresponds to the level of development of the forces of production, in close accordance with the material base of existence.

Both of these positions reveal that the expression of human nature, within a specific historical setting, or over a certain historical epoch, is more fluid than fixed. This notion of human nature still allows the claim that human nature has a motivating and decisive force in historical change. It must express itself, and find its outlet in a manner which is defined by the social context, and not simply by the content of human nature. The ways in which human nature is expressed in specific stages of capitalism show how the potential developments of individuality are affected by different stages in the development of capitalist society.

Bourgeois individuality

For Marx, the emergence of capitalism was dominated by the bourgeoisie, the class which was progressive in the sense that it was associated with the means of production that were superior to the feudal mode. Marx's own opinion of the revolutionary, and therefore historically progressive, nature of the bourgeoisie is nowhere better demonstrated than in the *Communist Manifesto*.

> The bourgeoisie, wherever it has got the upper hand, has put an end to all feudal, patriarchal, idyllic relations. It has piti-lessly torn asunder the motley feudal ties that bound man to his 'natural superiors', and has left remaining no other nexus between man and man than naked self-interest, than callous 'cash payment'. It has drowned the most heavenly ecstasies of religious fervor, of chivalrous enthusiasm, of philistine senti-mentalism, in the icy water of egotistical calculation. It has resolved personal worth into exchange value, and in place of the numberless indefeasible chartered freedoms has set up that single, unconscionable freedom – Free Trade. In one word, for exploitation, veiled by religious and political illusions, it has substituted naked, shameless, direct brutal exploitation. ([1847] 1968, p. 38)

Here Marx's enthusiasm for the revolutionary character of the bourgeoisie emerges, especially in the way that it succeeded in brushing aside the social relations of the previously dominant mode of production. This reflects Marx's confidence in his theory of change, as a description and as an explanatory model, but also raises the question of the role of human agents in the making of history. The underlying enthusiasm for the bourgeoisie stems from more than their capacity and action in supplanting feudal relations. Although this is important, and gives Marx reason to be optimistic about the *next* historical transformation, the more interesting feature is the way that Marx portrays the bourgeois individual as the key protagonist. There is no competition between classes within one mode of production, but a battle between modes of production, where the bourgeois is the representative of the capitalist mode of production. Given the advanced nature of that mode of production, bourgeois individuals are in one sense fighting a battle for the progress of humanity, a battle to enable human society to take advantage of its abilities and knowledge.[6]

In terms of individuality, bourgeois individuals can be expected to exhibit a high level of development consistent with the development of the forces of production under feudalism. The bourgeois individual is therefore a special case, representing both the movement of history and the specificity of a particular form of productive relations. It is to be expected that such expressions of individuality do not quickly emerge fresh and new with the triumph of capitalism, however. As Jean Baechler points out in *The Origins of Capitalism*, the bourgeois individual has an identifiable but long history:

> the genesis of the bourgeois is explained by several original features of Western evolution from the late Middle Ages: (a) an almost complete disappearance of ordered human interaction, (b) the formation of a social system adapted to this situation that did not include the merchant, (c) the re-birth of the cities, now stripped of every political and military function and, because of this, forcing their members into economic activities, and (d) the illegitimate nature of those activities forced the bourgeois either to assimilate into legitimate orders or to make his own values triumphant ... Thus did Western society produce this bizarre individual, the bourgeois, devoted exclusively to profit and fundamentally dissatisfied because his way of life was not recognized by society and because it was impossible for him to attain dignity without repudiating himself. (1975, p. 71)

Baechler thus sees change in individuals occurring before the revolutionary success of the class as a whole. He also stresses the importance of agency and contrasts the growth of self-motivation and self-understanding with the confining nature of existing institutions and values. The eclipse of feudal social interactions clearly places early bourgeois individuals in conflict with the classes whose values and interests were superordinate. In this sense, the bourgeois individuals were an important part of the description of feudal society. An understanding of their role is essential for an adequate account of feudalism, even though the bourgeoisie may not always have been a crucially determining influence on that social formation.

The bourgeois individual had to exist before the bourgeoisie as a class overcame the feudal social order. The explanatory dimension of the class analysis, with specific relation to the transition to capitalism, implies the bourgeois individual as an entity with a set of values and interests characteristic of new capitalist individuals. Moreover, those individuals would have to constitute a class not just in itself, but a class-for-itself. This has to be the case if the development from one social formation to another is not an historical accident. The ability to make history is one of the qualities of human action and agency that Marx claims differentiate capitalist relations of production from more or less primitive modes of production. Thus bourgeois individuality and the class attitudes of the bourgeoisie have explanatory significance. It gives an insight into the differences between the feudal and the capitalist individual. These attitudes or rubrics are indicative of the capitalist mode of production, and of the development of individuality in the history of human society. According to Gandy, Marx and Engels were well aware of the demands that the emerging capitalist order made on the individual: it 'produced a commercial class that lived by individualism, thrift and discipline' (1979, p. 155).

To live by such rubrics is to have an understanding of what they entail. The consciousness of these three rules or standards is not a settled issue, however, then or now. It is certain, on the other hand, that the consciousness of individualism, thrift and discipline is, for the bourgeois individual, a much more advanced one than that possible for the feudal individual. In the first place, the forces of production under capitalism provide a greater degree of autonomy. This extra dimension of human agency makes the concept of thrift a much more meaningful one, since it can, and must, incorporate the ideas of forgoing immediate monetary gain in order to reap a profit later. Thrift is an act not merely to secure the future, but materially to enhance it. Similarly discipline implies control, which requires understanding, and the understanding of the bourgeois individual is greater, whether it be of the self narrowly conceived, or of the capacity of humans *vis-à-vis* nature.

However, this positive development of individuality as a result of the historical progression from feudalism to capitalism is a one-sided development. Tempering his praise for the bourgeoisie in the *Communist Manifesto,* Marx remarks: 'The modern bourgeois society that has sprouted from the ruins of feudal society has not done away with class antagonism. It has but established new classes, new conditions of oppression, new forms of struggle in place of the old ones' ([1847] 1968, p. 36). There is no need here to restate Marx's grounds for believing that the economic formation of capitalism is exploitation of class by class, and that this will lead to further change, and the possibility of a more advanced mode of production. In terms of the development of individuality, Marx was equally certain that the 'freedoms' of capitalism, although real enough advances in comparison to the relations of inequality and exploitation under feudalism, were severely restricted. This was especially true of the key characteristic of capitalism – free competition.

> Hence, on the other side, the insipidity of the view that free competition is the ultimate development of human freedom; and that the negation of free competition = negation of individual freedom and of social production founded on individual freedom. It is nothing more than free development on a limited basis – the basis of the rule of capital. This kind of individual freedom is therefore at the same time the most complete suspension of all individual freedom, and the most complete subjugation of individuality under social conditions which assume the form of objective powers, even of overpowering objects – of things independent of the relations among individuals themselves. ([1857–8] 1973, p. 652)

Marx employs a number of crucial abstractions here. These are, in order of use: development, capital, liberty, individuality and material forces. The concept of development is used in a way that implies a distinction between the historical development of individuality and a progression through a series of modes of production. They are related, but they are not necessarily equivalent processes. Capital, of course, refers to the classification of the mode of production, and is the source, in this case, of the kind of 'liberty' which Marx is discussing. Thus the concept of liberty is not entirely dealt with at the level of abstraction, for Marx also implies that liberty is used as a mere abstract idea and falsely attributed to the nature of *social* existence under capitalism, when it can only really relate to the structurally delimited economic realm. Individuality, too, has an important status in this passage. Marx clearly had in mind a particular 'entity', an entity which cannot be equated with the idea of the abstract individual redolent of the various forms of philosophical individualism. This 'entity' is the abstraction from the existence of 'real, living human individuals' in actual historical circumstances, circumstances which can always be specified, even if this calls for variable levels of generality. Conceived in this way, Marx can counterpose individuality to the final concept he employs, namely, material forces. There is no argument, among Marxists at least, that material forces exist in society. A theoretical acceptance of the reality of material forces means that individuality has a status in history that has become equivalent to a material force.

It is vital, then, to examine Marx's characterization of that relationship. First, Marx talks disparagingly of the 'total subjugation of individuality to social conditions'. Thus his critique of capitalism is based to some extent on the importance of individuality. It is one of his criteria for proper human existence, and capitalist relations of production are to be criticized because they actually prevent adequate realization of human potentiality. This is some distance from the claim that social conditions *determine* the level and type of individuality. To underline this point, Marx distinguishes between the appearance and the reality of social conditions, noting how they may take the form of 'objective powers' that are 'independent of the relations among individuals themselves'. Capitalism subjugates individuality to the extent that it makes only *individualism* possible and permissible. Such subjugated individuality, thereby, does not appear to have any reciprocal influence on the social condition which works so directly upon it. This may well be labelled 'determination in the last instance by the economy', but it is the very condition from which Marx wished to see humankind freed. As Wood has pointed out, it is the *raison d'être* of Marx's entire theoretical and practical endeavour (1981, p. 112).

Notwithstanding the way that capitalism characteristically constrains the full expression of individuality, Marx has confidence in both individuality and the possibility for its full realization. This is because development of individuality has occurred and is still occurring, at once lessening the disparity between the alienated social existence of capitalist society and a society of free individuality, and sharpening the consciousness of the differences between the two. This is to distinguish between levels of individuality, or ways of understanding it. Individuality is an historically developing phenomenon; individuality relates to a form of existence in a particular society; individuality may also express the potential for a *different* form of existence in a particular society; individuality may denote a specific form of society.

On this basis, bourgeois individualism is the capitalist form of individuality. It is the partial and contrived form of individual existence consistent with the exploitative and one-sided nature of capitalist society. It is in a dialectically contradictory relation to free individuality, and the development of the forces of production under capitalism must mean the progressive working out of that relation.

Proletarian individuality

The counterpoint to the historically specific bourgeois individual is, in a number of ways, the proletarian individual. At its emergence, the term proletariat is not used to refer to a collectivity. Instead, it is a generic term, describing individuals by virtue of their situation under capitalism. They become the representatives of humanity much later, partly because of the way that capitalism robs these individuals of the social connections with their human powers and abilities. From within capitalist society springs the progenitor of the future, according to Marx. The proletariat is the agent of change and the basis for non-class relations of production. As Gandy asks:

> What is the proletariat like, by contrast, during the 'historical genesis' of capitalism? This includes industrialization (1770–1850 in England): young people from the country crowd into city slums to work long hours for low pay. This young proletariat lacks 'education, tradition, and habit.' These workers don't see capitalism as 'self-evident'. They want to smash it and build a new world. They are revolutionary as they pass through rapid capitalist development. (1979, p. 159)

There are a number of reasons why the proletariat is revolutionary in the early stages of capitalist development. The first cause stems from the lack of a unifying social milieu, the absence of a structure within which individuals might find a position that

141

identifies them as members of the community. This is liberty, albeit of a negative kind, but is important for its effects on views of how the world might be. Second, this is the period in which the economic structure is undergoing sea changes, with the consequence that other, social, structures are damaged and destroyed, casting certain sections of society – especially the proletariat – adrift. In one way, the link between base and super-structure, as it is fairly crudely represented, holds true. That is, the offsetting appurtenances of feudalism, like the reciprocal obligations of lord and serf, a degree of self-sufficiency and the advantages of community, are wiped away, leaving only the raw fact of exploitative relations of production. The capitalist mode of production, and capitalism as a tradition, have yet to take hold, making this form of society more open to the expectations and influences of individuals, if only in disorganized, ineffectual ways.

Finally, the proletarians are revolutionary individuals not merely due to their desire to smash capitalism, for this was a desire shared by other, even reactionary, groups in society. What makes the proletarians become revolutionary by definition is their position *vis-à-vis* other classes. In respect of the feudal ruling and peasant classes, proletarian individuality has moved far beyond feudal social relations and can no longer be accommodated by that society. Yet in the absence of self-consciousness as a class of capitalism, this early proletariat does not wish to entrench either the feudal or capitalist modes of production. Thus its members are revolutionary for their desire to remake the world, but they are not necessarily, or not yet at least, *progressive*. This is because they, unlike Marx, do not appreciate the superiority of the capitalist mode of production, and have not realized that it is the *ownership* of the means of production, not merely their character, which is at issue.

> Thus, while the refugee serfs only wished to be free to develop and assert those conditions of existence which were already there, and hence, in the end, only arrived at free labour, the proletarians, if they are to assert themselves as individuals, will have to abolish the very condition of their existence hitherto (which has, moreover, been that of all society up to the present), namely, labour. ([1845–6] 1970, p. 85)

The key phrase here is that the proletariat 'will have to' abolish labour, a condition of existence that has been the basic element 'of all society up to the present'. The abolition of labour is an idea almost too advanced to be conceivable, even now. Nevertheless, it has two levels of interest. Its deeper significance is the potent claim made about fundamental human nature. This is that humans are more than the sum of their productive and reproductive labours. This view is endorsed by other remarks in the *Grundrisse*. Capitalism may appear to enable a human to be a free wage-worker, and thereby produce value, but

> it is rather his power of disposing his labour, effected by exchange with him, which has value. It is not he who stands towards the capitalist as exchange value, but the capitalist towards him. His *valuelessness* and *devaluation* is the presupposition of capital and the precondition of *free* labour in general ... The worker is thereby formally posited as a person who is something for himself *apart from his* labour, and who alienates his life-expression only as a means towards his own life. (Marx, [1857–8] 1973, p. 289)

That is, the wage-labour relation of production brings with it an awareness of the power and value inherent in the *person*, *not* the relation, which is in the economic interest of both, but on entirely different terms.

As a surface phenomenon, the abolition of labour and the possibility of proletarians establishing themselves as individuals means the end of a conscious and practical distinction between labouring and non-labouring life activity. Such a distinction would be meaningless to wo/men able to assert themselves as individuals. The defining characteristic is no longer labour, but the condition of freedom. Such individuals would regulate their activity according to need and ability and decide for themselves the details of the realms of necessity and freedom. This is, of course, part of the vision of the future.

Given the different kinds of revolutionary consciousness and activity, the early proletarians, although singled out by Marx as potentially the most revolutionary force, were in the beginning unaware of their historical uniqueness and significance. It was only as a result of being under the crushing and apparent exploitation of the capitalist mode of production that they could generate an entirely new revolution, one that was simultaneously destructive of the existing economic and social realities and constructive of a new economic and social order. Marx argued that: 'The *surplus labour of the mass* has ceased to be the condition for the development of general wealth, just as the *non-labour of the few*, for the development of the powers of the human head'

143

([1857–8] 1973, p.705). Crucial to Marx's theory of change is an account of how this impinges on individuals. How quickly, that is, could individuals reject their past? Marx seems to indicate that the changes in the mode of production have swiftly brought the powers of individuals, and not just a few individuals, to a new pre-eminence in the development of capitalism. He saw:

> The free development of individualities, and hence not the reduction of necessary labour time so as to posit surplus labour, but rather the general reduction of necessary labour time to a minimum, which then corresponds to the artistic, scientific etc. development of the individuals in the time set free, and with the means created, for all of them. (ibid., p. 706)

This is a remarkable passage for three reasons. First, Marx indicates that it is distinct or unique persons who have a potentiality for being individuals. Second, those 'individualities' can be developed within capitalism. Third, one of the ends of social and political change is to permit just such a development of individualities. This leads to Marx's next point, where he claims that the existence and development of individuals and individualities by capitalist relations themselves are firmly within his model of a developing set of historical forces, and will bring about revolutionary change. 'Forces of production and social relations – two different sides of the development of the social individual – appear to capital as means, and are merely means for it to produce on its limited foundation. In fact, however, they are the material conditions to blow this foundation sky-high' (ibid.). The contradiction, for Marx, is between a mode of production and the developing powers of the individual; he is certain that it is the developed individual who will survive explosive social change.

Individuality and change through capitalism

Marx foresaw that capitalism would inevitably bring about the development of the individual of a kind capable of hastening the downfall of capitalism. This adds an important dimension to the conventional view of his theory of change, which usually focuses on class development and activity. The development of individuality in capitalism is, however, of no little consequence. As Marx argues in the *German Ideology*:

the division of labour implies the possibility, nay the fact that intellectual and material activity – enjoyment and labour, production and consumption – devolve on different individuals, and that the only possibility of their not coming into contradiction lies in the negation in its turn of the division of labour. It is self-evident, moreover, that 'species', 'bonds', 'the higher being', 'concept', 'scruple', are merely the idealist, spiritual expression, the conception apparently of the isolated individual, the image of very empirical fetters and limitations, within which the mode of production of life and the form of intercourse coupled with it move. ([1845–6] 1970, p. 52)

In other words, Marx is claiming that individual differentiation is part of individual development taken as a whole, but that the process has to be judged according to the conditions under which it takes place. Under capitalism, progress is occurring, but it is at the same time forced to express itself in ways that are as inadequate and contradictory as capitalist society. In this way, Marx is able to claim that the individualization of the isolated individual is the hallmark of the limited extent to which human development can be expressed. Nevertheless, he does not wish to underestimate these movements, nor is he slow to identify the material conditions which bring about those partial progressions. As such, the development of individuals is related to his class analysis of society, even if it does not automatically strengthen his class theory of change. As Marx states it, the proletariat, in contrast to the propertied class, is driven to anger rather than power.

The propertied class and the class of the proletariat present the same human self-alienation. But the former class finds in this self-alienation its confirmation and its good, its own power: it has in it a semblance of human existence. The class of the proletariat feels annihilated in its self-alienation; it sees in it its powerlessness and the reality of an inhuman existence. In the words of Hegel, the class of the proletariat is indignant at that abasement, an indignation to which it is necessarily driven by the contradiction between its human nature and its condition of life, which is the outright, decisive and comprehensive negation of that nature. ([1845] 1956, p. 51)

If the condition of life is 'an outright, decisive and comprehensive negation' of all that the proletariat is, then how can this be known?

Marx juxtaposes this negation with nature, but it is not clear whether he is referring to human nature, or the nature of the proletarian class as a whole. There are problems with the appeal to human nature, but it can be assumed that Marx was not alluding to some essence here. He was making a distinction within one notion of human nature as it is expressed in a particular historical epoch, given specific conditions. In this sense, then, the propertied class and the proletariat share the same basic human nature. They are equally affected by a mode of production that is exploitative and alienating, even though this shows itself in different ways and has a marked divergence in its impact. As Cohen points out, the bourgeoisie is content, whereas the proletariat is not, because: '1) the bourgeoisie, unlike the proletariat, cannot hope to escape its alienation; and 2) the bourgeoisie, unlike the proletariat, has no desire to escape its alienation' (1968, p. 213).

The individual member of the bourgeoisie, it is important to note, has undergone a change in capitalism, from what Cohen describes as 'he who is a most stupendously productive individual', to a capitalist who is variously miser, owner or consumer (ibid., p. 223). Capitalism leads to the degradation of the classes it brings into developed existence, powerless against the forces which first gave rise to the initial dynamism of the bourgeoisie. Alienation, from this perspective, is not explicable simply in terms of an absence of control over one's product and ultimately life. Rather, it is a measure of the frustration and diversion of the historical process, of the development of the forces of production, because the articulation of capitalist society has meant that 'the most stupendously productive individual' no longer has an equivalent role in society. Such individuals, Marx was pleased to observe about capitalism, had finally in effect become world-historical individuals. Marx's indictment of capitalism can also be seen as a reaction to the way that capitalism exploited, brutalized and degraded the most significant advance in the development of human potentiality since the discovery of metallurgy - represented by the bourgeoisie itself.

Marx acknowledged both the debt to the bourgeoisie and their consequent demise and alienation. Yet he is not concerned for their alienation on moral grounds, any more than he is for the alienation of the proletariat on those same moral grounds. Marx rejects the bourgeoisie as a class whose historical moment has been fulfilled. As such, it cannot help but restrain future, beneficial, ramifications of the existence of stupendously productive individuals. The mantle of progress and change has gone to the proletariat, not because of Marx's sympathy or outrage, but because the bourgeoisie is unable to carry history forward in a way that is consistent with the ends of 'artistic, scientific etc. development' of individuals. As Edgley states:

> the ideas of the bourgeoisie, progressive and revolutionary when the class is rising, have now become conservative and re-actionary. The bourgeoisie class position, originally cognitively liberating, is now a fetter on cognitive advance. The most general form of this cognitive deficiency is the historical outlook of the ruling class. As the class whose interests depend on the maintenance of the existing social system, their overall tendency is to represent that system as natural and its fundamentals not subject to change. (Edgley, 1983, p. 289)

The underlying interest here is that advance should take place, not merely in the material well-being of the working class, but in the process of cognitive development, as Edgley would have it, or in the 'stupendousness' of individual productive capacity in Cohen's account. In the *Holy Family*, Marx's concern for the transhistorical importance of a developing individuality is nowhere more clear. Here he appears in anguish over the manner in which the potential of the individual in capitalism is recognized yet reified, acknowledged but abstracted, seen but never properly understood.

> What a terrible mistake it is to have to recognize and sanc-tion in the Rights of Man modern bourgeois society, the society of industry, of private interest freely following its aims of anarchy, of the self-alienated nature and spiritual individuality, and yet subsequently to annul the *manifestations of the life* of that society in separate individuals. ([1845] 1956, pp. 164–5)

Marx is referring here to the way in which general historical truths are mistaken for aspects only of a particular society – in this case capitalism – while the nature of the society ought to be judged by those truths, properly understood. The manifestations of life to which Marx refers are the outcomes of the productive forces of the individual in capitalist society, not simply the basis for the assertion of self-evident human rights. With respect to the theory of alienation, Ollman is right to draw a distinction between

147

the existence of alienation, in some form and to some degree, and the applicability of the theory of alienation … Marx did not use the theory of alienation to understand the individual in capitalism but to understand capitalism from the standpoint of the individual. This is achieved by focusing not only on the individual but on those elements of his nature over which he has lost control and which are now controlling him. (1976, p. 53)

Ollman is not arguing that the individual *qua* individual provides the perspective on capitalism. Rather, the individual has dual reference points. Marx's criticism, echoed by Ollman, is that wholesale attempts to be bourgeois individualists, to assume 'rights' and live 'freely' cannot fully be accommodated, even though they are ostensibly encouraged. Capitalism, once founded upon a radical development of individualism, eventually becomes threatened by its earliest qualities – the drive to change and overcome, and assert the primacy of the individual agent over ossified feudal structures and strictures. For Marx, 'the revolutionary class becomes conservative' ((1847), p. 118). More specifically, Fritzhand claims that

> The ideals of freedom, equality, fraternity, universal develop-ment and happiness of each individual, just like the principle of *laissez faire*, began to play a merely apologetic role … Less and less was said about the harmony of the individual and social interests, while the thesis began to be voiced about an allegedly insurmountable antagonism between personal and social interests. (1980, p. 23)

Marx's own awareness of the disparity between the idealism and reality of individualist ideology is most marked when he identifies the exploitative and deceptive character of developing capitalist society. His powerful attack on individualism, however, is not simply aimed at overcoming individualism as a theory, or set of ideals. Instead, the attack is, as always, on capitalism and its association with individualist ideology, and this is not to be confused with the ideology itself.[7]

The connection between a capitalism which develops, and an individualist ideology which moves in tandem with that development, is crucial. Marx's critique of capitalism illuminates the varying demands made upon individuals, and how this affects their potential and ability to realize their capacities. At the same time, his critique exposes the inadequacy of life under capitalism.

Again, this is in terms of the potentialities and capacities of individuals, but it exposes also the individualism that capitalism generates. This simultaneous illumination and exposure puts a fresh perspective on bourgeois individuality (how it is *possible* to be an individual under capitalism) and bourgeois individualism (how one is *supposed* to be an individual under capitalism). As capitalism changes, so do the possibilities for, and suppositions about, the individual. What has to be distinguished, then, is the way that stages of individualism are implicitly recognized, and the relation of such stages to capitalism as a process of social change. For Ollman, Marxian analysis must always be a source of such differences, which become apparent as soon as the fluidity of capitalist relations is perceived:

> Each capitalist practice and institution reflects the alienated relationships of the whole system, but the more distinctive qualities of alienation – separation from and loss of control over one's immediate environment, mistaking human for inhuman agencies, manipulation by indifferent and/or hostile forces, etc. – exhibit differences of degree and form both between classes and through various stages in the development of capitalist society. (1976, p. 265)

Ollman's description does not necessarily rely upon the existence or otherwise of alienation (which is still a matter of dispute). More accurately, the 'distinctive qualities' are of capitalist social relations, and their growth and change lead to an expectation of changes in the way that they impinge upon individuals. Thus the development of capitalist society was bound to draw heavy criticism from Marx. On the one hand it deepened the exploitation of the individual proletarian and bourgeois. On the other, it began to negate the real progress achieved in capitalism's victory over feudalism.

But what is the materialist basis for the claim that capitalism as a mode of production has changed in such a way as to affect the impact and significance of individualist ideology or the character of individualism? It was Engels who highlighted the necessary distinction in the material analysis of society. He acknowledged that, in *Capital*, Marx's theory 'views modern capitalist production as a mere passing stage in the economic history of mankind': this should not prevent the more detailed understanding that there are 'two great and essentially different periods of economic history: the period of manufacture proper, based on the division of manual labour, and the period of modern industry based on machinery'

([1867] 1976, p. 111). Thus capitalist society may be just one more stage in the larger historical movement (and the last in human pre-history), but this does not mean that the description of capitalism can be straightforwardly achieved. The incidence of various forms or stages of capitalism, the shift from one to another, must also bring about adjustments in the lives of individuals.

That there are stages in the development of the productive forces within capitalism has a number of interesting implications. First, there is support for the idea that there is a variety of kinds of individuality in capitalism, and it is possible to distinguish between them. Second, the existence of kinds of individuality gives rise to different responses from Marx. He does not restrict himself just to the powerful attack on abstract individualism, to which commentators generally point as the best indication of his overall position or the trend of his thought.

First, Marx's critique of society is augmented by a developmental view of individuality which gives weight and breadth to a veridical portrayal of capitalist society. Thus the individualism associated with early capitalism, full of promise and creator of freedoms both positive and negative, is concomitant with an individuality of fruitful differentiation, beyond the feudal servitude of pre-conformist sameness. And the kinds of individuals to which Marx referred constituted a particular category in the first stage of the productive forces: 'in the period of manufacture the main productive force was the manufactory: a capitalist brought artisans under one roof, supplied raw materials, paid wages, and sold the product' (Gandy, 1979, p. 121). For Marx, the praise of early capitalism functions better to press home the debasement, degradation and provisionality of bourgeois individualism. The developmental aspect of individualism is retained, because Marx wishes to establish the starkness of the contrast between the ideals of individualism and the reality of its capitalist expression. This critique of the present is made even more potent by his refusal to invoke any return to the past, no matter how recent.[8] Thus he rejects, not the ideals of individualism in early capitalism, but the mode of production which was *bound*, in principle and in practice, to reject those ideals.

The theory of change in Marx's thought also displays the development of capitalism with a distinctly progressive character. However, the progression is *internal* to capitalism:

Bourgeois revolutions, like those of the eighteenth century storm swiftly from success to success; their dramatic effects outdo each other; men and things seem set in sparkling brilliance; ecstasy is the everyday spirit; but they are short-lived; soon they have attained the zenith and a long crapulent depression lays hold of society before it leaves soberly to assimilate the results of its storm-and-stress period. (Marx, [1852] 1973, p. 99)

There is development in the context of capitalism itself, and not in respect of feudalism alone. Marx is able to see this by virtue of the employment of the dialectical methods, which, 'in its rational form': 'includes in its positive understandings of what exists a simultaneous recognition of its negation, its inevitable destruction; because it regards every historically developed form as being in a fluid state, in motion, and therefore grasps its transient aspect as well' ([1867] 1976, p. 103).

This transient aspect contextualizes the movement from early manufacture to later developments in capitalist production. As Gandy demonstrates, the stages are linked, yet with quite distinct implications. 'In the period of machine industry, the main productive force is the mechanised factory. To these stages – bourgeois manufacture and factory organization – correspond two kinds of production relations: capitalist and communist' (1979, p. 121). The progression within capitalism, then, is in terms of the potential for post-capitalist society which is embedded in the actuality of factory organization. The capital realization process, for example: 'while it has the tendency to *heighten the productive forces boundlessly*, it *also and equally* makes one-sided, limits etc, the *main force of production, the human being himself*, and has the tendency in general to restrict the forces of production' ([1857–8] 1973, p. 422). Such change is crucial for Marx's theory of social change, wherein future society comes to exist as a possibility in the social formation it is to supersede, both at the level of human beings, and of productive power in general. His views on large-scale industry underline the claims that factory organization is an advance, within capitalism, over manufacture; and the negative aspects of each stage can readily be seen.

Thus large scale industry, by its very nature, necessitates variation of labour, fluidity of functions, and mobility of the worker in all directions. But on the other hand, in its capitalist form it reproduces the old division of labour with its ossified particularities ... This absolute contradiction does away with all repose, all fixity and all security as far as the workers' life station is concerned. ([1867] 1976, pp. 617–18)

151

Nevertheless, these same conditions show that each stage is also laden with potential for human 'progress', and progress is conceived of as *individual* development. As Marx goes on to say:

> But ... large scale industry ... makes the recognition of variation of labour and hence of the fitness of the worker for the maximum number of different kinds of labour into a question of life and death. This possibility of varying labour must become a general law of social development, and the existing relations must be adopted to meet its realization in practice ... the partially developed individual, who is merely the bearer of one specialized social function, must be replaced by the totally developed individual, for whom the different social functions are different modes of activity which he takes up in turn. (ibid, p. 618)

The contrast between the accounts of early and later capitalism provided by the critique of society and the theory of change is quite marked. The optimism over early capitalism from the point of view of individualism gives way to cynicism, but at the fully developed or factory organization stage of capitalism a renewed optimism appears, based upon a fresh set of opportunities for change. Thus capitalism is both criticized and applauded at every stage, but for quite different reasons. Constitutionally, capitalism is unable to respect and value the social relations it spawns, and the ways it achieves need satisfaction. 'It is destructive of all this, and constantly revolutionizes, tearing down all the barriers which hem in the development of the forces of production, and the exploitation and exchange of natural and mental forces' (Marx, [1857–8] 1973, p. 410).

This is not evidence of contradictions within Marx's thought, but does suggest a high degree of sophistication of the analysis of the individual as a concrete manifestation of life. Marx was aware, in other words, of the possible ways that an individual could exist in society, and these brought about changes to the array of needs and mental forces. Individuals would have greater mental forces at their disposal (such as their technological sophistication), greater cultural diversity, and richness in human social needs. At any point in the development of the productive forces, Marx was capable of distinguishing between the *content* of individual existence, and the *form* of that existence. Neither one nor both would uniformly attract praise or condemnation, because Marx's normative judgements tend to incorporate an attitude to the progression any stage

Individuality in capitalist society

Individuality in capitalist society

represented over a previous one, and the possibilities inherent in any stage for further development.

The development of capitalism brings with it a development of individuality as an historical prerequisite for social change. The question remains, however, as to the nature of that change, whether it is to be 'progress' toward communism or degeneration into barbarism. Both possibilities are consistent with Marx's critique of capitalist individualism, because it views the individual as object and subject. Although both cannot be said actually to exist, they are both *tendencies*, and Marx's aim is to expose the inadequacy of the former in order to facilitate the realization of the latter. As Kosik argues:

> There is a difference in principle, whether Man as an individual *disintegrates* in social relations, whether he is overwhelmed by them and deprived of his own appearance so that hypostatized social relations employ uniform and anonymous individuals as their instruments (in which case the transposition seems to represent the supremacy of the all-powerful society over the powerless individual), or whether the individual is the *subject* of social relations and freely *moves* within them as in human and humanly respectable surroundings of people retaining their own appearances, ie, of individualities. Individuality is neither an addition nor an unexplainable irrational remainder to which the individual is reduced after subtracting the social relations, historical situations and contexts and so on. (1967, p. 189)

Marx's account of capitalist individualism can be conceived as a critical appraisal of the extent to which the individual is hypostatized, and the ways in which the individual becomes or can become the 'subject' – a free agent, controlling circumstances, selecting from the range of alternatives open to people – of social relations. Indeed, on Ellen Wood's reading of the *Theses on Feuerbach*: 'Implicit in it is his idea of freedom as self-activity, self-creation, and individual self-realization – the reunification of subject and object by means of man's active participation in the world through use of all his faculties' (1972, p. 34).

Bourgeois individuality, in its various modes under capitalism, is just a moment in the process of the individuation of humanity. From this perspective, it is possible to go beneath the critical appraisal of capitalist individualism, where differentiation between persons is accompanied by a corrosive disunity of those persons (Keat, 1979, p. 137). What is revealed is the development of individuality that must continue to occur under capitalism. This claim does not rely upon an idealist notion of the inevitably 'progressive' nature of history, but upon Marx's materialist account of capitalism. First, and in comparative terms, 'modern industry never views or treats the existing form of a production process as the definitive one. Its technical basis is therefore revolutionary, whereas all earlier modes of production were essentially conservative' (Marx, [1867] 1976, p. 617). Second, and in more detail, Marx refers to the interaction of capital and labour.

> Capital's ceaseless striving towards the general form of wealth drives labour beyond the limits of its natural paltriness, and thus creates the material elements for the development of the rich individuality which is as all-sided in its production as in its consumption, and whose labour also therefore appears no longer as labour, but as the full development of activity itself, in which natural necessity in its direct form has disappeared; because a historically created need has taken place of the natural one. This is why *capital is productive; ie an essential relation for the development of the social productive forces.* ([1857–8] 1973, p. 325)

These quotations establish, on the one hand, that the material conditions for the constant transformation of social relations must *always* exist in capitalism, and on the other hand, that such transformations develop *specifically* the conditions for an all-sided individuality in practice and as a potential. Such an individuality is closer to the realization of fundamental human nature, as the relationship to the notion of wealth (explored further in Chapter 5) shows. It establishes, in a number of related ways, how a *general* historical development of the individual has taken place. First, the individual is the origin of the process of value creation: 'his life is the source in which his own use value constantly rekindles itself up to a certain time, when it is worn out, and constantly confronts capital again in order to begin the same exchange anew' (Marx, [1857–8] 1973, p. 283). Second, the kind of activity that individuals must undertake forms an attachment to the historical development of that stage of society. 'Since he exchanges his use value for the general form of wealth, he becomes a co-participant in general wealth up to the limit which, of course, turns into a qualitative one, as in every exchange' (ibid.). This connection with wealth for the purpose of 'the satisfaction of his needs is generally physical, social, etc.', and has a distinctive character and meaning for the individuals under capitalism (ibid., pp. 284, 705–6). Every individual becomes a part of the capitalist world order. They are vital to the creation of capitalist wealth, and can be excluded from it only as a matter of degree. The actual satisfaction of need is an open question: 'he is neither bound to particular objects, nor to a particular manner of satisfaction. The sphere of his consumption is not qualitatively restricted, only quantitatively. This distinguishes him from the slave, serf, etc' (ibid., p. 283).

This is a new freedom, an expansion of human possibilities. This is, for Marx, a phenomenon which 'falls outside the economic relation' (ibid.) Moreover, he went on to say that it corresponded to 'as yet no other developed relation before us' (ibid.). At the same time, he recognized that this unique relation intrinsic to capitalism between life as a source of value and life as a source of wealth gave individuals as consumers 'an entirely different importance as agents of production from that which they possessed eg in antiquity or in the middle ages, or now possess in Asia' (ibid.).

That importance, however, did not lead Marx to assume that he had identified the change and development which would be constitutive of a revolutionary individuality. This representation of human nature under particular circumstances remained bound, in his view, by other historical conditions. His focus remained on the effects on class conflict, and change was to be mediated by political action in the economic interests of the exploiting class. This commitment to the idea of the proletariat coming-to-be as a world-historical force persists, for good reason. As Edgley notes: 'As the class that needs no subordinate class to dominate, it is the only class that has the potentiality for classlessness and thus the power to effect the transition to a classless society. As such, its cognitive advantage will not be superseded by any other class' (1983, p. 289). The proletariat has a distinct 'cognitive advantage' because the individual members of that class have been subject to and revolutionized by the relentless technological achievement and innovation of capital and modern industry. They have acquired, in his words, more 'mental forces'. In their work experience, exploited and degraded though it is, it is they who have been forced to enlarge their competencies, to extend their capacities, to utilize to ever-higher degrees their faculties. They have been exposed, in both production and consumption, to what Marx refers to as 'the full development of activity itself'. R. E. Lane argues that the material conditions just do not exist, nor are they foreseeable, wherein any other group could benefit from the development of 'cognitive complexity' to any greater extent (1978, pp. 17–23).

Marx associated with this realization of human powers a quite remarkable general power – the freedom *not* to dominate and exploit, the freedom, that is, to exist without creating other classes. It is this power which provides normative superiority for the claim that the proletariat must successfully fight a class war, in contradistinction to the bourgeoisie, whose members earn praise because they are *technologically* superior.

The limitations of Marx's conception of social change stem from the insistence that cognitive advantage is not just necessary but also sufficient. Put another way, Marx overemphasized the importance of the working class strictly in terms of the forces and relations of production under capitalism. The proletariat continues to be derivatively defined. Even though they are to become world-historical individuals, the onset of such a history is dependent upon capitalism providing just the right conditions. Until the revolutionary moment, the focus perforce remains on the defensive reactions of the working class (not yet the proletariat). Cognitive advantage, along with the development of individuality as the development of activity itself, suggests that the proletarians ought to be seen not only as the future creators of history, but as key agents in the redefinition of existence in the present, outside, and in contrast to, the structural limitations of conventional work experience. It is true that Marx sometimes takes into account the implications of change under capitalism for the role and status of women in society, for example, but this is usually in (the narrow) terms of his definition of the economic sphere. Marx tended not to look in the opposite direction, as it were, to see the impact of the cognitive gains of individual development under capitalism outside the confines of waged work existence. The 'reserve army of unemployed' is thus understood in terms of its potential as wage-labourers, or in terms of its past status of productive employment. Women, when considered, are subsumed under the general category of exploited labour or seen as unpaid labour in the secondary service of capital.

Thus, from several perspectives, Marx's theory of change through class action is a relatively simplistic accompaniment to the historical materialist method for analysing society. Part of the reason for this stems from Marx's failure to pursue some of the implications of his own thought, and in particular the notion of a developing individuality of revolutionary potential. As will be seen in the next chapter, Marx viewed the development of the individual only as an indication of what s/he *would* be in communism, not what s/he could already do in the transition phase. The real key to change lay for Marx in the economic structure of capitalism. It is the way that Marx defined and refined his economic analysis which explains in part why his thought is usually regarded as so antagonistic to an account of the radical or revolutionary potential of developed individuality. In constructing a general model of capitalism, one that was explicitly to have relevance for *all* industrialized capitalist countries, Marx locked himself into a view of the relations specific to a capitalist *society* that approximated only to the early and middle stages of capitalism. Absent was an account of the changes in capitalist social relations from the middle stage of capitalism to decline, crisis and transition to post-capitalist social relations. Such change is a necessary corollary to Marx's dynamic and contradictory method of capitalism. The contradictions of capitalism would precipitate revolutionary possibilities, according to Markovic's account, only under the following conditions:

> (a) pure commodity production; (b) the existence of a class which, under conditions of commodity production *is* exploited and *an sich* is a potential revolutionary force, but which need not necessarily be aware of its social being and thus become a class *fur sich*; (c) a perfect market with the balance of demand and supply and without such disturbing factors as monopolies and the intervention of the state; (d) a closed national economy, without developed international collaboration and influences of the international market; (e) investments for profit without taking into account huge non-profit investments, such as armaments, and space programs. (1974b, pp. 67–8)

What is particularly striking about this version is the extent to which Marx relied upon and employed the concepts and models of bourgeois economics in order to construct his economic theory. It is no great surprise, then, that even a realist application of the model will skew the analysis of a given capitalist society toward the possibilities that are inherent in condition (b), the revolutionary status of the working class. The other four conditions amount to the standard *ceteris paribus* assumption of bourgeois economics, and so rule out detailed consideration of the ways in which capitalism might change, enter a quite different phase and transform the proletariat into a reformist rather than revolutionary class. As Gandy points out, this is what happened in England, for example, 'when its working class began to see capitalism in a new light':

England had begun industrialization around 1770, and after 1850 it had passed from the stage of rapid development into gradual growth. Then its proletariat became reformist. France and Germany, starting in the 1840s, continued rapid industrialization throughout the nineteenth century. The proletariat on the continent remained revolutionary. (1979, pp. 158–9)

It appears, therefore, that it is only in the early stages of capitalism that *either* of the bourgeois and proletarian classes is revolutionary. Marx was not unaware of this change in the nature of the proletariat, given his claim that 'the organization of the capitalist process of production, once it is fully developed, breaks down all resistance' ([1867] 1976, p. 899). Nevertheless, in Gandy's opinion, he does not seem fully to have appreciated that 'the silent compulsion of economic relations sets the seal on the domination of the capitalist over the worker' (1979, pp. 158–9). The incidence of this kind of change in capitalist production relations has not, of course, been confined specifically to the middle part of the nineteenth century and to Britain alone. Consequently, the impact on the proletariat as a revolutionary force depends upon the kinds of changes that have actually occurred. Unless those changes have accentuated Marx's stated conditions whereby the proletariat may become a class *fur sich*, then it may reasonably be concluded that his theory of change, in its predictive capacity, is severely weakened. Gandy provides a useful summary of the changes in industrial capitalism that have ensued:

In the twentieth century ... gradual industrial growth, developing technology, and rising wages split the working class into many strata. The factory proletariat, now a minority of the workers, divided into fractions: skilled operatives, unorganized labourers, industrial unions, craft associations, and labor aristocracies. New technologies produced pyramids of skilled, semi-skilled, and unskilled workers throughout the industrial sector ... During the twentieth century differences of income and status have divided the wage-earning class into countless strata, broken up class solidarity, and created different interests and views. (1979, pp. 160–1)

Such a pattern of development fails to conform to any notion of an increasingly unified class in clearer and more direct conflict with the forces of capitalism. With the proliferation of 'pyramids' of workers, quite the reverse has happened. Instead of class unity, capitalist society has seen workers accept its definition of individual life. It would appear a retrograde step, one difficult to reconcile with Marx's schema of historical development. As Gandy puts it:

'in the nineteenth century the proletariat was in society but not of it', whereas 'in the twentieth century the proletariat became an integral part of capitalist society' (ibid.). If this is the case, then the industrial proletarians have not only become totally dominated by capitalism, but they have also been separated from other workers, hence the perception of their collective degradation which may no longer even *appear* as degradation. W. P. Archibald, for example, asks the question: 'if workers look upon the conditions of their existence as self-evident laws of nature, if they are so alienated that they no longer aspire to fulfilling relationships and labour, where is the motivation for rebellion and revolution to come from?' (1983, p. 78). Further, strong doubts are raised about the existence of the proletariat in anything like the sense suggested by the writings of the early Marx. A. Gorz claims that 'for over a century the idea of the proletariat has succeeded in masking its own unreality', and goes on to point out that 'the proletariat which the young Marx saw as a universal force devoid of any particularized form has become a particularized individuality in revolt against the universal force of the apparatus' (1982, p. 67). Thus the notion of the proletariat is subject to criticism as an adequate description of reality even in the time of Marx's writing, both as a description of the way that social change would be brought about, and, perhaps more seriously, as an account of existing social reality.

In spite of these criticisms, there are some indications that Marx's analysis was capable of taking into account such changes in the composition and motivation of the so-called proletariat. Archibald identifies two arguments put forward by Marx to deal with this problem, thereby implying that he had some grasp of the difficulty of explaining the nature of the proletariat's revolutionary potential in strictly economic determinist terms:

> The first concerns what has become known as the 'immiseration' hypothesis ... the de-skilling process accompanying the division of labour and mechanisation greatly increases competition and lowers wages, which in fact tend toward, and even below, the limit of physical subsistence. Combination therefore becomes a matter of dire necessity. (1983, pp. 78–9)

However, the evidence for this kind of development is weak, and leads to a consideration of the second of his solutions, 'the counter trend in Marx's later writings':

> The argument can be summarized as follows. Wages may not in fact decrease. Indeed, they may even *increase*. However, even

these developments will not prevent workers from organising
and eventually making the revolution since their aspirations will
also increase and thereby remain unfulfilled as long as capitalism
persists. (ibid.)

This second version of the generation of revolutionary consciousness and action, it has to be observed, relies upon the character of the
individuals involved to a much greater extent than the bludgeoning
impact of immiseration. It does accord, on the other hand, with
Marx's view of the civilizing aspects of production, consumption
and the association with wealth. More directly, Marx was assuming
that the cognitive ability of the proletariat would be utilized to
generate a much more sophisticated understanding of the relative
position of the working class in highly developed and diversified
industrial capitalism. This represents a marked shift from the much
more direct link (in the first version of revolutionary response)
between the economy and social change, in favour of a much looser,
more open intertwining of the economic and superstructural in the
second instance. The question here is whether the individual in capitalism has wholly to be understood in terms of economic forces. If
individuality has not significantly developed in the early and middle
stages of capitalism, where Marx is most competent to judge, then
it is reasonable to assume that *all* the modes of individualism under
capitalism must remain rooted in the paradigm of 'determination in
the last instance by the economy'. In other words, to understand any
capitalist individual, economic determination must come into play.

There is, however, enough evidence to suggest that Marx did
indeed believe that the economy would cease to be the decisive
determinant, that it is vital to examine the individual in society.
This is to reaffirm the significance of history in the account of social
change to, within and from capitalism. Although such a history will
inevitably deal with the economic determinants of social change, it
was Marx's belief that capitalism brought with it the possibility of
the end of that period of history.

Class existence developed in ways that proved to be *less*
antagonistic to capitalism than Marx expected. Individuality, on
the other hand, develops along with capitalism, becomes potentially
more antagonistic to capitalism. It becomes a force for change, to the
extent that capitalism fails to fulfil the capacities and expectations it
continues to generate but must exploit. For example, when Marx
talks of the 'egoistic individual' one would expect that this would
be a mode of individual existence which should be overcome and
disappear. Instead, that very modern kind of individuality appears

160

to be a precursor to true communality. In the *Holy Family*, Marx has this to say of the egoistic individual:

> each of his senses compels him to believe in the existence of the world and the individuals outside him and even his *profane* stomach reminds him every day that the world *outside* him is *not empty*, but is what really fills. Every activity and property of his being, every one of his vital urges becomes a *need*, a *necessity*, which his *self-seeking* transforms into seeking for other things and human beings outside him. ([1845] 1956, p. 162)

Egoism, usually considered so synonymous with capitalism, is actually conducive to the development of a 'real' consciousness of the world, a piercing of the veils of ideology and appearance. Furthermore, egoism itself is instrumental (in all senses of the word) in leading the supposedly self-sufficient and abstract individual into association with others, into the recognition of the need for others and thus, implicitly or potentially, community itself. What this passage demonstrates is the way in which a development at the individual level has relevance in the larger historical setting. This reading of egoism becomes a possibility because living individuals are more than 'workers' or 'economic animals'. G. Petrovic similarly sees capitalism as the epoch where the change from an economistic definition of human individuals begins to take place:

> In the course of historical development, man's practical activity differentiates into different, apparently self-sufficient and opposing, 'forms,' 'kinds' or 'spheres,' and the lowest among the forms of his practical activity, material production for the satisfaction of immediate living needs, becomes predominant. During a whole epoch of his development, man is primarily an economic animal, and as such he is split into antagonistic social classes, into exploiter and exploited ... But even in this epoch other higher forms of practical activity also develop, and the possibility of overcoming their independence and mutual opposition gradually emerges. (1967, p. 113)

The *Grundrisse* provides a wealth of clues to his understanding of the complex patterns of development that were occurring under capitalist relations of production. The explicitly economic analysis and the 'structuralist' flavour of much of the later works are here intertwined with other themes that are redolent of the early Marx. Yet they do not indicate confusion or transition. Marx did not see the materialist analysis of capitalism ruling out a concern with and an account of the individual. Instead, as capitalism progressed, this

161

became much more of a requirement, as individuals become more aware of themselves, and their abilities, powers and needs. This kind of development is the direct outcome of Marx's view of the developing relations of production.

> When we consider bourgeois society in the long view and as a whole, then the final result of the process of social production always appears as the society itself, i.e., the human being itself in its social relations ... The conditions and objectifications of the process are themselves equally moments of it, and its only subjects are the individuals, but individuals in mutual relationships, which they equally produce and reproduce anew. (Marx, [1857–8] 1973, p. 712)

One of the direct outcomes of this 'long' view is, for example, that Marx talks of the worker as an *agent*, thereby accentuating the positive effects that labour under an advanced mode of production can have on the individual.

> He steps to the side of the production process instead of being its chief actor. In this transformation, it is neither the direct human labour he himself preforms, nor the time during which he works, but rather the appropriation of his own general productive power, his understanding of nature and his mastery over it by virtue of his presence as a social body – it is, in a word, the development of the social individual which appears as the great foundation-stone of production and of wealth. (ibid., p. 705)

Summary

For Marx, the individual has *always* been socially defined, both in reality and as a conception (*vide* the discussion on 'the Robinsonades') (ibid., pp. 83–4). Nothing new is being claimed – capitalism has not made possible the *social* individual, as distinct from any other kind of individual. There is no future composed of new 'social individuals', because no other kind of individual has ever been possible. Rather, the emphasis has to be on the context of *development*, for here is an example of the way in which the individual is and will continue to be changed. What the individual gains, by the development in human productive forces and the immersion in the productive process, is an increasing ability to perceive, understand and ultimately to exercise control over the determinants *and* possibilities of individual existence. 'Universal prostitution appears as a necessary phase in the development of the social character of personal talents, capacities, abilities, activities. More politely expressed: the universal relation of utility and use' (ibid., p. 163). Thus the increasing definitional power of the individual is reliant upon the developmental of social powers. Those social powers are intrinsic in their actuality to the individual, who becomes more autonomous to the extent that the 'general productive force' of the whole becomes appropriated and employed by the single participant. Further, the individual can only be said to have appropriated such forces if s/he can use those forces *outside* production for necessity.

> The capacity for enjoyment is a condition of enjoyment and therefore its primary means; and this capacity is the development of an individual's talents, and thus of the productive force ... Free time – which includes leisure time as well as time for higher activities – naturally transforms anyone who enjoys it into a different person. The man who is being formed finds discipline in this process, while for the man who is already formed it is practice, experimental science, materially creative and self-objectifying knowledge, and he contains within his own head the accumulated wisdom of society. (ibid., pp. 383–4)

All these points affect the view of the development of capitalism since the mid-nineteenth century. In the first place, there has been an unprecedented increase in that which can be seen as free time. For Marx, 'all *free time* is time for free development, [but] the capitalist usurps the *free time* created by workers for society, ie, civilization' (ibid., p. 634). Nevertheless, more and not less free time, and its enjoyment, have accompanied developing capitalism. Not only does the complexity of the development of the productive forces lend weight to the idea that the capacity as well as the talents of the individual have increased, but that such an increase is experienced and manifested is highly likely. Further, Marx refers, as he so rarely did, to the way in which individual persons could undergo change *within* a particular epoch. Such change is not deemed revolutionary, at least in the classical sense of proletarianization, but it would be difficult to regard the accumulation of the 'wisdom of society' as irrelevant or non-revolutionary. Capitalist individuals, in other words, are the created agents of world-historical change.

Notes

1 Although such reference is usually thought to be of a moral or ethical nature, these need not be the only grounds. Others could be, for

example, efficiency, utilitarian considerations, or the Nietzschean position. For an interesting discussion on this, see Wood, 1981, pp. 149ff.

2   The presupposition behind this quest is that certain kinds of revolutionary activity or solutions to transitional problems are ruled out. It is possible, of course, to ignore the difficulty of dealing with those who have been reared and have become, to all intents and purposes, *constitutionally* capitalist until the time comes to purge society of such people. Apart from ethical objections, it is sufficient to point out that the failure to come to terms with the reality of this problem is an obstacle to the growth of Marxist revolutionary movements among those antagonistic to violent practices and solutions.

3   Thompson, 1967, 1968, argues that dramatic changes were brought about by industrial capitalism; his research is supported by Hamilton (1978), and Clark (1968), where the changes for women highlight the early stages of capitalist development.

4   As Heller notes, 1976, pp. 41–2, 'needs are simultaneously passions and capacities (the passion and the capacity to appropriate the object) and thus capacities are themselves needs.' It is this combination which gives features of human nature the status of *powers*.

5   Of course, Marx was aware that a particular individual might achieve an accurate self-perception and self-understanding, but for all to do so would require a complete change in society.

6   A distinction can be made between class analysis relating to a critique of society, and a theory of class when it concerns a transition from one historical epoch to another. A class account of feudalism would then focus strictly on feudal classes, and lead to a critique which was not anachronistic or otherwise misleading. The history of feudalism could thus be presented as a history of class struggle. However, the class conflict explanation of the transition must take a different form, since the conflict is not between exploiter and exploited, but between forms of exploitation. The conflict is between the landed aristocracy and the revolutionary capitalist class. It is only where a truly revolutionary class exists that Marx can talk of the achievements of such a class, and this implies a separate account, based on his view of humanity and his belief in historical progress.

7   As Fritzhand, 1980, p. 23, remarks: 'naturally, the individualism of the second stage of the development of the bourgeoisie could not but be firmly condemned by Marx. This condemnation, however, should not be mechanically extended to the early individualism of the bourgeoisie, and thus to individualism in general.'

8   Thus Marx, [1857–8] 1973, p. 488, referred to 'the childish world of antiquity' which seems 'loftier', but which is in a state of 'closed shapes, forms and given limits'. Clearly this falls far short of the capacity of the human individual in either capitalist or communist society.

5 *The individual under communism*

The development of individuality under pre-capitalist modes of production shows that, compared to all other epochs, capitalism has unique characteristics. This has special significance for an analysis of the individual in society and history, highlighting the distinction between the forms of individual existence under the conditions of capitalism (class society), and the emergence of a historical stage which will bring about social conditions favourable to further individual development. Specifically, the actual existence of living individuals can reveal the extent of the possibilities in capitalist society, as much as it can demonstrate the limitations and depredations of that same society. Capitalism is a human but not yet humanized social product. Since it is still a limited and (pre-)historical one, the modes of individuality that emerge will be a mixture of the new and dynamic, and the partial and unsatisfactory.

Such a proposition is supported by Marx's intimations that capitalism was characteristically assisting in the quiet revolution of individuality, by encouraging developments that could only undermine the long-term interests of capital. The expressions of individuality within capitalism, then, are one of two kinds. One is a regressive, and the other a positive, form of the development toward the social existence of communism. In general terms, individuality has been characterized by an emergence of a more complex orientation to nature, self and others, and an increase in autonomy from forces and mystifications which constrained feudal individuals. Put slightly differently, capitalist individuality exhibits a high degree of cognitive complexity and greater personal independence. On the other hand, capitalist individuality is constrained by an objective dependence on the forces and relations of production, and a low level of communal understanding and awareness. Given his critique of feudal and capitalist societies, it is apparent that these kinds of changes indicate that Marx thought

165

that the individual in society had qualities and capacities which amount to *agency* and *autonomy*, with all the implications for a theory of social change.

With respect to the movement from one historical stage to another, there is a dialectical connection between the stages of society and the forms of individual existence that accompany a particular stage. However, this is not a claim that historical progression is in close tandem with or parallel to the development of human individuality. There is no logical reason why the stage of development of individual potentialities should exactly match the development of the forces and relations of production. Nevertheless, this does not exclude the coincidence within one historical stage of both difference and unity with respect to individual and society. Marx did put capitalism at the end of pre-history, so it bears within it the means by which the possibility of a future communist society can be created. Capitalism is the transition stage between feudalism and communism. From this perspective, the individuality that emerges, in all its forms, is indicative of the sometimes gradual, sometimes swift, movement from the rural servitude of feudal individuality through to the potential for communist individuality.

Ultimately, therefore, the question of the individual in capitalism, and of the nature and level of development that can be said to have taken place, must be put in the context of Marx's vision of individuality under communism. The application of the theme of human history as the progressive growth of human individuality provides a contrasting account of the post-capitalist individual.

Method in communism

The central axiom of communism is freedom. It is a vision of the future in which historical contradictions have been resolved in favour of humankind at the levels, uniquely, of both the conception and the notion of human nature. Thus the puzzle of the individual – in terms of the content and the role of the individual in social change – and the critical assessment of individual existence in all previous societies culminate in the account of the individual under communism. This is the society in which individuality loses all abstractness and conditionality. There is, for the first time, 'free individuality'.

The resolution of individuality and freedom puts communist society into an analytical category of its own, as this part of the examination of individuals in history will demonstrate. As a proposition, communism is both theoretical and practical, and has a multitude of entry points for examination, from the point of view of productive relations, politics, history, class, or human nature, to name but a few. Certainly Marx saw it in this way, partly because he so often talked of communism as a negativity, as an absence of class society or property relations. After all, he saw as one of his major tasks the provision of definitive critiques of existing society. Moreover, communism is singularly important in that it also represents the technical and theoretical resolution of all of those critiques. Freedom, then, is not the informing idealist backdrop, but a teleology and a practice. The victory of humankind will not be through conflict (since that would not be a new or different kind of change). The victory of humankind is represented as a freedom from conflict.

When Marx did refer to communism obliquely or incidentally, making no direct reference to the individual or individuality, his view of the individual under communism is always implicitly present, since s/he is a crucial part of the prognosis of human society. And yet, the writings themselves on communism do not appear to be of such central significance for an understanding and appreciation of his thought as a whole. Such writings are fragmentary, generally lack detailed development, and are relatively inconsequential when compared to the space and time devoted to the great issues of history, economics and politics, and their contemporary expression in capitalism and class conflict.

Nevertheless, the (practical) *idea* of communism continues to be the one feature of Marx's work which can capture and convey the essence of his contribution. Indeed, in *Insight and Visions*, R. Berki even goes so far as to claim 'that communism is the *only thing* that is important about Marx's thought' (1983, p. 1). Communism is the fulfilment of the history Marx discovers and explains in such depth; it is the resolution of the conflict between individual and society; it represents a means of political action, while also serving as a political end; and transforms the need for productive and reproductive labour into an interactive process of controlled creativity between free members of a community. Furthermore, it is the presentation of this kind of practical idea of communism as a possibility which sets Marx out as a unique thinker, because he generates a connection between such a possibility and a high level of scientific probability. Alternatively, as Berki puts it:

> The dominant message in Marx's thought is that the vision of communism and the insight into communism ultimately coincide, that they are essentially one and the same thing, real and ideal fused together. It is as a *fused* concept that communism provides the intellectual starting-point and central motive force of Marx's doctrines. (ibid., p. 5)

However, the examination of the individual under communism seems bound to be frustrated by the absences or silences in Marx's various accounts and writings: the relative lack of material explicitly concerning the individual is apparently compounded by Marx's ostensive reluctance to provide detail about communist society. As will be seen, there are a number of reasons for this kind of initial reading, but none can detract from the necessity of questioning Marx's opus closely on these points.

It is important to note that the early Marx relied upon the practical relevance of the idea of communism. He used it to organize an understanding of contemporary capitalism, and to explain the nature of historically significant human action. Communism is not an end-point, but a task that continually presents itself to humankind. In the *Economic and Philosophical Manuscripts*, Marx joins the notion of a human essence to historical development and communism:

> since for socialist man the *whole of what is called world history* is nothing more than the creation of man through human labour, and the development of nature for man, he therefore has palpable and incontrovertible proof of his self-mediated *birth*, of his *process of emergence* ... [Socialism's] starting point is the *theoretically and practically sensuous consciousness* of man and of nature as *essential beings*. It is the *positive self-consciousness* of man ... through *communism*. Communism is the act of positing as the negation of the negation, and is therefore a *real* phase, necessary for the next period of historical development, in the emancipation and recovery of mankind. *Communism* is the necessary form and the dynamic principle of the immediate future, but communism is not as such the goal of human development – the form of human society. ([1844] 1975, pp. 375–8)

There are a number of things to note in this passage. Rather than an optimistic gaze into a rosy future, there is an altogether different tendency – to look to the past, to respond to and organize it. Hence history produces a sense of what has been achieved in terms of the emergence of human society out of the natural order. It is this reading of history which gives Marx reason to talk of the possibility of communism, not as an imaginary entity, but as an interpretation of current reality, as a reordering of already existing historical products and forms. Further, Marx talks not just of the emancipation of humankind, but simultaneously of its *recovery*. As McLellan observes:

> Marx considered it evident that any future development was going to include a recovery by man of the social dimension that had been lost ever since the French Revolution levelled all citizens in the political state and thus accentuated the individualism of bourgeois society. (1981, pp. 110–11)

The notion of recovery is consistent with the positing of communism as the negation of the negation. This could mean, for example, that communism is the active utopia which brings about the close of pre-history. Or, more passively, communism is the result of the end of all basic contradictions, a sort of residual utopia. Both possibilities are inherent in the view that the negation of the negation constitutes an utopia of uncompromising and sharply defined dimensions.

However, as Allen Wood argues, a close relationship between the negation of the negation and the vision of the future does some violence to both aspects of Marx's thought.

> According to some of Marx's cruder critics ... Marx depicts communist society as one in which all sources of conflict, tension and discontent have melted away. And these critics suggest (quite properly) that such a picture is not only fantastic but also unattractive. Marx does hold that communism will do away with alienation, with the systematic social causes of unfulfilled, wasted human lives. And he does think that change and development in post-capitalist society will occur through conscious, collective human decisions rather than through destructive class struggles. But it is a caricature both of Marx's conception of humanity and his vision of communist society to suppose that he either predicts or desires a static society in which all the sources of human discontent have been done away with. (1981, p. 26)

Consequently, one is led to question the significance of the connection between the philosophical status of the negation of the negation and the vision of communism. The reading of the connection between the negation of the negation and the vision of communism is a source of controversy. There is some uncertainty about the extent to which his views on the future society can be taken seriously, either as political theory, practical politics, or prophecy. Berki's view of communism as a single theme is reiterated by L. Sekelj, for example, who finds that a single definition of communist society – 'as a full and free development of every individual' – holds true throughout Marx's productive output. However, he immediately undermines this claim by reintroducing the by now traditional distinction between the young and the old Marx: 'within the framework of this one concept there are two approaches and two versions of communism':

> Marx's first vision of communism in *Economic and Philosophical Manuscripts* contains an idea of communism as the end of history, of communism as a Hegelian absolute. In this vision of communism, Marx tends to understand it as a historical necessity which will end all basic contradictions, including the contradiction between human essence and human existence. Communism as a negation of negation is a utopia of total and final dealienation. It is an abolishment of every aspect of human alienation in relation to nature, as well as in relation to man and humanity. (Sekelj, 1984, p. 360)

In other words, Marx's historical approach is equated with a presumed historical outcome. Actually, Marx had already rejected the idealist understanding of the negation of the negation as 'the absolute positive, the self-supporting positive, positively based on itself' ([1844] 1975, p. 125). Communism cannot be a *residual* utopia, since that characterization rests on the Hegelian as distinct from Feuerbachian understanding of the negation of the negation. Whereas for Hegel it incorporated that which is true and embodies the movement of Absolute Spirit, Feuerbach saw the negation of the negation as a materially transcending movement in history, not a speculative one. As Marx noted approvingly: 'Feuerbach also defines the negation of the negation, the definite concept, as thinking surpassing itself in thinking and as thinking wanting to be directly awareness, nature, reality' (ibid.). In other words, the negation of the negation, as a 'definite concept', makes particular claims about agency and explanation in society, just as it is a description of historical process. Lucien Goldmann goes so far as to claim that Marx's approach is different and important precisely because it theorizes real human beings in history:

> Marx opposes to Hegel's error of inventing the real relation between subject and predicate the need for a scheme of thought which would be both positive and radical, and would see in real human beings and their social institutions (the family, civil society, the state) the genuine subject of historical action. (1981, p. 51)

The alternative version presents communism as 'the realm of freedom'; 'the concept of the free development of individuals based on the reduction of necessary labor to a minimum' (Sekelj, 1984, p. 360). Unfortunately, his separation of utopia as residue from utopia as creative space opens Marx's thought to several kinds of attacks. First, the Hegelian character of the early writings becomes a major flaw, because it leads to ahistorical analyses and claims of which the communist utopia of final and total dealienation is just one example. Second, the early version of communism, while more clearly identifiable and comprehensible as a vision of the future, constitutes too great a claim on the credulity of Marxists and non-Marxists alike. Sekelj seems to be suggesting that Marx's philosophical method produces an excess of romanticism, in contradistinction to the mature vision of communism, which is supported by a hard-headed materialism.

The choice between versions of communism is not one of simple preference. The validity of the vision of society reflects upon the validity of the discussion of the individual as a subject in history, as an agent and as a representation of human nature, and affects the possibility of describing these things. In a sense, conflicting interpretations are explicable from the point of view of the reception of the idea of communism. Depending on when actually Marx wrote his various comments, their import can be mediated by the notion of the 'early' and 'mature' years. On this view, a lurch into philosophical idealism is a regrettable but quite acceptable feature of the early works, and is seen to be a regular occurrence. The mature works, however, are preponderantly *not* about communism, and this is taken as evidence that the early works are indeed tainted by philosophical idealism, and that what little is said about communism should not be associated with the output of the young Marx on this subject. (As Levin (1984, p. 345) remarks, it should be no surprise that works on capital prove not to focus on a society without capital; rather, it should be questioned why anything at all is said

about communism.) This kind of approach makes it appear
that there are two kinds of communism in Marx, and that it
is proper to respond to them in respect of their chronological
emergence.

Is communism as the negation of the negation to be seen as an
early, and therefore confused, notion? Put another way, does the
reliance upon the philosophical expression prejudice the relevance
of the vision of communism as 'total and final dealienation', as
Sekelj seems to suggest? Marx himself made clear that communism
was *not* 'as such the goal of human development', but only its
'form' and 'principle'. The dangers of getting these confused were
quite apparent to Marx.

> It is above all necessary to avoid once more establishing
> 'society' as an abstraction over against the individual. The
> individual *is* the *social being*. His vital expression – even when
> it does not appear in the direct form of a *communal* expression,
> conceived in association with other men – is therefore an
> expression and confirmation of *social* life. (Marx, [1844] 1975,
> p. 350)

That Marx had this to say in the early writings argues against
the view that he constructed an idealist utopia which could
conceivably come to dominate the thoughts and existence of
individuals. Here Marx was careful to point out that it was
possible to construct a vision of the future which would repeat
the mistake of seeing the individual in isolation, distinct from
society, and dependent upon society as a prior structure. Some
take this to mean that Marx precluded himself from detailing
the future manner of social arrangements, as if it was enough
to state that communism meant emancipation, the development of free individuality, and the beginning of true human
history. Levin (1984, p. 345) is one who praises his 'prin-
cipled refusal' to be specific, but others feel free to expand
Marx's utterances into a full-blown vision of a Marxist humanist
future society. Marx's thought provides excellent support for
these approaches, but they do not manage to position the
vision of communism in his thought as a whole. They are
attempts to find a 'best fit' solution, a strange thing to have
to do with the ultimate resolution of history, the practical
outcome of human productive endeavour. Even Berki (1983)
has to conclude that communism is a problem for Marx's
thought, notwithstanding his generally successful demonstration
that communism represents a number of features of Marx's

methodology, and perhaps constitutes yet another feature in itself.

Not just the credibility, but also the philosophical integrity of Marx's vision of communism relies upon the structural features of communism as a practical idea. McLellan has identified three such features, and these were focused upon by Marx in his early writings.

First, he stressed that communism was a historical phenomenon whose genesis was 'the entire movement of history' ... Second, Marx stressed that everything about man – starting with his language – was social ... Marx emphasized, thirdly, that the stress on man's social aspects only served to enhance the individuality of communist, unalienated man, whom he described as 'total' or 'all-sided'. (McLellan, 1981, p. 116)

Although some like to present the emphasis on the social aspect of existence as a predominantly humanist element of Marx's thought (and this is seen as either a welcome or an unfortunate occurrence), it is in fact the key to his claim to be scientific.

Our method indicates the points where historical investigation must enter in, or where bourgeois economy as a merely historical form of the production process points beyond itself to earlier historical modes of production. In order to develop the laws of bourgeois economy, therefore, it is not necessary to write the *real history of the relations of production*. But the correct observation and deduction of these laws, as having themselves become in history ... leads at the same time to the points at which the suspension of the present form of production relations gives signs of its becoming – foreshadowings of the future. Just as, on one side, the pre-bourgeois phases appear as *merely historical*, i.e., suspended presuppositions, so do the contemporary conditions of production likewise appear as engaged in *suspending themselves* and hence in positing the *historic presuppositions* for the new state of society. (Marx, [1857–8] 1973, pp. 460–1)

Thus the *Grundrisse* continues the theme of the movement of history as the most important part of his analysis. It is within this schema that communism must always find its place. Communism has a unique place in Marx's thought because it

173

contributes to the historical analysis of capitalism, but is also the result of that analysis and that history. That is, communism must contribute to its own existence and sense. Admittedly, this creates difficulties of interpretation, but that does not necessarily mean that Marx was ambivalent about the future, as Levin describes it, although his account of the relevant influences is worth viewing.

> *Firstly*, Marx's ambivalence on the future is a consequence of the collision within him of the scientist and nineteenth century progress theorist ... *Secondly*, we can emphasize that Marx was primarily a theorist of capitalism, and his views on that have a higher status than his remarks on any earlier or later stage of production. There is, however, also a sense in which even Marx's remarks on communism are simultaneously about capitalism. As with all futurology, science fiction, and utopian literature, what purports to be about the future is actually more about the present. (1984, p. 345)

Levin's first point distinguishes between a scientist and nineteenth-century progress theorist. It is difficult to see, however, that these two things can be separated, especially in Marx's case. It was his science which encouraged him to endorse progress theory, rather than the two somehow being irreconcilable elements of his methodological inclinations. It also suggests that the scientist has a kind of purity denied to other kinds of theorists, and this again is a view discredited by Marx above all others. On the second point, Levin correctly draws our attention to Marx's expertise and specialization with contemporary society, and intimates that any discussion of other societal forms has only a second-class or derivative status. However, this begs the question of Marx's reason for developing a critique of *any* society. His commitment to a future radically different from the past, and his awareness of the mediating role of the present, point not to variations in the importance of Marx's comments but to their significance in the enterprise as a whole. Similarly, the idea that remarks on the future are actually to do with the present has its obverse – *all* Marx's work on capitalism has to do with its supersession by, at best, communism.

Levin makes a third observation concerning the fluctuating output on the subject of the future society (ibid.). This implies a distinction between Marx the politician and Marx the scientist, such that he sought to balance inspiration and scientific realism, to be 'scientifically acceptable while providing a vision to rival that of his utopian competitors' (ibid., p. 343). In other words, Marx's thoughts on communism do not stand among other versions of future society, but squarely between capitalist reality and utopian unreality. The invitation is to identify with clear-eyed scientists and be aware that Marx's political motivation led him to be intentionally emotional in his appeal at the expense of 'serious' theoretical argumentation.

However, this interesting pattern of thoughts on communism is open to different interpretations. As a subject, communism appears in the 1840s – 'the most optimistic decade of his life' – and then again in the 70s and 80s (ibid., p. 345). The significance of this return to the concerns of his early writing career should not be minimized. It offered, after all, the opportunity fully to incorporate his 'science', to re-tailor the emotional appeal, and to clear away lingering misconceptions. Yet none of this re-jigging is to be found in the texts. If anything, Marx is even more positive and focused in his remarks, because he is able to say what is *not* communism, as well as how it is to be conceived. It may be concluded then, that Marx's vision of communism as a 'hazy outline' does not arise out of a conflict between science and the need to proselytize, or as a response to the appeal of competing utopian visions (ibid., p. 343). Rather, the vision of communism represented a challenge to Marx, because it required him to operationalize the complex of ideas that he held about the study of history, society and social change in a way that unified instead of compromised his scientific and political commitment to a unique kind of social transition and order.

Marx's vision of the future society is differentiated from social utopianism to the extent that it does not rely upon a clear-cut recommendatory morality. Marx insisted that it be judged by other than prevailing bourgeois standards – a requirement that precludes the terms good and bad or good and evil, concepts of right and justice, as well as the ostensibly non-moral language of productive efficiency and instrumentality.[1] In what follows, some of the tacit and explicit features of Marx's thoughts on communism will be examined in order to draw out what it might mean to be an individual under communism.

Communism as the end of classes

Some of the descriptions of communism provided by the second-ary literature can be accepted without endorsing their associated conclusions. Ollman, for example, draws out a very useful six point description of communism, highlighting the changes in the orientation of every human to the natural and social environment (1976, pp. 67–8). It involves the end of the division of labour, an overwhelmingly social existence and the abolition of private property. Furthermore, events stem from action consciously intended to manipulate the environment, activities are internally organized, and all national, social, geographical, etc., divisions disappear. Communism could simply be described as a society of liberating absences. It is a society without the structural limitations of private property ownership, with its distorting and distorted relations of production. It is therefore a society without the straitjacket of class and represents the change from class conflict to class-free existence for all members of society. Conventionally, the vision of communism rests on the analysis of class, because it is the destiny of the working class to emancipate itself and transcend class society for the first time.

> The condition for the emancipation of the working class is the abolition of every class, just as the condition for the liberation of the Third Estate, of the bourgeois order, was the abolition of all estates and all orders ... The working class, in the course of its development, will substitute for the old civil society and association which will exclude classes and their antagonism, and there will be no more political power properly so-called, since political power is precisely the official expression of antagonism in civil society. (Marx, (1847), pp. 146–7)

This passage contains the grand claim about transcending class existence, and indicates the extent of its implications. The claim is central to Marxian analysis. It is important to distinguish, however, between the importance of class to Marx's critique of capitalism, and the significance of the disappearance of class. With the transition to communism, every other class is to be transcended: every individual is to be allowed an equal participation in the resultant association. The dissolution of classes is predicated on a dialectical understanding of the working out of contradictions. The solidarity and identification provided by classes is not lost to the newly classless individuals, but finds its real expression under communism. On the other hand, the destructive features of class existence – the role-boundedness, hierarchy and divisiveness – lose their structural foundation and stimulation. Thus individuals become emancipated in the dual sense of being freed from restrictions to human interaction, as well as finding that human interaction can be generally less brutal and diminishing than under class society.

These are monumental claims. Communism does not entail a transformation of capitalist class relations into another form of the social and economic class genre. Therefore, post-capitalist society will be free of contradictions with respect to humanity. There may still be an endless dialectical continuation of social contradictions, but they will be limited and resolvable within the new form of social organization. The difference, for Marx, is that communism does not set humankind and human beings in opposition to one another. This distinction between kinds of contradictions is exemplified by Marx's thoughts on political power. Under capitalism, he urged the proletariat to realize and exercise its political power as an offensive weapon against the bourgeoisie. In communism, that power does not arise in conflictual form, and ceases to have the same brutalizing effects on the lives of individuals, since the fundamental antagonisms that underlie class societies must no longer be reflected in social relations. Thus the demands on individuals change. Competitive responses become less necessary or appropriate, and are displaced by a development of other strategies for conflict resolution. Power and politics remain, but the emphasis shifts to the challenges of successful organization and the achievement of solutions to problems, rather than the crude necessities of victory and advantage which characterize capitalist political struggle. As I. Walliman notes:

> For Marx communism is not the end of history. Rather, it is the beginning of a new type of history – consciously directed history. It is made possible by the elimination of 'mechanisms' such as exchange, commodity production, and the resulting involuntary division of labor which hitherto propelled it. As long as these mechanisms are absent, Marx sees no reason to believe that communism will be an unstable social condition despite the presence of some scarcity. (1981, p. 119)

There is room here for admitting the continuation of contradictions without being tied to the idea that contradictions are inherently destabilizing and must always bring about a revolutionary restructuring of society (although Elster (1985) takes a

177

different view). In Marx's opinion, there was every justification for making these kinds of claims and predictions. Within the concept of the 'course' of 'development' of the working class lies the Marxian interpretation of history up to the then state of capitalist society, and the extrapolation of the tendencies that were entailed within that theory. In *Socialism: Utopian and Scientific*, for example, a 'sketch of historical evolution' provides a three stage history, culminating in the proletarian revolution as the 'solution of the contradictions':

> the proletariat frees the means of production from the character of capital they have thus far borne, and gives their socialized character complete freedom to work itself out. Socialized production upon a predetermined plan becomes henceforth possible. The development of production makes the existence of different classes of society thenceforth an anachronism. In proportion as anarchy in social production vanishes, the political authority of the state dies out. Man, at last the master of his own form of social organization, becomes at the same time the lord over Nature, his own master – free. (Engels, 1970, p. 682)

This freedom is a complex matter, involving the lack of certain things, like economic determination and state authority, and the addition of powers over nature, society and the self. The course of development of the working class includes the overcoming of the proletariat itself. The proletariat is a 'class' only because other classes exist. It is not a class in sociological terms, since it does not share the same empirical properties as capitalist classes. The proletariat cannot be defined in a non-class way, cannot be 'beyond class' unless a post-capitalist society has at least been 'thought'. Communism provides such a conceptual future, a means by which class society and class categories can be superseded. The proletariat is a 'class' only inasmuch as it cannot continue to be defined as a class after the transition to communism. Unlike all other classes, before or after a transition from one mode of production to another, the proletariat gives rise to no other class in contradistinction to itself, either in capitalism or communism. Thus Marx was making a claim about the historical progression toward the end of classes, not as a specific social arrangement, but as the *lack* of certain features of all previously existing societies. As Marx points out in the *German Ideology*:

Communism is not for us a *state of affairs* which is to be established, an *ideal* to which reality [will] have to adjust itself. We call communism the *real* movement which abolishes the present state of things. The conditions of this movement result from the premises now in existence. ([1845–6] 1970, pp. 56–7)

Individuals and nature in communism

As a practical idea, communism has its context in the reality of the present as much as it is predicated on the movement toward a quite different future. Since it is a future without classes, it must therefore be a future consisting *solely of individuals*. They could not be described as anything else, even though they may have a common, collective identity – an identity as humanity. They cannot be class beings, and neither can their association be merely natural, in an Aristotelian sense. In terms of communism being progressive, but also offering something very new, Marx was uncompromising in his formulation:

Communism differs from all previous movements in that it overturns the basis of all earlier relations of production and intercourse, and for the first time consciously treats all natural premises as the creatures of hitherto existing men, strips them of their natural character and subjugates them to the power of the united individuals. (ibid., p. 86)

To call these 'united individuals' communal beings, for example, would be inadequate. This would be tantamount to referring to them as herd animals, thereby equating members of communist society with the lack of differentiation of the earliest forms of society, where freedom existed only in the sense that all were equally subjected to the vagaries of nature, where development of individuality had yet to spring from the development of the social relations of production.

By contrast, communism is the unique combination of unity and individuality, where each is not collapsed into the other. Under communism, all individuals are free to pursue their own development, to differentiate themselves in the context of a truly social existence. That development may very well depend on others and on decisions concerning the distribution of resources and opportunities. Far from being seen as a limitation on Marx's claim, or a reality which makes that claim dubious, the freedom to develop is presented here as indicative of emancipation from the artificial, exploitative and divisive form of social organization which previously constructed these outcomes. Nevertheless, Marx does not altogether suggest that communism is a society that achieves every thing for every single individual, as Walliman points out:

> Although communism enables individuals to associate freely, it cannot be conceived of as providing *the* social environment conducive to the peculiarities of an individual. Thus, individuals cannot be compared with a plant which, in order to grow, must be provided by nature with water, soil, sunshine, and the like. Communism must not be envisioned as a society in which each individual has a claim to be nurtured according to the peculiarity of his person. (1981, p. 108)

As a society, therefore, communism cannot be described and specified in the way that those in the present might like. Communism is a society composed of a collection, not just of individuals, but *individual lives*. Those lives cannot be laid out in advance, before communism exists. Even under capitalism, as Engels remarked in a letter to Bloch, 'we make history ourselves, but, in the first place, under very definite assumptions and conditions' (Engels, [1890] 1970, pp. 427–8). If this is true for capitalism, then the freedom offered by communism is one in which the conditions and means for individual self-expression are open-ended and even more complex. Nor are the conditions of freedom and the means to freedom easily specifiable. At the very point at which detail is demanded, Marx tended to respond with the methodological principles which concern not the imagination but the need for the recognition of current reality and action. In this Marx seems at his most un-utopian, because the emphasis is not on resolution of conflict in the future but on dealing with it in the present.

However, this does not always mean that the form of post-capitalist society finds no expression. In the *Economic and Philosophical Manuscripts* (1844), Marx created an extremely powerful set of images of communism, and these images had strong connections with both his early humanist and Feuerbachian thought and the emerging science of society that was soon to receive greater attention in the *German Ideology*.

> *Communism* is the *positive* supersession of *private property* as
> *human self-estrangement*, and hence the true *appropriation* of
> the *human* essence through and for man; it is the complete
> restoration of man to himself as a *social*, i.e. human, being, a
> restoration which has become conscious and which takes place
> within the entire wealth of previous periods of development.
> (Marx, [1844] 1975, p. 348)

The first thing to note is that communism is presented in two
ways. Without the already existing reality of capitalism, it would
be difficult for Marx to begin to describe the future society. Also,
communism cannot simply be seen as a negativity, as an absence
of the capitalist social order. Thus it is not implied that the
removal of private property ownership would coincide with the
cessation of human self-estrangement. This is because Marx saw
that communism was not solely a reaction to capitalism, but was a
creative and active social movement with specific tasks to achieve.
These tasks are described as 'appropriation of the human essence'
and the supersession of private property. Such tasks are related
very definitely to real individuals in actual historical conditions in
terms of restructuring society. Those tasks also have to be seen in
the context of the way that those conditions came to exist, and the
wider meanings of the various conflicts. The key to this passage
is the historical basis upon which communism can be conceived
and achieved. It is also interesting to observe how it is pervaded
by Feuerbachian humanism.

Communism, as the solution to the riddle of history, is
above all a neat and tidy outcome. The view of history is
both long- and short-term, and the attitude to humankind is
all-embracing, forgetting nothing. Hence Marx refers to the
'complete restoration of man to himself as a *social*, i.e. human,
being', thereby implying that past history has systematically
distorted a once-social/human existence into something partial
and contradictory. What is unclear, however, is the point at
which humankind did not *need* to be restored. The 'complete
restoration of man to himself' bespeaks an established unity that
has been broken apart, and one is entitled to wonder if Marx
saw this ancient unity in anthropological or idealist terms.

Immediately following this remark, Marx signalled a new order
of thought, one that is distinctly historical-materialist in flavour.
Instead of implying the estrangement of an abstract social being
(for the assumption that humans are always social *animals* remains
intact), Marx refers to a *conscious* restoration 'which takes place

within the entire wealth of previous periods of development'. If there has been development, and this is to constitute a conscious part of the change to communism, then it is not an abstract social being that has been in conflict with society, but all living individuals as both individuals and representatives of humankind. That is, the members of ancient society, feudal society and capitalist society all suffered human self-estrangement, or whatever term is desired to describe the conflict between existence and being, and so on. Under capitalism, private property ownership is of special note because it is a productive relation which estranges, more thoroughly than any other, humankind from highly sophisticated human productive activity. Alienation is the term to reflect this historical form. But Marx looked toward the end of alienation in so far as it was the most recent and virulent development in the history of self-estrangement. What makes communism different from all other developments is that this movement is in accordance with the progress achieved by previous modes of existence. It has no need to set itself against the human achievements of these societies; in fact it cannot, because the move to communism is dependent on the wealth of human social development thus far attained.

The introduction of the historical element into the account of human essence or nature is quite significant for the humanist tenor of the *1844 Manuscripts*. It means that Marx cannot easily be accused of philosophical idealism. He seems about to fall into the trap of regarding individuals in an abstract fashion, but manages to circumvent this error while still being able to produce transhistorical generalities. This is achieved by presenting communism as a creative political praxis, not merely as a reaction to and rejection of an earlier social existence. Individuals are conceived, no matter what their historical position, in definite and concrete relations, and this allows Marx to draw out the regularities, the necessities and the certainties of human social existence. This is equally true of his account of communism. Above all, individuals in communist society are subject to the kinds of objective realities under which humans have always had to toil. Furthermore, the achievement of the most recent form of development in human society – the capitalist system of private property – is *necessary* as a precursor, but must be defeated.

We have seen how, assuming the positive supersession of private property, man produces man, himself and other men; how the object, which is the direct activity of his individuality, is at the same time his existence for other men, their existence and their existence for him. Similarly, however, both the material of labour and man as subject are the starting point as well as the outcome of the movement (and the historical *necessity* of private property lies precisely in the fact that they must be this starting point). So the *social* character is the general character of the whole movement; *just as* society itself produces *man* as *man*, so it is *produced* by him. Activity and consumption, both in their content and in their *mode of existence*, are *social* activity and *social* consumption. (ibid., p. 349)

The elements of this passage link the essential features of Marx's political, economic and philosophical enterprise. Aware that communism is a movement which has *positive* tasks, tasks that humans must set for themselves and others, he then began to talk of the character of the relations between people under communism. Again, there is a strong connection between individual existence under capitalism and in the future society. Communism is possible, as a solution to private property ownership, only once private property ownership has led to its own overcoming. This is not a philosophical concept, but an activist notion, indicating that consciousness of the real conditions of existence has to develop. Moreover, it is at the same time a recognition of the fundamental features of *any* society – 'the material of labour and man as subject'. Thus Marx identifies the material base of society, and draws from it the principle that the general character of society is its social character. If this is so, then communism is the recognition that social production can be the medium for the expression of individuality, not just for the single individual, but also for all other individuals. This can only occur in communist society, where all the implied social relations are subject to conscious human purposes. As Wood notes, 'human control can only be collective control, and only in communist society can this control be exercised by and for all members of society' (Wood, 1981, p. 52). Marx has another way of making this argument, in the course of a large claim not just about communism but the proper way to conceive of the relationships between three nodal points – humankind, nature and society.

This communism, as fully developed naturalism, equals humanism, and as fully developed humanism equals naturalism; it

183

is the *genuine* resolution of the conflict between man and nature, and between man and man, the true resolution of the conflict between existence and being, between objectification and self-affirmation, between freedom and necessity, between individual and species. It is the solution to the riddle of history and knows itself to be the solution. (Marx, [1844] 1975, p. 348)

Marx redefines the understanding of nature. He demonstrates that our view of the objective or external world bears directly on the way that humans conceive of themselves and their place in the world, i.e. society. No longer is nature to be seen as a separate reality, an environment with its own forces and rules in respect of and within which humans must move and respond. Once society has emerged, even in its primitive form, then nature is changed and enlarged. Society is, as Aristotle claimed, a natural association, but Marx alters this understanding by insisting that the relationship between society and nature is a flexible one, depending upon the mode of production. Nature thus has a special character beyond its external or concrete presence and reality. It is also the objective mediation, between individuals and in relation to their consciousness of themselves as individuals. For Marx, this relationship is an ever-present reality *and* a potentiality, requiring human society to respond to that fundamental reality by reorganizing itself, such that both humankind and nature can bring to fruition all the dimensions of that relationship. The human and the natural, it follows, are coextensive social realities, even though the form of society may not truly reflect this. The view of nature, therefore, is a reflexive one, containing both ontological and teleological aspects. The intervening variable is, of course, the history of that relationship, wherein various modes of production entail a specific way of combining and conceiving the social and the natural. For this reason, Marx pinpointed in capitalism the foundation of its objective relevance and superiority, and presented it as the key to progress both naturalist and humanist.

The positive supersession of *private property*, as the appropriation of *human* life, is therefore the positive supersession of all estrangement, and the return of man from religion, the family, the state, etc., to his *human*, ie, *social* existence ... economic estrangement is that of *real life*. (ibid., p. 349)

That is, communism returns to the individual his or her human existence, unlocking all the bonds of structure, ideology and institution. Close attention to the text, however, reveals an interesting terminological point. Marx is constantly referred to as a humanist on the basis of these writings, and he does reiterate his concern that a *human* existence is the promise and goal of communist society. Marx's meaning is clear. *Human* means *social*.

> The *human* essence of nature exists only for *social* man; for only here does nature exist for him as a *bond* with other *men*, as his existence for others and their existence for him, as the vital element of human reality; only here does it exist as the *basis* of his own *human* existence. Only here has his *natural* existence become his *human* existence and nature become man for him. *Society* is therefore the perfected unity in essence of man with nature, the true resurrection of nature, the realized naturalism of man and the realized humanism of nature. (ibid., pp. 349–50)

Thus there should not be any thought that Marx relied on the notion of an essence, an abstract human nature on which to found his humanism. When Marx equated naturalness with humanness, and humanity with *sociality*, he expressed, in an extremely succinct fashion, the more famous but subsequent formulation of the basic premiss of historical materialism to be found in the *German Ideology* ([1845–6] 1970). Sociality entails the wealth of productive power of human society, the sum and substance of social relations.

The character of communist individuality

On the basis of the discussion thus far, the term communism must be a synonym for society. Marx's claim about the true nature of society as the perfected unity of humankind and nature is equivalent to the notion that communism is the genuine resolution to the conflict between humankind and nature. Transposing these terms in the previous quotation gives us the following: 'the *human* essence of nature exists only for *communist* man'. There is, of course, the crucial difference between the original conception of the nature/human unity, and the historically achieved unity under communism. Humans will have a consciousness of that unity, such that it will appear to them as freedom. This is borne out by the way in which wo/men are to be considered emancipated by communism.

The supersession of private property is therefore the complete *emancipation* of all human senses and attributes; but it is this emancipation precisely because these senses and attributes have become *human*, subjectively as well as objectively. The eye has become a *human* eye, just as its *object* has become a social, *human* object, made by man for man ... Need or enjoyment have therefore lost their *egoistic* nature, and nature has lost its mere *utility* in the sense that its use has become *human* use. (ibid., p. 352)

This is not emancipation of an abstract human individual. 'Human' in this sense does not relate to a person at all, but to the quality of the social interrelationships, and this quality or character is governed by the type of social organization that exists and is historically possible. This will prevail until the realization of the communist movement, whereby individuals are able to develop themselves beyond the confines of a utilitarian orientation toward themselves, others and nature.

Only through the objectively unfolded wealth of human nature can the wealth of subjective *human* sensitivity – a musical ear, an eye for the beauty of form, in short, *senses* capable of human gratification – be either cultivated or created. For not only the five senses, but also the so-called spiritual sense, the practical senses (will, love, etc.), in a word, the *human* senses, the humanity of the senses – all these come into being only through the existence of *their* objects, through *humanized* nature. The *cultivation* of the five senses is the work of all previous history. (ibid., p. 353)

Marx was excited about the future, since humankind has been cultivated over long historical time. Humans are now uniquely prepared to exercise their faculties at a very high level of sophistication. Furthermore, they are capable of using their senses in new ways. The senses become more than the interface between the subjective and the objective. 'The whole of history is a preparation, a development, for "*man*" to become the object of *sensuous* consciousness and for the needs of "man as man" to become [sensuous] needs' (ibid., p. 355). This version of human history is the proper conception of human nature, a human nature which contains a developed wealth that can be realized only by the communist movement as it takes over the means of production and places them under

conscious control. This truly social control is a permissive
control, allowing the senses to attain a subjective as well as
an objective character simultaneously and diversely. That is, a
'society that is *fully developed* produces man in all the richness of his being, the *rich* man who is *profoundly and abun-
dantly endowed with all the senses*, as its constant reality' (ibid.,
p. 354). If this is the constant reality of communism, then,
Marx expected such a society could be profoundly advanced
in what it could demand from its members, just as they
would not merely experience the enjoyment of their senses
and faculties, but also be able to extend those faculties in
hitherto unexpected fashion and degree. Above all, communism is the defeat of the social effects under a capitalism of
manipulated scarcity (not, it should be noted, of scarcity itself),
and Marx clearly looks beyond the situation where sense is
restricted by being 'a prisoner of crude practical need' (ibid.,
p. 353).

> We have seen what significance the *wealth* of human needs
> has, on the presupposition of socialism, and consequently
> what significance a *new mode of production* and a new *object* of
> production have. A fresh confirmation of *human* powers and
> a fresh enrichment of *human* nature. Under private property
> this significance is reversed ... for private property does not
> know how to transform crude need into *human* need. (ibid.,
> p. 358)

The centrality of needs to this account of communism is
not just a feature of this early writing. In Volume I of *Capital*, Marx had cause to refer to needs again, as one of the
key defining aspects of humankind – i.e. 'distinguished from
all other animals by the limitless and flexible nature of his
needs' ([1867] 1976, p. 1068). More importantly, communism
is no different from other forms of social organization in that
it leads to changes in human nature. The difference lies in
Marx's certainty that communism will bring about a distinct
enrichment. Human nature expresses itself in society, according
to circumstances, and that circumstance can lead to a further heightening of human powers. As Gandy puts it, 'the
acquisitive, stunted, cringing person of today will undergo a
transformation'; communist consciousness will develop in the
course of revolutionary struggle, and, ultimately, 'the New Man
and New Woman emerge after generations of change' (1979,
pp. 94–5).

However, the emergence of these new individuals raises difficulties and objections. How could Marx claim that the 'acquisitive, stunted, cringing person of today' was going to be a member of the working class whose historic mission it is to form, sustain and drive the communist movement to victory? It is not enough to argue that human nature is malleable – this much is clear from the historical materialist critique of society – or to insist that human nature, as the ensemble of social relations, automatically adjusts itself in accordance with the change in the structure of society. As Geras demonstrates with great clarity, these kinds of views cannot be sustained and do violence to Marx's thought (1983). Nor do they deal adequately with the development within capitalism which Marx thought so valuable for future society. What is required is a closer look at the connections between the development of the forces of production and the development of individuality.

Exchange, production, and the universal individual

In order to see just how communism could come about, it is necessary to examine the processes which prepared the individual for the future, and the transition to that future. Marx dealt in detail with the activities of consumption and production, and the way that they related to individuality in capitalist society. The role of exchange was especially important, for this made the activity of consumption, already universal, into a *uniform* universality. In the process, the social bonds of earlier forms of social organization were subjected to enormous strain, leading to a great loss of existing communality, and the destruction of established social relationships.

> In the money relation, in the developed system of exchange (and this semblance seduces the democrats), the ties of personal dependence, of distinctions of blood, education, etc. are in fact exploded, ripped up (at least, the personal ties all appear as *personal* relations). (Marx, [1857–8] 1973, p. 163)

Marx noted but obviously did not mourn the passing of all of these ties. He was careful to indicate that such personal relations as existed are by no means the models for future society, because they are every bit as partial and flawed by the feudal mode of production as the relations that supersede them. In their place appears a spurious freedom, a sham individualization:

individuals *seem* independent (this is an independence which is at bottom merely an illusion, and it is more correctly called indifference), free to collide with one another and to engage in exchange within this freedom; but they appear thus only for someone who abstracts from the *conditions*, the *conditions of existence* within which these individuals enter into contact (and these conditions, in turn, are independent of the individuals and, although created by society, appear as if they were *natural conditions*, not controllable by individuals). (ibid., pp. 163–4)

This separation of individuals into supposedly autonomous decision-makers constitutes a new social reality. The room for manoeuvre appears great, since the mechanisms which mediate social interaction are impersonal and non-discriminatory. Actual social relations (which Marx never fails to treat with the utmost seriousness) begin to reflect these characteristics. Individuals may be liberated from the relations of personal dependence that were a feature of feudal society, but the development that does occur is distorted and blocked by the ways and means of expressing that individuality.

The reciprocal and all-sided dependence of individuals who are indifferent to one another forms their social connection. This social bond is expressed in *exchange value*, by means of which alone each individual's own activity or his product becomes an activity and a product for him; he must produce a general product – *exchange value*, or, the latter isolated for itself and individualized, *money*. On the other side, the power which each individual exercises over the activity of others or over social wealth exists in him as the owner of *exchange values*, of *money*. The individual carries his social power, as well as his bond with society, in his pocket. (ibid., pp. 156–7)

The universality of individuality is the contribution that the dominant capitalist mode of production makes to the development of society. This is a significant achievement, as far as Marx's vision of the future is concerned. That vision is always rooted in the consideration of the present. The problems with the capitalist development of individuality reveal deeper aspects of his communism. Thus his criticism is that capitalist practice cannot realize its own ideals, cannot fulfil the interesting and legitimate possibilities it creates for humans. First, the 'independence from persons of the social character of things' has to be on a 'basis of alienation where the relations of production and distribution stand opposed to the individual, to all individuals, at the same time subordinated to the individual again' (ibid., p. 160). There is no other way that *all* the individuals in society can proceed (ibid., p. 164). The costs are high.

> Activity, regardless of its individual manifestation, and the product of activity, regardless of its particular make-up, are always *exchange value*, and exchange value is always a generality, in which all individuality and peculiarity are negated and extinguished. (ibid., p. 149)

Exchange, predicated on the universality of individuality, ultimately entails a denial of individuality and peculiarity. Ironically, this is exactly the kind of accusation that is levelled at Marx's vision of communism, that he would impose a collective sameness. Even though the individual is in close connection with, and appears to have control over, money, in fact s/he is prevented from self-expression and real social contact. 'Individuals come into connection with one another only in determined ways'; they become 'ruled by *abstractions*, whereas earlier they depended on one another' (ibid., p. 164). Thus, in the second place, individuals are devoid of the relative richness of relationships before the complete development of the system of exchange. The incidence of money as 'pocketed' social power produces *comparison* in place of real communality and generality (ibid., p. 161).

Nevertheless, 'the reciprocal relations of production separated from and autonomous of individuals' has its obverse and more positive significance (ibid., p. 164):

> In the case of the *world market*, the *connection of the individual* with all, but at the same time also the *independence of this connection from the individual*, have developed to such a high level that the formation of the world market already at the same time contains the conditions for going beyond it. (ibid., p. 161)

Part of those conditions concerns the individualization of the members of capitalist society. This is not just in terms of the individual as an interesting and worthwhile social product. The development of exchange has meant that the *productive* capacity of the individual has been enhanced, as a result of the destruction of the ties that preserved but also restrained what Wood refers to as 'the relentless tendency of human beings to develop and exercise their capacities to dominate nature and creatively shape it to satisfy human wants and express human aspirations' (Wood, 1981, p. 29). It is precisely this kind of growth in capitalism that Marx felt was essential if his vision of communism was to be a credible alternative – a society which, in other words, set no unrealistic demands on the individuals within it. The regularity of capitalist exchange may be anathema to the symbiosis of primitive communism, but that does not necessarily amount to a diminution of the human individual. The individual of primitive communism could not create the kind of social existence Marx had in mind under post-capitalist communism: such an individual could not even hope to contend with such an advanced communistic social existence.

Marx's realistic demands relate to a particular kind of individual, who shares the abilities and faculties that are consistent with the mode of production in question. Such individuals also reflect the complexity of the historical development that has taken place.

> Whenever we speak of production, then, what is meant is always production at a definite stage of social development – production by social individuals. It might seem, therefore, that in order to talk about production at all we must either pursue the process of historic development through its different phases, or declare beforehand that we are dealing with a specific historic epoch ... However, all epochs of production have certain common traits, common characteristics. *Production in general* is an abstraction, but a rational abstraction in so far as it really brings out and fixes the common element and thus saves us repetition. Still, this *general* category, this common element sifted out by comparison, is itself segmented many times over and splits into different determinations. Some determinations belong to all epochs, others only to a few. [Some] determinations will be shared by the most modern epoch and the most ancient. (Marx, [1857–8] 1973, p. 85)

There are two 'rational abstractions' to note. The most obvious concerns production, while the other centres on social individuals. For Marx, 'all production is appropriation *on the part of an individual* within and through a specific form of society' (ibid., p. 87; italics added). In this way, production is either an abstraction which generalizes about humankind, or it specifies the details of individual existence. Therefore, production presupposes social individuals.

But what special meaning is to be attached to Marx's use of the term 'social' individuals? According to him, individuals have never been anything *but* social individuals. It seems unrealistic to assume that only certain kinds of production give rise to social individuals, given that all production involves a co-ordinated and co-operative appropriation of nature. There is a temptation to treat social individuality as a special term and equate it with communist existence. This is to say that the true social individual appears solely after the creation of communist society. But Marx did not claim this. For that eventuality he chose the term *free* individuality. Moreover, in his vision of future society, he did no more than specify the *kind* and *degree* of appropriation that would characterize individuality under the post-capitalist mode of production.

> Man appropriates his integral essence in an integral way, as a total man. All his *human* relations to the world – seeing, hearing, smelling, tasting, feeling, thinking, contemplating, sensing, wanting, acting, loving – in short, all the organs of his individuality, like the organs which are directly communal in form, are in their *objective* approach or in their *approach to the object* the appropriation of that object. (Marx, [1844] 1975, p. 351)

This is a description of the optimum kind of appropriation, one that permitted and encouraged the full sensuousness of human faculties in their activity. All these relations to the world pre-exist communism, and therefore so too does social individuality. The term 'social' individuality accentuates the material connections of human beings to their social nature and the socializing activity of the production and reproduction of human existence in its particular form, and its transhistorical generality.

Within the framework of individuality and production can be seen the importance of Marx's developmental approach. As Wood puts it, 'the development or "self-genesis" of man in history is for Marx fundamentally an expansion of man's productive powers' (1981, p. 33). For Marx:

> The act of reproduction itself changes not only the objective conditions – eg transforming village into town, the wilderness into agricultural clearings, etc – but the producers change with it, by the emergence of new qualities, by transforming and developing themselves in production, forming new powers and new conceptions, new modes of intercourse, new needs, new speech. (1964, p. 93)

These two processes – the changes in objective and human conditions – are inseparable, or are elements of the same historical interplay of one upon the other. On this basis, Marx is able to extrapolate beyond the relative efficiency and potential material abundance of capitalist society, notable for two features which imply their own transcendence:

(1) that individuals now produce only for society and in society;
(2) that production is not *directly* social, is not 'the offspring of association', which distributes labour internally. Individuals are subsumed under social production; social production exists outside them as their fate; but social production is not subsumed under individuals, manageable by them as their common wealth. (Marx, [1857–8] 1973, p. 158)

The first feature confirms the universality of individuality as well as the universally social character of production. The system of exchange brings every individual to the same level of objective relation. However, as the second feature highlights, such universality is a poor or crude levelling of the potential inherent in social production standing over individuals, and production, *by individuals*, for society. In the juxtaposition of individual and social production, Marx was critical of a mode of production which made individuals subservient. A very important ranking is being assigned here. Both individuals and social production, equally, are historical products, yet Marx claimed that it was the position of *individuals* vis-à-vis the production process which is the major concern in the organization of society. This brings into question what Marx saw as the overall driving force in the course of historical development. Wood wants to argue that 'human history (on Marx's theory) is most intelligible in terms of the fundamental human aspiration to develop and exercise the productive powers of society' (1981, p. 30). However, Wood appears to confuse what is the *product* of a long historical developmental process with an essential and motivating quality of human nature. There is very little evidence to support such a view, which would in any case lend enormous weight to an 'aspiration', as if this could be some kind of drive of the species. Marx is much better understood as claiming that the development and exercise of the productive powers of society is an interactive process, continually escalating in complexity, and constantly changing the actual and possible form of social arrangements, which in turn reflect the alterations in productive relations and the individuals who are contained within them. Marx, in a footnote in Vol. I of

Capital, neatly summarized this method and order of comprehension:

> Technology reveals the active relation of man to nature, the direct process of the production of life, and thereby it also lays bare the process of production of the social relations of his life, and of the mental conceptions that flow from those relations. ([1867] 1976, p. 493)

At the same time, Marx had also argued that the interactive process of individual and productive powers would lead to a very specific outcome. If this were not the case, then there would be no means of differentiating between the forms of society and their relevant modes of production. Although he asserted that there existed earlier, communal forms of society, this did not mean that they formed the basis for the conception of communist society. He was careful to make explicit other distinguishing features of superficially similar social formations. Of earlier varieties of communal society, he wrote: 'Great developments can take place here within a specific sphere. But there can be no conception of a free and full development either of the individual or the society, since such development stands in contradiction to the original relation' ([1857–8] 1973, p. 487). That original relation is the productive relation, which is not under the command of the individuals in primitive communist society. This presupposes that there was to be an historic overcoming of that obstacle. Whatever one takes to be the driving force in historical development, Marx saw this outcome as the direct subjection or 'subsumption' of social production to individuals. Furthermore, Marx did not refer to any class in this respect, but confirmed his view of the historical development of powers within individuals. That development culminated in the possibility, even necessity, of seeing social production as no more than a faculty of individuals in society. As a faculty, rather than a drive or need, social production is something like other individual abilities, such as whistling or singing; these faculties have no power over us, and our use of them can be entirely in accordance with the effect we might wish to produce by their exercise. We come to judge them by criteria of quality, not just of efficiency or necessity. So Marx envisioned social production and the power of individuals.

Now at this point, it may well be that human aspirations can exercise and extend the productive powers of society, but this can be so only at the end of pre-history or the beginning of true history (as Marx variously called it) and *not* at the beginning of that process. The development of humankind and the development of individuals are complementary under a given mode of production. However, that complementarity does not necessarily entail an equivalence or congruence of the 'interests' of humankind and individuals. Communism is envisioned precisely because it reorganizes the relationship between individual development and the conscious control by individuals of social production under capitalism. There, the development of humankind is falsely set against individual realization of human capacities, such that the specific circumstances of the vast potential of masses of individual lives become a condition for the continued development of the whole society.

Capitalist production, when considered in isolation from the process of circulation and the excesses of competition, is very economical with the materialized labour incorporated in commodities. Yet, more than any other mode of production, it squanders human lives, or living labour, and not only blood and flesh, but also nerve and brain. Indeed, it is only by dint of the most extravagant waste of individual development that the development of the human race is at all safeguarded and maintained in the epoch of history immediately preceding the conscious reorganization of society. (Marx, [1873] 1959, p. 88)

This shows the manner in which the development of the individual and that of humanity may not be complementary. One way of seeing the contradictory nature of capitalism is to counterpose the social misuse of individual faculties with the necessity, for Marx, of preserving just that potential of individuals in their social life. Capitalist society, although at a high level of development, fails to take advantage of the abilities of the individuals of which that society consists. It is as if humans themselves are being treated as part of that nature which must be totally suborned and dominated by the capitalist mode of production. Just as nature is seen as an objective reality to be overcome and manipulated, so are the products of wo/men's labour. So, ultimately, are individuals themselves, whether they are wage-labourers or dependent upon breadwinners in a variety of ways.

On another level, however, the fact that wo/men produce what they do in the ways that they do is an indication of the development of humankind. They participate in and assist the continuation of 'capitalist progress'. In so doing, they make more possible a communist existence. Marx noted the contribution that individuals were making by identifying the difference between the natural and the social, by highlighting the uniqueness of the relation of humans to the given world and of humans to products of labour. At the same time, he was acutely aware that naming reality was not the solution to the massive discrepancy between the developmental advantages accruing under capitalism and actual existence under that same mode of production.

> The belated scientific discovery that the products of labour, in so far as they are values, are merely the material expressions of the human labour expended to produce them, marks an epoch in the history of mankind's development, but by no means banishes the semblance of objectivity possessed by the social characteristics of labour. (Marx, [1867] 1976, p. 167)

Thus Marx distinguished clearly, and in more than one place, between humankind as a whole and the life of the individual. The development brought about at the level of humankind Marx most definitely wanted realized for all individuals. Indeed, Marx argued that this was the *drift* of historical development. For him, capitalist development, and especially the incidence of surplus-labour, for example, must lead to specific changes in productive forces, and therefore social relations.

> Thus it gives rise to a stage, on the one hand, in which coercion and monopolization of social development (including its material and intellectual advantages) by one portion of society at the expense of the other are eliminated; on the other hand, it creates the material means and embryonic conditions, making it possible in a higher form of society to combine this surplus-labour with a greater reduction of time devoted to material labour in general. (Marx, [1873] 1959, pp. 818–19)

The development under capitalism has a twofold importance for communism. First, the supersession of capitalism as a limiting and increasingly anachronistic form of social organization can be assumed (even though it is not to be deemed *automatic*; nor is there any necessity to make moral judgements about the desirability of change). Second, the new social formation will be characterized, quite significantly, by a reduction in the amount of necessary labour. This Marx saw as a good, but not because he thought material labour ought to be avoided as much as possible. Far from it, since Marx viewed work as an essential human activity, the proper analysis of which allowed him to construct his critique of capitalism. Marx was indicating a deeper interest in the possibilities for individuals under communism. More time meant greater opportunities, not just for leisure, but to realize human potential in an active and positive way. In this sense, labour under communism was to be doubly liberating, developing each individual in the act of working, while at the same time detaining the worker for as short a time as possible, in order that further fulfilment could be experienced in the remainder of the day. Explicitly, only under communism can material production be such a liberating activity.

> The work of material production can achieve this character only (1) when its social character is posited, (2) when it is of a scientific and at the same time general character, not merely human exertion as a specifically harnessed natural force, but exertion as subject, which appears in the production process not in a merely natural, spontaneous form, but as an activity regulating all the forces of nature. (Marx, [1857–8] 1973, p. 611–12)

When dealing with future society, Marx is concerned with the way that the pre-existing split between the individual and humankind as a whole can be overcome, such that the development of one is also the development of the other. For this to come about, the two points in the quotation above must hold. They reveal much about Marx's view of the new individual under communism and the relationship between the individual at present and as s/he might or can be. Both are related by virtue of the need for individuals to transform the mode of production by participating in and contributing to the development of the forces of production. This involves the transition from individuals as particular beings, isolated from all others, into individuals who increasingly act in terms of a wider humanity on the way to a fully developed communist individuality. This comes about through the changes to themselves, as individuals develop their cognitive complexity and their all-round ability to interact with nature and others, but simultaneously involves the extension of capitalism, both geographically and technologically. This dual development is crucial to communism as a solution to capitalism and to communism as a possibility for humanity, in the following way:

The result is: the tendentially and potentially general development of the forces of production – of wealth as such – as a basis; likewise, the universality of intercourse, hence the world market as a basis. The basis as the possibility of the universal development of the individual, and the real development of the individuals from this basis as a constant suspension of its *barrier*, which is recognized as a barrier, not taken for a *sacred limit*. Not an ideal or imagined universality of the individual, but the universality of his real and ideal relations. Hence also the grasping of his own history as a *process*, and the recognition of nature (equally present as practical power over nature) as his real body. The process of development itself posited and known as the presupposition of the same. (ibid., p. 542.)

In order for Marx to be able to claim that *his* view of the individual under communism was not just another piece of utopian idealism, there had to be a means to connect the existence of all humans to the historical materialist manifestation of capitalism. Marx was confident that this was already achieved by the world-dominating social and economic order that is capitalism. Therefore, universality of human nature has been made into an objective reality composed of individuals in relation to capitalist relations of production, so that it is reasonable for Marx to claim that the communist individual, in so far as s/he has developed from the capitalist individual, truly is a universal representative of humanity, while also being a real living human under specific conditions of existence. *Relations* have become universal, and so too has the individual.

On being an individual

At this point the definition of the individual warrants further scrutiny. Marx's account of the way that the development of the productive forces establishes universality brings about changes in the conception of the individual and their relation to circumstances. There are, now, *ways* to be an individual, for Marx, and he appears to invert the conventional (eighteenth- and nineteenth-century) perceptions when perceiving the individual in the context of historical development. For example, he castigated bourgeois economists for failing to see the difference between a 'barrier' and a 'sacred limit' (ibid.), and in so doing, highlights their crude understanding of the individual.

The bourgeois economists are so much cooped up within the notions belonging to a specific historic stage of social development that the necessity of the *objectification* of the powers of social labour appears to them as inseparable from the necessity of their *alienation vis-à-vis* living labour. But with the suspension of the *immediate* character of living labour, as merely *individual*, or as general merely internally or merely externally, with the positing of the activity of individuals as immediate general or *social* activity, the objective moments of production are stripped of this form of alienation; they are thereby posited as property, as the organic social body within which the individuals reproduce themselves as individuals, but as social individuals. The conditions which allow them to exist in this way in the reproduction of their life, in their productive life's process, have been posited only by the historic economic process itself. (ibid., p. 832)

On the one hand, individuals have *always* been social; they are individuals only when the backcloth of society provides dimension and meaning. This is not a profound point of Marx's, even though it still seems to elude some otherwise sophisticated thinkers. Beyond this common-sense level is the historically based claim that there are qualitative differences between the individuals that one sees under various modes of production. Thus 'individual' to the bourgeois economist implies the isolation of each person in the productive process. Marx, however, shows that such an individualness is just an appearance, that a quite particular social individuality is entailed. This leads to the necessarily dual apprehension of the 'historic economic process' and the definite conditions of existence for specified individuals. Awareness of the limitations on social individuality of a certain mode of production is possible because Marx provided the means to at least 'think' outside our own mode. Moreover, it is conceivable to contemplate the single individual under certain circumstances, some of which s/he has been able to choose, without assuming an abstract separateness. These latter perspectives are not a major concern of Marx's, but they do appear at those important points at which he made negative judgements about the human effects of capitalist production. For example, in the case of the variation of labour, Marx saw that

the contradiction between the revolutionary technical basis of large-scale industry and the form it takes under capitalism ... does away with all repose, all fixity and all security as far as

199

the worker's life-situation is concerned ... [and] bursts forth without restraint in the ceaseless human sacrifices required from the working class, in the reckless squandering of labour-powers, and in the devastating effects of social anarchy. This is the negative side. ([1867] 1976, pp. 617–18)

Implicitly, the potential of each individual is crippled and stifled by industrial capitalism, as s/he is required to exercise the attribute of labour-power under conditions of sacrifice rather than as a contribution to social production. There are two facets, then, to the way that Marx saw the relationship between individuality and the mode of production. The 'negative side' restricts individuality, but Marx was careful to point out that something like the variation of labour need not have such a consequence under communism. Indeed, the social reorganization of large-scale industry would solve a problem for the working class as a whole, while facilitating the growth of each single individual.

This possibility of varying labour must become a general law of social production, and the existing relations must be adapted to permit its realization in practice. That monstrosity, the disposable working population held in reserve, in misery, for the changing requirements of capitalist exploitation, must be replaced by the individual man who is absolutely available for the different kinds of labour required of him; the partially developed individual, who is the bearer of one specialized social function, must be replaced by the totally developed individual, for whom the different social functions are different modes of activity he takes up in turn. (ibid., p. 618)

Thus Marx looked forward to a significantly different kind of person under communism. A central feature of his conception has to do with the development that humankind has undergone in previous epochs. The solutions to history offered by communism are not restricted to reactions to the inadequacies of capitalism, or any other particular epoch. Therefore, Marx's claim that individuals should be 'absolutely available' is more than a structural requirement imposed upon each person. It is also a statement about the capabilities of the human individual in general – 'there is a devil of a difference between barbarians who are fit by nature to be used for anything, and civilized people who apply themselves to everything' (Marx, [1857–8] 1973, p. 105).

This is a theme to which Marx returns later in the *Grundrisse*, in the course of an attack on Smith's version of labour as a curse, drawing attention in the process to the nature and need of the individual in capitalist and, by extension, communist society.

> It seems quite far from Smith's mind that the individual 'in his normal state of health, strength, activity, skill, facility', also needs a normal portion of work, and of the suspension of tranquillity. Certainly, labour attains its measure from the outside, through the aim to be attained and the obstacles to be overcome in attaining it. But Smith has no inkling whatever that this overcoming of obstacles is in itself a liberating activity – and that, further, the external aims become stripped of the semblance of merely external natural urgencies, and become posited as aims which the individual himself posits – hence a self-realization, objectification of the subject, hence real freedom whose action is, precisely, labour. (ibid., p. 611)

It should be noted here that Marx was prepared to suggest that there is some 'normal' level of work. This is by no means an absolute standard, but one which does relate to the 'normal' state of the individual concerned. Thus the reference point is the individual in society. Moreover, Marx argued that labour itself, as well as the social perception of labour, has changed with the progression through the historical epochs. Therefore, to the extent that labouring activity has changed, so too have the individuals who undertake that activity. This perception contributes to the view that work is more than a simple or normal need, but can become under communism a liberating activity, because it allows the direct and explicit expression and meeting of the needs *in general* of the individual. Furthermore, labour is not just a passive response to need.

> A. Smith considers labour psychologically, as to the fun or displeasure it holds for the individual. But it is something else too, in addition to this *emotional* relation with his activity – firstly, for others, since A's mere sacrifice would be of no use for B; secondly, a definite relation by his own self to the thing he works on, and to his own working capabilities. It is a *positive, creative activity*. (ibid., pp. 613–14)

That is, individuals do not labour only for reasons that are utilitarian, or that reflect the necessary nature of labour. The need to labour is as individual as it is general. This is an abstraction that holds across historical epochs, and in respect of the variety of modes of production. After all, this is a principle that serves to reinforce Marx's belief that the forces of production will continue to be developed. The difference between the reality of capitalism and the vision of communism is that Marx invested labouring activity with added dimensions. Labour was, could be, *positive* and *creative*. There is no *need* to labour once it becomes a faculty of a free individual. By claiming that it was not solely need-related, Marx transforms human needs into definite social powers, with a potency that makes it conceivable that they could bring about change in society.

In the *Grundrisse*, Marx highlighted two practical senses in which the changes in the conditions of labour could contribute to the efficacy of the individual and thereby the power to exert a transforming influence on society. A crucial element of the capitalist mode of production is reconceptualized in terms of its relevance for the evolutionary advance it secures.

> The capacity to consume is a condition of consumption, hence its primary means, and this capability is the development of an individual potential, a force of production. The saving of labour time [is] equal to an increase of free time, i.e. time for the full development of the individual, which in turn acts back upon the productive power of labour as the greatest productive power. (ibid., p. 711)

Although Marx is critical of capitalist consumption, he was prepared to examine it for its impact on humankind, and not just individuals in the narrow sense. For him, it indicated a further way in which labour power constituted a progressive force, developing capitalism toward the ultimate resolution of its internal contradictions. On the other hand, the increase in free time brought about the more immediate transformation of individuals under capitalism, as they became fitted for a different perception of their relationship with society.

> Free time – which is both idle time and time for higher activity – has naturally transformed its possessor into a different subject, and he then enters into the direct production process as this different subject. The process is then both discipline, as regards the human being in the process of becoming; and, at the same time, practice, experimental science, materially creative and objectifying science, as regards the human being who has become, in whose head exists the accumulated knowledge of

society ... When we consider bourgeois society in the long view and as a whole, then the final result of the process of social production always appears as the society itself, i.e. the human being itself in its social relations ... in which they renew themselves even as they renew the world of wealth they create. (ibid., p. 712)[2]

Even under capitalism, labour, as the production of wealth, suddenly takes on a new and more intriguing meaning. Marx makes clear the dual nature of the historical progression which takes place even within an historical epoch. The fundamental activity of labour itself undergoes great changes, but so too do the individuals who are the present subjects of this activity. Not only can capitalism be seen in a new light, but the prospects for individuality under communism become much more sharply delineated:

> when the narrow bourgeois form is peeled away, what is wealth, if not the universality of needs, capacities, enjoyments, productive powers, etc., of individuals, produced in universal exchange? What, if not the full development of human control over the forces of nature – those of his own nature as well as those of so-called 'nature'? What, if not the absolute elaboration of his creative dispositions, without any preconditions other than antecedent historical evolution which makes the totality of this evolution – i.e. the evolution of all human powers as such, unmeasured by any *previously established* yardstick – an end in itself? What is this, if not a situation where man does not reproduce himself in any predetermined form, but produces his totality? Where he does not seek to remain something formed by the past, but is in the absolute movement of becoming? (Marx, 1964, pp. 84–5)

These are remarkable passages, not least for their similarity with the Nietzschean theory of change as a process of continual becoming through transfiguration (Nietzsche, 1968, 708, 784–5; Nietzsche, 1966, II, 2, 12). Here Marx produced a complex image of the way that the individual operates both as a single being and a member of humankind. There is always the sense of history, and Marx made explicit the way that history has at last to be put into a human social context. In other words, history makes the future possible, but it is up to humans actually to make the future. Thus Marx wanted to end the hitherto defining role of history and society, and for human individuals to be responsible for the process which had for so long been beyond their conscious control, even though they had always been its progenitors. In this way humans would become the new individuals that a continually transformed society, detached from a determining history, allowed them to be.

There are two further aspects which deserve attention. First, Marx referred to the *dispositions* of individuals. In so doing, he perceives in capitalist society the qualities required of a communist social order. Marx did not claim that communist individuals would be made aright and anew by an appropriate social structure. Instead, the relevant dispositions are a matter of historical creation and record. They are not of his imagination or desire. Communist individuality is thus a projection of present possibilities, not the inevitable outcome of the model order.

Second, the communist individual can be confined to no particular form, but 'produces his totality'. Again, this signifies that Marx envisaged a social individuality of a certain variety. The communist individual does not expect or demand fulfilment and self-realization in terms of his or her own needs, capacities and enjoyments, as if an obligation existed on the part of others or society. It is the bourgeois individual who roams society in search of the niche or series of connections which will secure these things. Under communism, however, the new individual experiences needs as a human, not as a 'private' individual. The communist variant of social individuality incorporates the understanding that, to be an individual, the appropriate social conditions have to be created that are consistent with what are also experienced as personal needs. This is a view first put forward by Marx in the *1844 Manuscripts*, and from which there appears no significant deviation:

> Since the essence of *man* is the *true community* of man, men, by activating their own essence, produce, create this human community, this social being which is no abstract, universal power standing over against the solitary individual, but is the essence of every individual, his own activity, his own life, his own spirit, his own wealth. Therefore, this *true community* does not come into being as the product of reflection but it arises out of the *need* and the *egoism* of individuals, i.e. it arises directly from their own activity. ([1844] 1975, p. 265)

The relationship between the dispositions of the human individual and the nature of the community underpins and defines the character of individuality under communism. The status of the individual (as a necessarily social being) can thus be analysed, while avoiding the pitfall of relying on abstract notions. Materialism, in particular, connects two things: Marx's view of the social individual; and the justification for augmenting his critique of capitalist society with a theory of change. In the *Holy Family*, Marx reiterates the point made earlier, that 'the final result of the process of social production' is 'the human being itself in its social relations', in the following way:

> If man derives all his knowledge from the sensible world and from his experience of the sensible world, then this is to say that the empirical world should be arranged in such a way that man experiences and assimilates there what is really human, that he experiences himself as man ... If man is formed by circumstances, these circumstances must be humanly formed. If man is, by nature, a social being, he only develops his real nature in society, and the power of his nature should be measured not by the power of private individuals but by the power of society. (Marx, [1873] 1959, p. 243)

The validity of this kind of claim does not rest upon any moral consideration, or upon a rights argument. Marx is making a logical claim that society, since it is human in its basis, should be human in other senses and ramifications as a matter of consistency, or avoidance of contradiction. That is, the values which inhere at the fundamental level should be maintained throughout. The first sense is a constant or fixed requirement, whereas the second refers to the variable, socially defined comprehension of what it means to be human.

Given Marx's reputation as a class theorist, one could be forgiven for concluding that the second sense of human must relate to class existence. This holds true for his account of, for example, the rising bourgeois class with its historic mission to transform feudal production relations and secure the predomination of the capitalist mode of production. However, these were 'the conditions that have existed hitherto, when one class always ruled, when the conditions of life of an individual always coincided with the conditions of life of a class' (Marx, [1845–6] 1970, p. 31). In Marx's opinion, industrial capitalism had produced a special kind of class. It is possible to argue about the qualities of this class – about whether it did have an actual or theoretical revolutionary potential – but it is not possible to mistake its singular novelty as a class without a logical counterpart and successor. This is generally overlooked, or the proletariat is regarded as the 'last' class. For Marx, capitalism will be followed either by socialism or barbarism, *not* a new class situation. The proletariat is not a class when it is considered in isolation, as it would be after the collapse of capitalism. The proletariat is another term for humanity under specific conditions of production and reproduction. Under capitalism, it is degraded humanity. Under communism, the proletariat simply *is* the pattern of life of the constituent individuals.

If Marx's view of what is human cannot be reduced to a class view of the future, and some kind of utopian vision of the future is ruled out as abstract nonsense, then Marx has to rely on the quasi-ideal of the all-round development of the individual. As the following extract demonstrates, Marx appeared to be aware of the difficulties of vaunting communism without contradicting or vitiating the methodological process which led him to appreciate its desirability.

> The all-round development of the individual will only cease to be conceived as an ideal, as vocation, etc. when the impact of the world which stimulates the real development of the abilities of the individual comes under the control of the individuals themselves, as the communists desire. (ibid., p. 32)

Marx could not, while developing and professing the new science of historical materialism, countenance an idealist appeal, however much the form and content of the ideal accorded with his desire for a certain kind of world. Nevertheless, Marx was here dealing with his version of what 'ought' to be the future for humankind in general and individuals in particular. Necessarily, then, the notion of the all-round development of the individual denotes two things: a set of specifiable characteristics which are common to individuals *qua* individuals; and the material existence of the conditions relevant to that individuality. Pertinent inquiries, then, are bound to focus on the extent to which Marx did provide information on these two criteria. Certainly, he seemed well aware of the importance of establishing the credentials of the underpinnings of his vision of the future: 'if we did not find concealed in society as it is the material conditions of production and the corresponding relations of exchange prerequisite for a classless society, then all attempts to explode it would be quixotic' (Marx, [1857–8] 1973, p. 159). The next section examines the concept of wealth, and shows how Marx used it to reveal the prerequisites for communism, not just in capitalist society, but in all societies to the present.

Wealth and communist individuality

The classless individuality of communism may have similarities with earlier societies, but cannot stand comparison at the structural level. If individuals are no longer to be forced into restrictive classes, institutional and work-related roles, but are free to shape their own personal and social existences, then it must also be the case that the structure of society will have become the joint product, rather than the overall producer of individuals. If so, the difficulty of referring to a future which has yet to be created arises. A focus on wealth and the basis of wealth in society provides a connecting link between past history and possible future and facilitates an exploration of how free individuality can be comprehended as a material achievement even before the onset of communist society.

The impossibility of describing, in specific detail, a new social formation in the language of the present has meant that structural features are for the most part negatively defined. Marx resisted the Rousseauian impulse to legislate and thereby structure the future for the greater good. Instead, he looked to the conditions that must exist in every epoch of human history when he wanted to give some idea of the kind of existence that could reasonably be expected under communism. Again, the points are stated in the negative. Communism will be *unlike* all previous societies, in that it will be devoid of the contradictions of exploiter/exploited, employed/unemployed, and owner/non-owner of private property.

Nevertheless, communism still shares the concerns of those epochs. 'Wealth' takes on a special meaning, and continues to be of prime importance to communism. By claiming that 'all previous forms of society – or, what is the same, of the forces of social production – foundered on the development of wealth' (ibid., p. 540), Marx establishes three things. First, wealth appears in all societies, because it springs from the activity of individuals in specific conditions of productive existence. Second, wealth is conceived in terms of the values of that society (of which production for material existence is fundamental). Third, wealth incorporates the possibility of development. It refers not to a fixed stock of that which is valued, but to the creation of that which is valued. Taken together, these aspects of wealth indicate that Marx incorporated an assessment of the capacities of individuals into his account of the differences between societies and the nature of individuality under communism. Hence the development of wealth comes from changes in productive existence, the tendency to generate more rather than less wealth in society, and leads to 'new powers and expanded intercourse on the part of individuals' (ibid.). Thus wealth is at once the product of society and of history as a whole, and each transition from one epoch to another brings about (1) a new level of wealth, which is a new expression of the powers of individuals, and (2) an advancement in the material base bringing about that new level of wealth: 'there was not only a development on the old basis, but also a *development of this basis itself*' (ibid., p. 541). Communism is at the end of this process as it has occurred so far in history. It resolves the conflict between the developing forces of production and the mode of production, by bringing together wealth creation and the creators of wealth for the first time. For Marx, communism signals not quite an end, but a 'flowering' of this process:

> The highest development of this *basis* itself ... is the point at which it is itself worked out, developed, into the form in which it is compatible with the *highest development of the forces of production*, hence also the richest development of the individuals. (ibid.)

The development of the individual gets a slightly different treatment here. It is not so much that the individual becomes all-rounded; rather, s/he is enriched as fully as is possible. Marx thus remained unspecific about the character of the individual in communist society, while creating at the same time the strongest sense that a great deal could be expected in such a society. In A. Heller's view, the message conveyed by Marx's concern with the production of wealth in society could not be clearer: 'the precondition of "human" wealth is only the basis for the free development of all the capacities and senses of the human being, the free and many sided activity of every individual' (1976, p. 38). This representation, while it might accurately reflect the Marxian vision, also reflects the hopes and possibilities of pre-communist society. These are demands which reflect dissatisfaction with the present. In other words, what is understood by 'free' and 'many-sided' must depend largely on the perceptions of the present, not on the concrete form of these terms in the future.

However, the fact that his descriptive terms are rooted in the preconceptions and images of bourgeois society does not entirely prevent Marx from explicating what he had in mind. In the *Grundrisse*, for example, he suggests that wealth has ultimately to be conceived in terms of the impact that it has on individuals in a given society. Moreover, such an understanding is derived in part from an incisive view of the nature of capitalist society, in part from his overall historical approach to the development of the individual.

Thus the old view, in which the human being appears as the aim of production, regardless of his limited national, religious, political character, seems to be very lofty when contrasted to the modern world, where production appears as the aim of mankind and wealth as the aim of production. In fact, however, when the limited bourgeois form is stripped away, what is wealth other than the universality of individual needs, capacities, pleasures, productive forces etc, created through universal exchange? (Marx, [1857–8] 1973, pp. 487–8)

To the extent that the individual is no longer the product of society, Marx was prepared to acknowledge the superiority of capitalism over pre-capitalist modes of production. But that superiority is a temporary one indeed. For him, the achievement of capitalism has to be understood from a standpoint beyond bourgeois perceptions. 'Wealth' in capitalism actually refers to the historic possibilities open to the individual under communism. There, through universal exchange, no limits would be placed other than those set by the needs and abilities individuals can bring to bear (scarcity may thus be accommodated here). Existence is not to be seen as conflict between forces set in opposition to one another: humans versus nature; individual versus society; need versus satisfaction. Instead, the wealth of humankind means to be faced by a combination of daunting challenges and exhilarating freedoms.

Mastery over nature is not enough; Marx also dares humankind to take control over its own (human) nature. That is, humankind is the responsibility of every individual in the course of their own life. Individualistic decisions with an exclusive focus on the self become a poor form of the choices of the free individual, who will always choose with full awareness as a member of humankind. It becomes impossible to live for oneself in the liberal-bourgeois expectation of a greater social good arising magically or mysteriously. Second, Marx enjoins human individuals to express their full potential, without limitation, taking into account only that such potential has been brought into existence by historical progression. This can be seen, even by those sympathetic to Marx, as an invitation to disaster, because there may be potentialities which are more destructive than constructive, that require control or diminution.

In any event, the manifestation of the creative potential of each individual serves as its own teleological justification. On the other hand, Marx does overcome the difficulty of escaping the need fully to describe the individual life under communism by pointing out that there can be no 'predetermined yardstick' for the development of human powers. This is especially so since communist individuality is not a static form of expression. The communist individual, in the free expression of (human) powers, must also constantly be changing.

Embedded in this conception, then, is the notion of progress. This is a special kind of progress, however. It will be remembered that the above definitions come about through the development of wealth and the development of the *basis* of wealth. Up to and including capitalism, these aspects of development have constituted historical progress, in so far as the forces of production have constantly revolutionized the mode of production, bringing in its train changes to the relations of production and the form of social organization in general. In communism, that process of development continues as far as the individual is concerned. Indeed, development appears to be enhanced, because Marx precludes the operation of those elements which hitherto restricted the expression of potential, or the exercise of the full range of human powers. Moreover, Marx insists that the development of such human powers is *the* end in itself. Communism, however, permits but is not transcended by the development of the forces of production. This society can, apparently, accommodate all manner and extent of changes. As such, it cannot be the facilitator of individual expression and the constant process of creation and re-creation Marx referred to as 'becoming'. The concept of society, certainly civil society, becomes evacuated of all content.

While the promise of such a society seems vital, and the form of that society crucial, an examination of the life of the individual in post-capitalist society indicates that it is only the individuals who could really be said to exist in any meaningful sense. Civil society could not. The term 'social individual' thus takes on a more pronounced meaning. 'Society', under communism, must reside exclusively in the activity of individuals. Far from the individual disappearing under communism, the opposite appears the more likely possibility. If individuals are constantly involved in expressing and developing human powers, and are deliberately seeking to break free from their present being, then the notion of a settled society, which captures the basic activities and form of individual existence, is untenable. Society is, after all, a useful abstraction only so long as a mode of production does condition human existence. As soon as the Marxian revolution to communism takes full effect, individuals are not subject to any ordering or unifying power. It might be argued, therefore, that communism is not a defining society, but an *absence* of social definition.

If this is the case, then the load that has to be carried by the individual is considerable, but there is evidence to suggest that Marx believed the individual to have the necessary capability and power for this new form of association with others. In the *German Ideology* he claimed that

> by the overthrow of the existing state of society by the communist revolution ... the liberation of each single individual will be accomplished in the measure in which history becomes transformed into world history ... *All-round* dependence, this natural form of the *world-historical* co-operation of individuals, will be transformed by this communist revolution into the control and conscious mastery of these powers, which, born of the action of men on one another, have till now overawed and governed men as powers completely alien to them. ([1845–6] 1970, p. 55)

Implicitly, society up to and including capitalist society is, in the Aristotelian sense, a natural phenomenon. Marx, however, goes beyond this formulation. If social existence is natural existence, then a communist existence is distinctly post-natural. This puts Marx's claim about the control and conscious mastery of human productive powers into perspective. Society is that condition where 'the action of men on one another' has been a mysterious and uncontrollable process. When individuals are no longer 'overawed and governed', society in the conventional sense ceases to exist. For this to occur, there has to be a radical change in the mode of production, and once more, this is a change that is not a natural one. It is not a natural working out of the contradictions inherent in the existing productive stage. All that is natural in the change process, for Marx, is the manifestation of crisis in the bourgeois system and the accompanying universalization of the conditions of existence for humankind. In effect, there is no available or ready-made agency of historical change, the mantle of which used to lie on class conflict. Such an occurrence is ruled out by Marx's insistence on universalization - humankind cannot struggle against itself.

Nevertheless, there is the task of overcoming the structural limitations and dominance of the capitalist mode of production. Marx's brief reference to the role of the dictatorship of the proletariat in this respect is illuminating of capitalist society, not of change processes themselves. The notion of a proletarian dictatorship is indicative of the extensive controlling mechanisms in capitalist society. These instruments of class power must be removed from the exploiting classes and used against the expected backlash from those classes. Capitalist institutions, it has to be assumed, must be subordinated to wholly anti-capitalist ends and means, otherwise capitalism will inevitably reassert itself. Even more fundamental questions are begged by the notion of the dictatorship of the proletariat. The transition from one mode of production to another has its precedents, but such transitions always involved one class displacing another, and the dictatorship of the proletariat covers the transition from class rule to non-class association. The withering away of the state, the end of its transmission and monitoring of roles and expectations, must be displaced by a phenomenal growth of new forms of human association. A withering state, a remnant of a divided society, cannot conceivably achieve such a result. What, then, gives force to the process of change, if the dictatorship of the proletariat is confined to performing the last rites to a dying capitalist mode of production? Rather than an agency of change (usually presumed to be the proletariat), it can be concluded that there are instead only *agents* of change. Those agents are individuals.

> Thus things have come to such a pass that the individuals must appropriate the existing totality of productive forces, not only to achieve self-activity, but, also, merely to safeguard their very existence. This appropriation is first determined by the object to be appropriated, the productive forces, which have been developed to a totality and which only exist within a universal intercourse. From this aspect alone, therefore, this appropriation must have a universal character corresponding to the productive forces and the intercourse ... The appropriation of these forces is itself nothing more than the development of the individual capacities corresponding to the material instruments of production. The appropriation of a totality of instruments of production is, for this very reason, the development of a totality of capacities in the individuals themselves. (ibid., p. 92)

Individuals must bring about the appropriation of productive forces, and so bring about the end of capitalism, but they do so without such an aim specifically in mind. Instead, such action is under condition of the full development of the productive forces, and in the context of their own need to realize their powers as they have so far developed. Furthermore, the actions of individuals to bring about the end of natural society are also carried out on the basis of the needs of individuals to continue to develop their powers. Thus there is no appeal to any moral code or notion of abstract right, just the claim that the powers of individuals can be freed, and that those powers will seek to express themselves. The result of such action to achieve self-activity is communism, not as a society *per se* but as the transcendence of society, as the highest stage of development conceivable by Marx. 'Only at this stage does self-activity coincide with material life, which corresponds to the development of individuals into complete individuals and the casting-off of all natural limitations' (ibid., p. 93).

The downgrading of the importance of civil society to the new individual, or its apparent disappearance as a dominating and conditioning reality, means that social life itself has undergone an immense change. For Marx, social interconnections do not cease to be of crucial significance to the individual, but the relationship between the two changes. The analogy would be between food and the starving person, and food as one of many meals when that person is well-fed. In the first case, food is merely vital, whereas in the second it is also a contrived and controlled part of existence and is subordinated to other aspects of human wants and needs. The way to understand the relationship between social life and society is to see it not as natural or even social, but as historical, as relating to a specific phase of the development of individuals.

The alien and independent character in which it presently exists *vis-à-vis* individuals proves only that the latter are still engaged in the creation of the conditions of their social life, and they have not yet begun, on the basis of these conditions, to live it. It is the bond natural to individuals within specific and limited relations of production. Universally developed individuals, whose social relations, as their own communal relations, are hence also subordinated to their own communal control, are no product of nature, but of history. The degree and universality of the development of wealth where *this* individuality becomes possible supposes production on the basis of exchange values as a prior condition, whose universality produces not only the alienation of the individual from himself and others, but also the universality and the comprehensiveness of his relations and capacities. (Marx, [1857–8] 1973, p. 162)

The transition from civil society (in which the conditions of life are a constant preoccupation) to communism (in which individuals actually create those conditions) involves two things. First, Marx claimed that natural social existence was not a transhistorical absolute, even though it was original and basic. Thus, what was natural could be overcome, until it made sense to conceive of human existence in other terms altogether. It is for this reason that Marx adopted the historical approach, in order to capture the process as well as progress of change from natural to world-historical social existence, from the absolute to the relative. Second, the conception of wealth takes on an increasingly human and not merely material meaning. Whereas in previous societies wealth referred to any number of physical, social, material, or spiritual properties, wealth in the transition from natural to human or world-historical social existence can be understood only in terms of free individuality.

This is the significant product of the development of wealth, and its real achievement is measured, by Marx at least, in terms of its universality and comprehensiveness. On one level, communal individuality as a product of wealth has to be a concrete possibility for *all* individuals. On another level, that individuality has to be composed of the richest possibilities for *each* unique individual. These points are expressed by Marx in a number of ways. In the *German Ideology*, there are positive statements about the difference between state and society under capitalism and the expectations of a 'real community'.

> Only in community [with others has each] individual the means of cultivating his gifts in all directions; only in the community, therefore, is personal freedom possible. In the previous substitutes for the community, in the State, etc. personal freedom has existed only for the individuals who developed within the relationships of the ruling class, and only in so far as they were individuals of this class. The illusory community, in which individuals have up till now combined, always took on an independent existence in relation to them, and was at the same time, since it was the combination of one class over against another, not only a completely illusory community, but a new fetter as well. In a real community the individuals obtain their freedom in and through their association. (Marx, [1845–6] 1970, p. 83)

Marx refers to the necessity of the community, pointing out that all communities to date have been illusory and lacking in universality and comprehensiveness. Thus far, societies have been external realities, or forms of social organization which stood above them. With the development of communist individuality, however, the conditions exist whereby social interaction loses its apparent predominance and becomes the creation of individuals in association – it is a product like any other material product and holds no special powers over its creators. In effect, society becomes theoretically and practically secondary to the individuals who express their abilities in association.

If there is no overriding importance that should be attached to society, then communism is logically precluded from demanding a particular kind of social expression from each person. Unlike capitalist society, there ceases to be a division between 'the personal and the class individual' (ibid., p. 84). It is generally assumed, on the basis of Marx's insistence on the social nature of human beings, that the resolution of history – the overcoming of capitalism and the onset of communism – brings about a complete socialization of the capitalist individual. This view is contradicted by Marx in two ways. First, his view of the transition to communism contains descriptions of the proletarian class in revolution which go far beyond the notion of a class individual with a personality 'conditioned and determined by quite definite class relationships' (ibid.):

> the communal relationship into which the individuals of a class entered, and which was determined by their common interests over against a third party, was always a community to which these individuals belonged only as average individuals, only in so far as they lived within the conditions of existence of their class – a relationship in which they participated not as individuals but as members of a class. With the community of revolutionary proletarians, on the other hand, who take their conditions of existence and those of all members of society under their control, it is just the reverse; it is as individuals that the individuals participate in it. (ibid., p. 85)

Here the emphasis is quite clearly on the quality of individuality which can be experienced under class society when compared to post-class existence. This is quite anti-collectivist in tenor, and the suggestion is that the superiority of the proletarian movement resides in its ability to draw upon the full range of powers of individuals, rather than restricting them and allowing only an 'average' kind of social expression. It is not the collectivity of

proletarian existence that holds great promise, but the exten-
siveness of proletarian individuality that is so remarkable and
powerful. For Marx, a 'combination of individuals' is the best
way to describe the revolutionary proletariat, rather than any
notion of class or collectivity (ibid.).

The second instance where Marx contradicts the notion of the
individual becoming a totally socialized integer is to be found
on one of the rare occasions that he compares actual communist
life with the existing norms of capitalism. Although he had high
expectations of the nature of communist existence, he did not
presume to impose barriers to behaviour in order to see those
expectations realized. Communists, therefore,

> do not put to people the moral demand, love one another, do
> not be egoists, and so forth; on the contrary, they are very
> well aware that egoism, just as much as self-sacrifice, is in
> definite circumstances a necessary form of the self-assertion of
> individuals. Therefore, the communists by no means want ...
> to do away with the 'private individual' for the sake of the
> 'general,' self-sacrificing man. (Gandy, 1979, p. 94)

Marx (and Engels) does more than separate himself from
vulgar interpretations of communism and the implications for
the individual. He also demonstrates that his method did not need
to rely upon the approaches and imperatives of earlier thinkers.
Although the spirit of the Enlightenment remains a strongly
pervasive influence, Marx did not exhibit the excessive optimism
of utopian romantics, nor did he revert to the repressive prognosis
of those who saw egoism as a destructive but irremediable feature
of human existence. Marx remained resolutely uncritical of human
faculties and capabilities, and his main purpose appears to be one of
relativizing rather than judging the development of individuality
in human history. When the context is a future social order, such
relativizing must be restricted to maintaining an openness toward
possibilities. It would have been possible for Marx to consider the
likely shape and extent of the problems confronting the association
of communist individuals, but this would have involved the kind
of abstract procedure of which he was always most critical.
Moreover, no single individual could achieve anything of use,
since the problems of communism must logically arise out of
its actual existence, not its theoretical postulation. That existence
presupposes association, not private speculation.

In other words, Marx could not possibly know of the difficulties
between individuals that might arise under communism. This is

consistent with a future existence of free, self-determining and responsible individuals, even if it does imply a certain quiescence about the quality of their interaction. Marx was certain that the development of the individual that had so far preceded communism was to be regarded as an achievement in its own right. He did not regret particular aspects of the human animal, even if he felt that some were overemphasized and others underexpressed in certain societies. Marx's methodological approach dictated that individuality was always a totality as an historical product. As such, it was not a question of the appropriateness or otherwise of that individuality as he saw it developed and developing, but a question of bringing individual existence into close correspondence with the existence of individuality.

> In the present epoch, the domination of material conditions over individuals, and the suppression of individuality by chance, has assumed its sharpest and most universal form, thereby setting existing individuals a very definite task. It has set them the task of replacing the domination of circumstances and of chance over individuals by the domination of individuals over chance and circumstances. It has not, as Sancho imagines, put forward the demand that 'I should develop myself', which up till now every individual has done without Sancho's good advice; instead it has called for liberation from one quite definite mode of development. (Marx, [1845–6] 1970, p. 117)

Significantly, Marx signalled freedom from a certain mode of *development*, not production, thus indicating how individuality is entailed by a productive mode. Marx was not an ultra-rationalist, seeking to maximize the output and efficiency of the community. Despite the need to make such improvements, more important ends were at issue: namely, the 'free development of individuals':

> this development is determined precisely by the connection of the individuals, a connection which consists partly in the economic prerequisites and partly in the necessary solidarity of the free development of all, and, finally, in the universal character of the activity of individual in the basis of the existing productive forces. (ibid.)

Summary

Taken together, the possibilities for post-capitalist society adumbrated by Marx bespeak a new individuality which is fully reconcilable with pressing social demands. However, the kind of individuality implied by Marx means that it is the hitherto uncontrollable and unavoidable exigencies of life that come under the sway of the individual, instead of the reverse order being maintained and the details revised. Where the individual was dominated and subjugated in pre-communist societies, there Marx installs freedom alone. He did not suggest that other social, moral, or material imperatives could substitute for the practical realization of human powers.

This picture of total freedom is generally said to be diluted somewhat in Volume III of *Capital*, where Marx talked of the realms of necessity and freedom ([1873] 1959, p. 820). On the contrary, this differentiation between what individuals will and may do in communist society is a final confirmation of the importance of an account of individuality in Marx's social and political thought. Many of the elements of his thought that appear to be quite diverse, and for some quite contradictory, do find their resolution. Marx referred to human nature (usually associated with the youthful philosophical zeal of the early works) and accompanied this with the notion that there is an appropriate interplay between nature and human nature. This residue, as it were, of the early Marx does not minimize the recognition of the strong, although not in this case determining or conditioning, impact of the mode of production on human existence. This concerns the way in which humans can never be truly freed from the basic realities of subsistence and reproduction, as if Marx was particularly cautious about too much optimism for the future for humankind.

Yet, for all the strenuous insistence that the realm of necessity is unavoidably the basis for the realm of freedom, Marx ultimately showed that the first priority is the reduction of the time devoted to precisely that activity. Not only freedom of individuality, but freedom for the continued development of individuality remains a central feature of Marx's vision of communism: the beginning of 'that development of human energy which is an end in itself, the true realm of freedom' (ibid.). The communist individual, therefore, is unique in that s/he will be able to express the full range of capabilities and powers. On the other hand, such individuals will owe the nature of their existence to the development of individuality that has been brought about in earlier stages of human history. Thus, for Marx, the communist individual is realization and confirmation of that history. This is the closest Marx comes to an absolute version of freedom – the ability to live without being fettered by the past or in thrall to the future.

Notes

1 As Lukes, 1985, pp. 146–7, puts it, 'all that it holds to be irrelevant to the project of human emancipation'. Lukes makes this argument in respect of Marxist consequentialism, but it is interesting to note that his approach to the relationship between Marxism and morality has some similarities with the earlier discussion of the place of the individual in Marx's thought.

2 It seems that Marx is indicating a rich society, beyond and inclusive of the direct production process. The construction of society is not, therefore, all necessary labour, but must be said to include all these other (personal) pursuits.

6   *The new individual*

The thought of Karl Marx, examined from the perspective of his views on the individual in society, reveals a critique of individualism that must be put in the context of a much more extensive account of the development of individuality in history and society. Individuality is an important attribute of historical change and offers a better means of understanding the individual in any society.

Marx has wrongly been seen as an 'anti-individual' thinker. Although very antagonistic to liberal-individualism in his approach to the question of the individual in society, Marx was not a philosophical anti-humanist who denied the significance of the individual. Nor did he propose a kind of methodological individualism. The puzzle of the individual is a genuine one. Marx's view of the individual has strong affinities with humanist accounts; his contribution was to extend humanism into historical materialist method, rather than to transcend humanism or desert it as a theoretical possibility altogether. Through the connections between humanism and Marxian thought and between humanism and individualist thought, Marx actually shared some of the concerns of individualism, even though he proved to be its most implacable critic. Of particular relevance are issues of the existence or otherwise of the historical subject, the problem of individual intersubjectivity, and the relationship between the individual and human nature. Marx's criticisms of some forms of individualist and humanist social theory can thus be separated. First, his criticisms do not amount to a full specification of the meaning or practice of scientific socialism. Second, the particular issue of the individual, and the role of the individual in theory, society and history, remain fully to be theorized. The fate of the individual in social explanation is thus far from settled. Without a more developed theory of the individual, Marxism cannot offer a credible vision of the future or an effective political practice for the present.

Accounts of the individual offered by individualist thought represent the major ideological challenge to Marxism. Marxian thought is counterposed to a variety of approaches to the individual; it is clear that the divisions between forms of individualism are manifold and that Marxian thought is by no means equidistant from all possible versions. Liberal social theories produce a number of claims against Marx, using the notion of the individual to generate and support those social and political analyses. These approaches pose theoretical and political demands on Marxian thought.

Of those accounts, methodological individualism in its many guises offers the most prominent challenge, but its premises and practice often amount to no more than another form of abstract individualism of the kind so successfully attacked by Marx, especially in the *Grundrisse*. Interestingly, ethical individualism demonstrates a number of affinities with humanist and Marxist concerns. Ethical individualism could be interpreted in a relativist fashion, giving it a different character to the abstract idealism of methodological individualism. Moreover, ethical individualism is chiefly concerned with the question of autonomy. This resonates with the Marxian interest in human emancipation, presented here as autonomy under given circumstances of human construction.

Ultimately, individualist theories of society can be separated from claims about the importance of the individual. That is, the argument that a theoretical concern with the individual must by definition be non-Marxian does not hold. Indeed, the overlap indicates that it is Marxian thought which has much more to offer to the analysis of the individual in society than individualist theories themselves. Consequently, autonomy can be treated as a social phenomenon and a theoretical framework with significance for a study of the individual from a Marxian perspective. Human nature and history provide a framework which shows both the importance of autonomy for the individual and the requirements for a proper understanding of them. In practical terms, a number of things are needed: an account of the impact of the mode of production on the individual; an account of the (relative) meaning of autonomy to and for the individual; and a sketch of the mediating links between the conditioning influences on the individual. Only with an examination and understanding of these factors is it possible to consider the existence and nature of the individual in society.

Within the limits of his own ideological purposes, then, Marx established some crucial differences between his and the individualist accounts of the individual. Rather than the liberal-individualist focus on an abstract essence or a notion of the atomized individual,

221

Marx's view is that there is a certain *potential* to be an individual, according to the mode of production and the historical stag∘ ∘f development. Thus Marx was able to transcend what we recognize as *individualism* with its Kantian autonomy of self, the reliance on abstract rights and the formal institutions of the state in favour of a much more sophisticated understanding of the potential for *individuality*. Having taken as part of his basic methodological premiss actual individuals, Marx consummated his critique of society and history with an account of real individual living.

If the individual is to be considered for a central role in Marx's account of social existence, then the individual must have a specific place in the transition from one society to the next. For this reason, Marx's theory of change proves to be an illuminating testing ground for the proposition that the individual is an intrinsic part of a radical account of society, since it is almost universally accepted that the impetus for social change cannot be explained by reference to the individual, but must be in terms of classes or groups or economic circumstances. This is to take issue with the economic determinist view of social change, with the support of the instances within the Marx–Engels corpus which suggest a multi-causal determination of social change, which, combined with the inevitable uncertainty that such an admission entails, effectively rules out last-ditch determinism altogether. In any event, Marx was highly critical of the way that the capitalist mode of production did succeed in determining the life and consciousness of the individual, and looked forward to a situation where such social forces were under human control. In other words, he wanted social change which would bring about the possibility of autonomy from determining social forces. Only in a society where wo/men had control of and responsibility for their circumstances could free individuality express itself and flourish.

Nevertheless, the tension between autonomy and determinism in Marx's thought remains. In general terms, this tension has resulted in a downgrading of the significance of the development of the individual with an active and purposive consciousness. In the Marxian account, this is best exemplified by the inherent difficulty in explaining how a strict historical or economic determinism could ever produce and give way to full human emancipation, self-realization and equality, since these things imply both autonomy and agency.

Theorizing the individual in the account of social change means incorporating the individual without invalidating the central elements of Marxian analysis. It is axiomatic that such an account must be historical materialist and that change is a constant. When applied to the theory and the concept of human nature and the relationship to history in particular, this approach produces the basis for understanding the way in which individuals come to be in any form of social organization. Far from being any kind of determinist, Marx is better understood as presenting a theory of human nature in terms of a potential for social expression. It is just as legitimate, in theoretical terms, to speak of limits to such a human nature, but it does not rule out the possibility of change in human nature. In this respect, Marx's theory is more sophisticated than those placed at some point on the nature/nurture spectrum. Ideas of fixity and malleability presume a mutual exclusivity and rigidity to the content and form of human nature and thereby fail to apprehend the historical character of human nature as it is revealed under differing social circumstances. Using Marx's method it is possible to do three things: first, distinguish that which is fundamental from that which is dependent upon historically specific circumstances; second, explain how that which was or may presently be regarded as fundamental may itself undergo change; and third, explain how what is fundamental attempts to reach its potential.

Crucial to this enterprise is the distinction between conceptions and notions of human nature, referring respectively to a transhistorical nature and to a nature as it emerges under specific circumstances. This distinction conceives of the individual in society reflecting a fundamental human nature which was the result of earlier social formations and developments, and the impact of the current mode of production. Marx applied such a distinction in his critique of society and in his theory of change. Given Marx's belief in a progressive movement of history, the two interconnect over long historical time and within each historical epoch. This means that Marx understood human nature to have a developmental as well as potential character. Each new society created new potentialities, to the extent that humans became highly individualized in society. That is, they were differentiated from other herd animals by virtue of the development of the capacity for individuality - a multi-faceted collection of many abilities and faculties, like language, imagination and numeracy, for example.

The emergence of this capacity produces a dramatic change in human social evolution, because history and human nature must be *twin* forces in the construction of the individual in society. This is the basis for a logic of historical development which theorizes the interaction of these two forces. The dialectical movement through successive stages of production, applied to the emergence and subsequent development of individuality, reveals a developmental connection between the individual, individuality and social change in a very fruitful way. It means that there can be a parallel focus on the development of humanity in history and the development of individuals within a specific society. At the same time, it facilitates a comparative analysis of different modes of production, thereby highlighting the differences and similarities between the lives of individuals in society, and the way that developments within a mode of production can contribute to change across a series of modes of production. An examination of the evidence for the claims about the place of the individual in Marx's thought allows the insights offered within one mode of production to add to the insights provided by the others. The individual, from this perspective, does not seem quite so puzzling after all.

Primitive existence, sketchily known, highlights the minimal impact that the mode of production can have had on human nature in respect of the dominating influence of nature. In feudal modes of production, individuality was a crucial factor in the development of society and human potential. Individualization appeared in its early forms, as individuals began to perceive themselves in new relationships to nature, productive activity and other humans. At base, this was an extension of an existing historical process of growth away from a narrow animal existence into what we recognize and Marx termed as human social beings. Far from implying some essentialist movement of history, Marx presented such development as arising out of the interaction between the mode of production and the increasing cognitive and physical skill and complexity of feudal individuals. In keeping with his view of contradictions, feudal society not only saw the development of the rudiments of bourgeois individualism, but in so doing it also brought about the conditions which would lead to the destruction of feudalism. In this process, the development of the feudal individual was a vital part.

Non-economic factors also play a role in the construction of the individual's perceptions and life. Here belief, superstition and religion stand in the way of the forms of knowledge and ways of knowing that are integral to capitalism. Of most significance is the material change in the connection between nature and human nature. Under feudalism, nature to a very large extent ·proscribed and prescribed the extent to which human nature could be expressed. However, this connection changes with increasing human control and understanding of the natural world. As feudal individuals began to place parts of nature under their command, so the potential of human nature had more opportunity for expression. At the same time, greater demands were placed on human cognitive and social resources. Even in pre-capitalist societies, it was the enhanced self-consciousness and powers of individuals that enabled material forces to bring about structural change. Indeed, it was the developing powers of individuals which created the possibility of further social and material progress.

The duality and reflexivity of the relationships between individual, natural and productive circumstances in feudal society prefigured the nature of individual existence in the capitalist society which was to occupy so much of the attention of Marx. There was a decisive increase in the power of individuals in society to structure and control their environment in accordance with their developed needs and capacities. Effectively, individuals began to have an impact on their own societies and their own lives. In other words, the developing feudal individual previewed capitalist individuality, with implications for the problem of social change. The powers of individuals were perceptually as well as concretely related to labour activity, and the changing nature of labour was directly connected to the changes that were brought about in the labouring individuals themselves. This had positive effects on the individuals concerned, from which two conclusions are to be drawn. First, Marx saw that an enhancement of individual capacity had taken place. Second, Marx must have had in mind a superior notion of human development because he saw the development that had taken place as only partial and one-sided. Thus, even when considering the feudal mode of production, Marx validated the argument that human progress took place and was to be located in and judged by the development of complex skills and cognitive capacities within individuals.

Associated with these changes was an associated change in the needs of individuals. Whereas the emergence of new skills and capacities could demonstrate progress after the event, the creation of new needs formed the basis of the explanation for one of the reasons that change took place at all. When combined with needs, the capacities of humans, under all modes of production, prove an irresistible force for social change. Marx characterized this combination by the term wealth. Wealth develops, and with it individuality. Thus the claims that Marx made on behalf of the historical movement of economic structures apply with equal force to the historical movement of individuality.

An examination of pre-capitalist modes of production might produce a somewhat scant picture of the feudal individual, but each mode of production also reveals an account of the concrete possibilities for the display of human capacities. Furthermore, the distinction between particular historical expressions of individuality and individuality as a transhistorical abstraction is demonstrated by the contrast between the paucity of feudal social relations and the way that the developing needs and capabilities of feudal individuals prove to be a force for change. A society may be judged harshly for the kind of individual existence it permits; but it may simultaneously provide evidence of and forces for progress.

Ultimately, the enduring character of feudal existence is crucial for any understanding of individualism under capitalism. It was not Marx's argument that feudal individuality was totally destroyed by the victory of the capitalist mode of production. Rather, it underpinned and helped to bring about that change in the mode of production. The feudal individual was not stranded by historical change; the feudal individual outgrew feudal society long before structural change could be effected.

Marx's analysis of capitalism is a searching account of the individual and individuality. Capitalism is the most important of the modes of production, because it is this social formation which supposedly anticipates the end of pre-history. As such, it reveals new characteristics relating directly to that unique status, particularly with regard to individuals. Where individuality has developed, then these are indications of human social progress. On the other hand, where there is degradation of the capacities and lives of individuals, this is the precursor of further social change. Furthermore, there is a discernible pattern of progress of individuality *within* capitalism deserving of historical materialist examination. On this basis, the conventional perception of Marx and of his critique of capitalism too easily dismisses the significance of the capitalist experience of individuality.

The transition to capitalism involves a conceptual and social as well as economic transmutation in the lives of individuals. Massive change takes place to people as subjects as well as objects, and feudal nature was not simply and unproblematically discarded. Even a preferred development, from the superstitious emotionality of the feudal individual to the more rational and autonomous capitalist individual, involves loss, e.g. of intimacy, to individuals and to society. This relatively underdeveloped feature of Marx's thought highlights the cost of progress, and shows that feudal nature is nevertheless a part of the formation and ultimate content of capitalist nature.

Analysis of the historical character of early capitalism augments the logical and social significance of the transition. Marx introduces two parallel histories of human nature, one relating to the impact of fundamental human nature on society, and the other providing an account of what it means to be human under specified historical circumstances. The belief in progress is an inherent element in Marx's view of history. It surfaces most noticeably in his account of early capitalism, where humanity flowers. The impression is given that humans are endowed with powers capable of bringing about swift and beneficial social change. By implication, human nature is an emancipatory force, and one which allows for a flexibility of expression under varying conditions. This view stimulates some interesting questions concerning the roles of classes and of human nature in this kind of change. Class conflict cannot be a uniform phenomenon and no such model will suffice as an explanation of future social change.

The change from feudalism to capitalism was likely to be change of a quite different order to that of the transition from capitalism to communism. Part of this difference lay in the way that labour had changed under capitalism, drawing out and extending what were nascent powers of human beings. However, the question of slumbering powers threw into doubt the force of Marx's Sixth Thesis on Feuerbach – the empirical placement of human individuals within a social milieu does *not* of itself constitute human nature at all levels of understanding. Further insight into the way that human nature has a changing potential for individuality is provided in the relationship with nature that develops under capitalism. As control over nature increased, so did the capacities and powers of humankind come to fruition. It was in this way that feudal nature gave way to capitalist nature and that the freedom to realize human capacities came to be an imperative.

The uniqueness of capitalism called for a singular approach. It is to be found in Marx's claim that an account of capitalism must necessarily be an account of the human history which preceded that mode of production. The lasting nature of some of the remnants of past societies cannot be rejected as residual in an unimportant way. For example, the relationship with nature changes, but new mystifications of that which is 'natural' are created. Similarly, a range of descriptions of capitalist individuality are possible, and these will change with the development of capitalist society. Distinctive aspects of individuality are associated with Marx's critique of society, his vision of society and his theory of change. Capitalism made individuals, but what assumptions about human nature are implied? These aspects and questions yield the fullest possible picture of the capitalist individual, illuminating the relation of individuality to historical change and the extent to which the individual is an agent of historical change.

There is a special connection between the development of human nature and the growth of capitalism. First, the idea that the potentiality of human nature is a simple function of the mode of production must be modified. The history of human nature is not directly equivalent to the history of modes of production. The connection which does exist is mediated by the changes in the notions of human nature. These are immediately associated with every mode of production. Changes in human nature at this level may or may not persist if there is a change in the mode of production. Given Marx's view of humans and production, humankind develops as a result of the interaction between human nature (as a conception) and nature. Capitalism is unique in that it provides the conditions under which humanity finally attains a dramatically new practical and cognitive relationship with nature. As a mode of production, it is the most assiduous developer of human needs and potential, even if it is in a one-sided way. Humankind develops the ability and consciousness of control over nature. Moreover, this is not a *local* development, since capitalism is the first universalizing mode of production. This means that a stage development of universal significance within human nature had occurred. Human nature, therefore, has an existence which, by virtue of the drive and potentiality and new powers that reside within each individual, gives it a force in history. This implies the logical possibility of humans universally rich in needs, culture, powers and choices. Individuals of this kind must be regarded with the capability of being agents of historical change.

In terms of social relations, there is a tension between the progress that takes place on the grand scale of individuality and the exploitative nature of capitalism. The individuals created by a progressive capitalism may come not to need conditions of existence which also limit and deny human potential. Thus, part of the maturation of the capitalist mode of production will be the growth and maturation of those forces that are most antagonistic to social relations not offering the *all-rounded* development of human faculties.

The extent of that development in early capitalism is best seen by counterposing individualism and individuality. First, the individual emerged as an historical entity properly differentiable from nature and society. The propensity to understand and control as a conscious choice is increased, even if the practical realization of that ability is denied and thwarted in capitalism. In other words, Marx appreciated the value and importance of selfhood and egoism to the individual. Second, individualism shared some of these features, especially on the ideological level. Thus individualism, often seen only as ideology, as mystification, is in addition and in concrete terms a notion of human nature in the service of the capitalist social order. Isolated individuals were falsely assumed to be the prime source of reality and their activities and motivations were to be explained in terms of instrumentality. The modern age may well be known as the age of individualism, but this is misleading, according to Marx, because the content of humanity is not yet taken as the fundamental reality. As a result of the false ontology of the abstract individual, capitalist individualism actually diminished each individual person. The tension between the notion of human nature appropriate to capitalism and the potential in the conception of human nature produces specific stages of capitalist development with consequences for expressions of individuality.

At first, the bourgeois form of individuality represents the progressive movement of history. It existed before capitalist society was dominant, and introducing new values and interests. Bourgeois individuals were instrumental in making history; they had more control over the economic and social environment and so experienced a greater degree of autonomy. Effectively, Marx acknowledged the development associated with bourgeois individuality and with capitalism. Concomitantly, his critique of this burgeoning of human powers reveals how he attached value to individuality and to liberty, not to the values that the bourgeoisie attached to their activities. Individuality was treated *as a material force* by Marx. Consequently, individuality continued to develop as a material force, despite the hostile environment created by the further development of capitalism. Free individuality is in dialectical contradiction with bourgeois individualism.

For Marx, this contradiction is played out in the development of the proletariat. As the proletariat developed into a class, its rebelliousness did not transform itself automatically into a world-historical revolutionary force. For that to occur, Marx argued, it was necessary to abolish labour. This means that

Marx's original epistemological claim concerning the primacy of subsistence organization no longer holds. The organization of social production ceases to be a *natural* imperative and might now become one which is increasingly subservient to human choice and control. Accordingly, humans must be more than the sum of their productive and reproductive labours. The proletariat is thus conceptualized by Marx in quite a problematic fashion. He implied that the proletariat would collectively provide the possibility and reality of free individuality, but placed the proletariat in the following situation. It is capitalism which must develop in the proletariat the ability to see the need for the abolition of labour and an entirely new basis for productive social relations. However, the impact of capitalism, as we have seen, is to individuate its members, which may well drive them into a collectivism which is merely a reflection of the acknowledged deficiencies of individualism. It is not necessarily the case that collective action in the pursuit of economic interests creates an historically new social force of the sort required for the transition to communism. It is conceivable that the development of capitalist individuals is related to his class analysis, but this does not plausibly strengthen the class theory of change. Instead, classes suffer differentially from capitalism in terms of their experience of individuality. The proletariat bears the contradiction between its human nature and the conditions of life that are available to it, while the bourgeoisie, once stupendously productive and able to express its human nature, experiences a decline in its effectiveness, until its members can be no more than exploiters who are a restraint on future social and individual development.

Incorporated into this reading of the classes is a commitment to the importance of cognitive progress within society and within humanity. This throws into sharp relief the difference between bourgeois individuality and bourgeois individualism. This is the contrast between how it is possible to be, and how one is supposed to be an individual in capitalism. The potential and form of individuality changed within capitalism. Crucially, the early promise of capitalism, and its association with revolution and the progress of humankind, are not fulfilled on the grand historical stage. The progress that occurs is internal to capitalism, in the shift, for example, from the period of the manufacture to the machine age. The connotations of the internal changes are manifold. On a theoretical level, they support the claim that capitalist social relations and therefore bourgeois individuality are not fixed. In practical terms, this internal progress anticipates the possibility of communist relations of production and it requires the further development of partially developed individuals into more able and flexible individuals.

Capitalism is predicated upon both the development and the degradation of the individual in society. The progress of the capitalist mode of production increasingly sharpens the contrast between the development of all-sided individuality that it relies upon and the possibility of controlling those faculties. As individuality is made more complex and rich, so does individuality begin to approximate to a realization of fundamental human nature. It was Marx's belief, however, that this could not occur under capitalism. Nevertheless, he intimated that a new kind of freedom arises. This freedom falls outside the realm of economic relations, since individual life in a developed capitalist society is quite unlike the life of a slave or serf. There is a qualitative leap from these relations of economic and social exploitation, since the developed capitalist individual gains the freedom to conceive of and enter into social relations which are not based on domination and exploitation. This historic achievement has taken place only within capitalism and is the source of the normative superiority of the proletarian revolutionary movement.

However, Marx's concentration on the labour process led him to assume that the cognitive advantage of the working class was sufficient as well as necessary to bring about the class conflict to end all such conflicts. In so doing, inadequate attention was given to developments beyond the economic sphere. Rather than making positive moves toward revolutionary change, the designated agent of historical change (the proletariat) was becoming reformist, and certainly did not experience the predicted immiseration which would galvanize consciousness and forge it with action. Nevertheless, non-class change was taking place, namely, the development of individuality with a revolutionary potential. This is associated with a more loose and open intertwining of the mode of production and social relations. As the exploited class became less antagonistic to capitalism, so did individuality begin to mount a strong challenge. Out of a highly individualistic idea Marx drew a material justification for the advancement of true communality. Egoism, the ideological prime mover for individualist theories of society, was reconceptualized by Marx as a creative force leading to association and the recognition of others' needs. Furthermore, capitalist development led to individuals being much more aware of their powers and needs, to the point at which they began to develop the sophistication and capacity of an historical agent.

It is in these respects that capitalism is the progenitor of communism. The historical movement of individuality has a high status, partly as the result of a particular kind of exploration of Marx's thought and partly as a corrective to the overemphasis on the inevitability of class conflict that pervades political readings of his work (Forbes, 1989). Capitalism is a dramatically new kind of social formation. It is a human, rather than natural, product. However, it remains a social product that is falsely naturalized, regarded as natural. Within this mode of production, human individuality is elaborated to the point at which this falsehood is perceived and experienced. It is this which makes plausible any claims about humanizing capitalism. Of course, such a humanization entails the transformation of capitalism into a communist social organization, an organization for individuals.

The climax of individual expression in Marx's social and political thought lies in the analysis of individuality and communism, with its underlying emphasis on freedom. Here was a mode of production which Marx took to be both possible and probable. For him, communism was based upon the full depiction and final resolution of the logical and historical puzzles of human social existence. For humanity, it was the end of a long struggle, but it was also a new beginning.

These arguments are important because they raise the issue of the relevance of communism as theory and practice. Moreover, they impinge directly upon the questions of whether the individual can be an historical agent and whether the individual subject is a representative of human nature. Communism is best understood as a continuing task, not as an endpoint, that it served as an interpretation of current reality and that it was part of the explanation of the movement of history. Nowhere is there evidence which rules out the need for an account of the individual. As such, some of the descriptions of communism can be endorsed, while rejecting the conclusions that communism is idealism, moralism, or just plain polemics. It is better understood as an umbrella term for the complex set of ideas and arguments Marx had about history, human nature and social change. It unified his social and political commitment to a unique kind of social transition.

The most outstanding difference between communism and all other social formations is the absence of classes. This would be a major liberation, with individuals no longer set against other individuals by class conflict. The oppositional relation that existed between humankind and human beings in class society would cease to exist. Thus communism as the end of classes is the act of solving the contradictions which crush and mutilate individuals. In practical terms, the end of conventional political power results in quite different and less damaging demands being made upon individuals under communism. The proletariat is not in fact a 'class' in any of the senses that pertain to pre-communist existence. It is more positively understood as composed of individuals with no need to be defined by virtue of a conditioning class position.

The future, therefore, is to consist solely of new individuals. Such individuals would have to forge new relationships with nature. There is only a superficial similarity with primitive communal or herd existence in this respect. The development of individuality is in terms of control over nature, society and self, and these three elements are either absent in earlier epochs, or only partially developed. Moreover, communism is not about individuals of this or that kind, defined by this or that role or activity, but about the *lives* of real individuals. The objective existence of free individuals would be transparent at any one time, but there would always be objective possibilities for change and the recognition and realization of other potentialities. Although communism is a neat and tidy outcome for Marx, it is not just an absence of alienation or powerlessness. It is also a positive movement, an interaction of human powers and historical and social possibilities which produces the uniqueness of communism. This entails the mutuality of humanity and nature. Marx looked forward to a situation where a *human* existence could take the place of what we have always experienced merely as *social* existence.

Communism is a synonym for society. Therefore, a developed human nature will realize itself as communist existence, bringing about a further enrichment of human nature. As a result, communist individuality would be particularly rich and diverse, notwithstanding the problem of how such individuals could emerge from a mode of production which was so stunting and stultifying in its impact on social relations.

The preparation of the individual for the future and the grounds for the transition to that future are an accomplishment of capitalism (Forbes and Street, 1986). Exchange and production created a universal individuality for the first time in history. If so, social individuality is not the novel product of communist society. Nor is social individuality the equivalent of communist individuality. Social individuality actually *precedes* communism, since it is an historic possibility in all social formations. Marx assumed that this was the only kind of individuality which could possibly exist. Brought to a high level of development

233

by capitalism, it prefigures the communist expression of such individuality. This development is understood in terms of the production process. Increases in cognitive complexity stem from the active relation of wo/man to nature encapsulated in the level of technology. The interactive nature of the production process means that human faculties are being extended and that this in turn affects social development.

For Marx, the development of individuals within a production process was not necessarily associated with the development of human nature. Development within capitalism of human individuals could produce pressure to change capitalism. Its gains for some individuals could not continue to outweigh its costs for humankind as a whole. Communism overthrows this natural and then artificial division between the individual and humankind. It is the positive solution to the contradictions of capitalism and the partial expression of individuality it encourages. At the same time, it is a new or self-defined possibility for humanity. That is, the universality of human nature as individuality becomes an objective reality, and the communist individual is a true representation of humanity. Just as relations are universal, so too are individuals.

Communist individuality is thus not merely a reaction to past inadequacies but a practical exploration of true human liberation. For Marx, humans are constantly in the movement of becoming, as they re-create the wealth of their society and themselves. Individuals become what a continually transformed society allows them the freedom to be, rather than being the inevitable outcome of an order belonging to a model future. The historical and human foundations of individual existence mean that communist individuality can also be seen as a projection of possibilities inherent in capitalist society. This may take a variety of actual forms, according to the ways that individuals create and express themselves. Crucially, needs are experienced as human, not as the wants and motivations of the private or isolated individual. Above all, Marx saw free individuality as relating to the all-round development of each person. This kind of development emerges as the major principle of his view of individuality, and the one criterion upon which societies could be judged. It was a provisional ideal and a political vocation in Marx's theoretical practice.

There are material grounds for believing that a transition to communism could take place. Free individuality is already a material achievement of human history, even before it is objectively and fully realized in a particular society. The extent of individuality and the quality of its expression is related to wealth. Wealth is a relative concept with respect to the values it assigns and recognizes in each society, and is developmental in its nature. In other words, wealth is the creation of that which is valued. As far as Marx was concerned, wealth included individuality. It was the extension and articulation of human powers which Marx saw as the goal of human social existence, and it was communism which was the mode of production capable of bringing about that kind of enrichment of individuals. The new individual, therefore, is a constantly changing human product. This means that progress and wealth development is the goal of communism, because the development of wealth cannot destroy communism in the same way that it led to the collapse of all earlier social formations. Humankind, once it is continually overcoming itself in the process of realising and enriching its individuality, is no longer in a struggle against itself. Consequently, there is no society which is over and above individuals as an abstraction, just as there is no abstraction of self and human nature, no particular kind of social expression which can be demanded from each person. On this reading, no individual could be regarded as a totally socialized integer, submerged in a collectivized existence. Therefore, it is not the collectivity of a proletarian class existence that holds the promise of free individuality under communism, but the development of a new individuality which can assert itself with equal confidence in both communal and private respects.

Freedom from all the defining assumptions of individual existence is intrinsic to this view of individuality. Marx assumed that freedom was a human capacity as much as a necessity for individuality to emerge out of social and natural relations. Furthermore, that capacity for the exercise of freedom established the grounds for the continued development of individuality, until such time as a future society would not have to stand in the way of the full expression of free individuality. It is in this stage of human history that fundamental human nature is entirely in accordance with human nature under specific circumstances. Those circumstances must be of human construction, under conditions of a freedom brought about by an expression of free individuality.

Marx can properly be described as a theorist of individuality. His most basic premiss concerned the existence of real human individuals, and the relevance of this to an understanding of the individual under different modes of production has been demonstrated. Contrary to popular as well as some scholarly views, Marx had a great deal to say on the subject of the individual. It is important to be reminded of the various ways in which the individual may appear in a Marxian account of social existence: as a real, producing and reproducing individual; as ideological construct, i.e. role bearer; as historical subject; as part of a change process, i.e. revolutionary agent; as a member of a class; as an exemplar of a theoretical dispute between Marx and 'individualist' thinkers; as an expression of human nature under given conditions; as an expression of human nature viewed from the long historical perspective.

Humankind could be developed to such a degree that it constituted a powerful enough historical force for the destruction of social organizations which restricted the full realization of human capacities and abilities. This argument has been pursued mainly from the historical perspective, since no strong moral case for the development of humankind toward free individuality arises out of this reading of Marx. It is concluded, therefore, that it is not possible to argue that there *should* be a change to a society of free individuality. It leaves relatively intact Marx's prediction that such a change *would* occur. His prediction, however, is partly a logical one about historical development and partly a preference for that which is, after all, no more than a possibility.

There are very good grounds for rejecting the interpretation that Marxian thought is based upon the premiss that the theoretical concept of the individual is to be transcended. This challenges the conventional view that consciousness of the true nature of society, and the real basis for proper human existence, relates only to class existence, and not individual existence. There is no real dispute about the prime importance of class struggle in the past, even though the developmental aspects of human nature predominate in this account of historical change. No lengthy justification for downgrading the importance of class analysis is necessary. On logical and practical grounds, the class conflict approach is quite inadequate as an explanation for any future transition to communism. The absence of a compelling account of the move from class to non-class existence is of central importance. Such a change has no historical precedent to draw upon, and the usual theoretical arguments are at best tenuous. Marx's rejection of individualistic thought indicates a belief in free individuality as a powerful and creative historical force.

Whatever its basis, Marxian thought does not itself *produce* the premiss that the notion of the individual in society, or in the good communist society, will or ought to be transcended. There is a less strong case that the individual is a central feature of Marx's account of social existence. He is usually understood to make individuals subject to historical processes rooted in material needs, to conceive only of collectivities, and to place historical significance on class antagonisms as the material expression of development arising out of objective social forces which are not under individual control. However, his antagonism to those theories in which the individual is of theoretical and practical importance is not necessarily the same as a rejection of any consideration of the individual.

Nevertheless, Marxian thought cannot be dismissed as an outmoded anti-individualism. His method can be applied to the puzzling individual to good effect. The method of analysis emerges unscathed and its ability to generate a challenging analysis of the individual is demonstrated. It opens the way for further study of contemporary existence and the experience of individuality, offering as it does a powerful vision of the future, on the basis of a consideration of the new individual rather than the conventional categories of class, economics and the politics of the state. If the basis of individual agency has already been developed and has become a part of fundamental human nature, then the new individual has to be regarded as an historical agent of singular importance for future transitions from one form of society to another, and for an understanding of contemporary societies.

It is also clear that the individual cannot be viewed in the usual or straightforward way. Examinations of 'human nature' have often been tied to a methodology which denies one or other of the essential features of a proper examination of the individual in society. Thus there are psychological accounts, cognitive accounts, ethical accounts and materialist accounts. Each of these approaches has its inadequacies, just as they are to be valued for their attempts to find answers to the crucial question of human nature and its relation to social existence. In the light of their mixed success, the Marxian framework remains at the very least a very open framework for analysis. That is, a dialectical and historical account of human nature and the individual offers the greatest chance for properly analysing all the features of human existence we at present recognize, while remaining open to the introduction of new insights and perspectives. For this, individuals will always be necessary; and new individuals always possible.

Bibliography

Aers, D. (1988), *Community, Gender and Individual Identity: English Writing 1360–1430* (London: Routledge).

Althusser, L. (1969), *For Marx* (Harmondsworth: Penguin).

Althusser, L. (1970), *Reading 'Capital'* (London: New Left Books).

Althusser, L. (1976), *Essays in Self-Criticism* (London: New Left Books).

Archibald, W. P. (1983), 'Psychic alienation in Marx: the missing link?', *Praxis International*, vol. 3, no. 1.

Avineri, S. (1968), *The Social and Political Thought of Karl Marx* (Cambridge: Cambridge University Press).

Baechler, J. (1975), *The Origins of Capitalism*, (Oxford: Blackwell).

Berger, J. and Offe, C. (1982), 'Functionalism vs. Rational Choice? Some Questions Concerning the Rationality of Choosing One or the Other', *Theory and Society* Vol. II, No. 4 (July).

Berki, R. (1983), *Insight and Vision* (London: Dent).

Berry, C. (1983), 'Conservatism and human nature', in Forbes and Smith (eds), op. cit., pp. 53–67.

Bhaskar, R. (1979), *The Possibility of Naturalism: A Philosophical Critique of the Contemporary Human Sciences* (Hassocks: Harvester).

Bloch, M. (1962), *Feudal Society*, 2 volumes, 2nd edition (London: Routledge & Kegan Paul).

Bottomore, T. (ed) (1981), *Modern Interpretations of Marx* (Oxford: Basil Blackwell).

Burke, J. P., Crocker, L. and Legters, L. (eds) (1977), *Marxism and the good society* (Cambridge: Cambridge University Press).

Carling, A. (1986), 'Rational-choice Marxism', *New Left Review*, 160, pp. 24–62.

Carver, T. (1987), 'Logic and the social individual in *Capital*', paper delivered at the annual meeting of the American Political Science Association, September.

Clark, A. (1968), *The Working Life of Women in the Seventeenth Century* (London: Frank Cass).

Cohen, G., (1968), 'Bourgeois and proletarians', *Journal of the History of Ideas*, vol. XXIX, no. 2, pp. 211–30.

Cohen, G. (1978), *Karl Marx's Theory of History* (Oxford: Clarendon).

Connolly, W. (1981), *Appearance and Reality in Politics* (Cambridge: Cambridge University Press).

Coole, D. (1988), *Women in Political Theory* (Brighton: Wheatsheaf).

Dawe, A. (1970), 'The Two Sociologies', *British Journal of Sociology*, vol. 21, pp. 207–18.
Delphy, C. (1984), *Close to Home* (trans. and ed. D. Leonard) (London: Hutchinson).
Dobb, M. (1963), *Studies in the Development of Capitalism* (London: Routledge & Kegan Paul).

Edgley, R. (1983), 'Philosophy', in McLellan (ed), op. cit. (London: Fontana).
Eisenberg, L. (1972), 'The *human* nature of human nature', *Science*, vol. 176, no. 4031, p. 123.
Elster, J. (1980), 'Reply to comments', *Inquiry*, 23, pp. 213–32.
Elster, J. (1982), 'Marxism, functionalism and game theory', *Theory and Society*, 11, pp. 453–82.
Elster, J. (1983), 'Reply to comments', *Theory and Society*, 12, pp. 111–20.
Elster, J. (1985), *Making Sense of Marx* (Cambridge: Cambridge University Press).
Elster, J. (1986), *An Introduction to Karl Marx* (Cambridge: Cambridge University Press).
Engels, F. (1968), 'Ludwig Feuerbach and the End of Classical German Philosophy' and 'Socialism: Utopian and Scientific', in *Karl Marx and Friedrich Engels: Selected Works in One Volume* (London: Lawrence & Wishart).
Evans, M. (1975), *Karl Marx*, (London: Allen & Unwin).

Forbes, I. (1983), 'Marx and human nature', in Forbes and Smith (eds), op. cit., pp. 20–35.
Forbes, I. (1989), 'Marxian individualism', in *Approaches to Marx*, M. Cowling and L. Wilde (eds) (Milton Keynes: Open University Press).
Forbes, I. and Smith, S. (1983), *Politics and Human Nature* (London: Frances Pinter).
Forbes, I. and Street, J. (1986), 'Individual transitions to socialism', *Theory Culture and Society*, vol. 3, no. 1, pp. 17–33.
Fritzhand, M. (1980), 'Individualism and collectivism', *Dialectics and Humanism*, no. 3, p. 23.
Fromm, E. (1976), *To Have or to Be* (London: Sphere Books).

Gandy, D. R. (1979), *Marx and History* (Austin, Tex.: University of Texas Press).
Gellner, E. (1964), *Thought and Change* (London: Weidenfeld & Nicolson).
Geras, N. (1983), *Marx and Human Nature: Refutation of a Legend* (London: Verso).
Goldmann, L. (1981), 'Philosophy and sociology in Marx's early

writings', in T. Bottomore (ed.), *Modern Interpretations of Marx* (Oxford: Blackwell).

Golubović, Z. (1983), 'Marx's concept of man vs. a Stalinist ideology of the "New Man"', paper delivered at the 6th annual meeting of the International Society of Political Psychology, July.

Goodwin, B. (1978), *Social Sciences and Utopia* (Hassocks: Harvester).

Gorz, A. (1982), *Farewell to the Working Class* (London: Pluto Press).

Gould, C. (1978), *Marx's Social Ontology* (London: MIT Press).

Gouldner, A. (1974), 'Marxism and social theory', *Theory and Society*, 1, pp. 17–35.

Gouldner, A. (1980), *Two Marxisms* (London: Macmillan).

Hamilton, R. (1978), *The Liberation of Women: A Study of Patriarchy and Capitalism* (London: Allen & Unwin).

Hassan, I. (1985), 'The Culture of Postmodernism'. *Theory, Culture and Society*, Vol. 2, No, 3, pp. 119–31.

Hearn, J. (1987). *The Gender of Oppression* (Brighton: Harvester).

Heller, A. (1976), *The Theory of Need in Marx*, (London: Allison & Busby).

Hindess, B. and Hirst, P. Q. (1975), *Pre-Capitalist Modes of Production*, (London: Routledge & Kegan Paul).

Hobsbawm, E. (1964), 'Introduction', in K. Marx, *Pre-Capitalist Economic Formations*, E. Hobsbawm (ed.) (London: Lawrence & Wishart).

Howard, D. and Klare, E. (eds) (1972), *The Unknown Dimension* (New York: Basic Books).

Hyppolite, J. (1969), *Studies on Marx and Hegel* (London: Heinemann).

Inquiry (1986), Symposium on *Making Sense of Marx*, no. 29.

James, S. (1984), *The Content of Social Explanation* (Cambridge: Cambridge University Press).

Kamenka, E. and Neale, R. S. (eds) (1975), *Feudalism, Capitalism and Beyond* (London: Edward Arnold).

Keat, R. (1979), 'Individualism and community in socialist thought', in J. Mepham and D. Hillel-Ruben (eds), *Issues in Marxist Philosophy*, Vol. III (Hassocks: Harvester).

Kiernan, V. (1983), 'History', in McLellan, op. cit.

Kosik, K. (1967), 'The Individual and History', in N. Lobkowicz (ed.), *Marx and the Western World* (Indiana, Ind.: Notre Dame University Press).

Lane, R. E. (1978), 'Waiting for Lefty: the capitalist genesis of socialist man', *Theory and Society*, vol. VI, no. 1.

Levin, M. (1984), 'On the adequacy of Marx's vision of communism', *Praxis International*, vol. 3, no. 4.

Bibliography

Levine, A., Sober, E. and Wright, E. O. (1987), 'Marx and methodological individualism', *New Left Review*, vol. 162, pp. 67–84.
Loewenstein, J. (1980), *Marx against Marxism* (London: Routledge & Kegan Paul).
Lukes, S. (1973a), 'Modes of individualism reconsidered', in J. O'Neill, op. cit.
Lukes, S. (1973b), *Individualism* (Oxford: Blackwell).
Lukes, S. (1985), *Marxism and Morality* (Oxford: Clarendon).

Macfarlane, A. (1978), *The Origins of English Individualism* (Oxford: Blackwell).
MacIntyre, A. (1968), *A Short History of Ethics* (London: Routledge & Kegan Paul).
McBride, W. L. (1977), *The Philosophy of Marx*, (London: Hutchinson).
McLellan, D. (1981), 'Marx and Engels on the future communist society', in J. P. Burke, L. Crocker and L. Legters (eds), *Marxism and the good society*, (Cambridge: Cambridge University Press).
McLellan, D. (ed.), (1983), *Marx: the First Hundred Years*, (London: Fontana).
Marcuse, H. (1965), 'Repressive tolerance', in R. P. Wolff and B. Moore, Jr, (eds) *A Critique of Pure Tolerance* (Boston, Mass.).
Markovic, M. (1974a), *From Affluence to Praxis*, (Michigan, Mich.: Michigan University Press).
Markovic, M. (1974b), *The Contemporary Marx* (Nottingham: Spokesman).
Marx, K. [1844] (1975), 'Economic and philosophical manuscripts', in Marx, *Early Writings*, op. cit.
Marx, K. [1845] (1956), *The Holy Family* (Moscow: Foreign Language Press).
Marx. K. [1845] (1968), 'Theses on Feuerbach', in Marx and Engels, op. cit.
Marx, K. [1852] (1973), 'The Eighteenth Brumaire of Louis Napoleon', in *Surveys from Exile* (Harmondsworth and London: Penguin and New Left Review).
Marx, K. [1859] (1968), 'Preface to *A Contribution to a Critique of Political Economy*, in Marx and Engels, op. cit.
Marx, K. [1875] (1968), *The Critique of the Gotha Programme*, in Marx and Engels, op. cit.
Marx, K. [1847] (1968), *Manifesto of the Communist Party*, in Marx and Engels, op. cit.
Marx, K. (1847), *The Poverty of Philosophy* (London: Lawrence & Wishart).
Marx, K. [1857–8] (1973), *Grundrisse* (Harmondsworth: Penguin)
Marx, K. and Engels F. [1845–6] (1970), *The German Ideology*, C. J. Arthur (ed.), (London: Lawrence & Wishart).
Marx, K. [1867] (1976), *Capital*, Vol. I (Harmondsworth: Penguin).

Marx, K. [1873] (1959), *Capital*, Vol. III, F. Engels (ed.), (London: Lawrence & Wishart).

Marx, K. (1964), *Pre-Capitalist Economic Formations*, E. Hobsbawm (ed.) (London: Lawrence & Wishart).

Marx, K. (1967), *Writings of the Young Marx on Philosophy and Society*, L. Easton and K. Guddat (eds) (New York).

Marx, K. and Engels, F. (1968), *Karl Marx and Friedrich Engels: Selected Works in One Volume* (London: Lawrence & Wishart).

Marx, K. (1972), *Karl Marx: Economy, Class and Social Revolution*, Z. A. Jordan (ed.) (London: Nelson).

Marx, K. (1973), *Political Writings*, Vol. 1, *The Revolutions of 1848*; Vol. 2, *Surveys from Exile*; vol. 3, *The First International and After* (Harmondsworth: Penguin).

Marx, K. (1975), *Early Writings* (Harmondsworth: Penguin).

Marx, K. (1977), *Karl Marx: Selected Writings*, D. McLellan (ed.) (Oxford: Oxford University Press).

Morgan, R. (1982), *The Anatomy of Freedom* (Oxford: Martin Robertson).

Neale, R. S. (1975), 'The bourgeoisie, historically, has played a most revolutionary part', in Kamenka and Neale, op. cit.

Nietzsche, F. (1966), *Beyond Good and Evil* and *Genealogy of Morals*, in *Basic Writings of Nietzsche*, W. Kaufmann (ed.), (New York: Modern Library).

Nietzsche, F. (1968), *The Will to Power*, W. Kaufmann (ed.), (New York: Vintage Books).

O'Brien, M. (1983), *The Politics of Reproduction*, (London: Routledge & Kegan Paul).

O'Neill, J. (1969), 'Hegel and Marx on history as human history', in Hyppolite, op. cit.

O'Neill, J. (ed.) (1973), *Modes of Individualism and Collectivism* (London: Heinemann).

Ollman, B. (1976), *Alienation*, second edition (Cambridge: Cambridge University Press).

Ollman, B. (1977), 'Marx's vision of communism: a reconstruction', *Critique*, no. 8, pp. 4–41.

Parkin, F. (1979), *Marxism and Class Theory* (London: Tavistock).

Petrovic, G. (1967), *Marx in the mid-twentieth century* (New York: Anchor Books).

Petrovic, G. (1983), 'Marx's concept of man', in Bottomore, op. cit.

Philp, M. (1985), 'Michel Foucault', in *The Return of Grand Theory in the Human Sciences*, Q. Skinner (ed.) (Cambridge: Cambridge University Press), pp. 65–82.

Pocock, J. G. A. (1975), 'Early modern capitalism: the Augustan perception', in Kamenka and Neale, op. cit.

Rawls, J. (1973), *A Theory of Justice* (Oxford: Oxford University Press).

Roemer, J. (1982), 'Methodological Individualism and Deductive Marxism', *Theory and Society*, no. 11, pp. 513–20.

Roemer, J. (ed.), (1986), *Analytical Marxism* (Cambridge: Cambridge University Press).

Rousseau, J.-J. (1973), *The Social Contract and Discourses* (London: Dent).

Sawer, M. (1977), *Marxism and the Question of the Asiatic Mode of Production* (The Hague: Martin Nijhoff).

Schaff, A. (1980), *Alienation as a Social Phenomenon* (Oxford: Pergamon Press).

Sekelj, L. (1984), 'Marx on the state and communism', *Praxis International*, vol. 3, no. 4.

Sève, L. (1975), *Marxism and the Theory of Personality* (London: Lawrence & Wishart).

Sève, L. (1978), *Man in Marxist Theory and the psychology of personality* (Hassocks: Harvester).

Street, J. (1983), 'Work and Human Nature', in Forbes and Smith, op. cit.. pp. 131–145.

Sweezy, P., Dobb, M., Takahashi, K. *et al.* (1976), *The Transition from Feudalism to Capitalism*, (London: New Left Books).

Tawney, R. (1926), *Religion and the Rise of Capitalism* (London: Murray).

Thompson, E. P. (1967), 'Time, work discipline and industrial capitalism', *Past and Present*, no. 38.

Thompson, E. P. (1968), *The Making of the English Working Class* (Harmondsworth: Penguin).

Tucker, D. F. B. (1980), *Marxism and Individualism* (Oxford: Blackwell).

Walliman, I. (1981), *Estrangement: Marx's Conception of Human Nature and the Division of Labour* (Westport, Conn.: Greenwood Press).

Warren, M. (1988), 'Marx and methodological individualism', *Philosophy of Social Science*, vol. 18, pp. 447–76.

Watkins, J. (1973), 'Ideal types and historical explanations', in O'Neill, op. cit.

West, F. J. (1975), 'On the ruins of feudalism - capitalism?', in Kamenka and Neale, op. cit.

Wetherly, P. (1988), 'Marxist functionalism - some "problems" considered', paper delivered to the Political Studies Association Annual Conference, April.

Williams, R. (1976), *Keywords* (London: Fontana).

Wood, A. (1981), *Karl Marx* (London: Routledge & Kegan Paul).

Wood, E. M. (1972), *Mind and Politics* (Berkeley, Calif.: California University Press).

Index

245

state xix, 81–2, 106, 116, 171, 178, 184, 212, 214, 222, 237
Street, J. 233
structuralism 3, 9–11, 13, 25–6, 28–9

Tawney 75, 77–8, 81–2
theoretical anti-humanism 2–5, 7–8, 11–14
Theses on Feuerbach 4, 153
Thompson, E. P. 101, 164
Tucker, D. F. B. 25, 34

utopia 170–2, 175

Walliman 177, 180
Warren, M. 24–6, 34
Watkins, J. W. N. 18–19, 22–3, 25
wealth 90–1, 117, 143, 154, 160, 162, 181–2, 186–7, 189, 193, 198, 201–17, 225, 234, 235
West, F. J. 89–90
Wetherley, P. 25
Williams, R. 2–3
women 156, 164
Wood, A. 23, 129, 140, 164, 169, 183, 190–3
Wood, E. M. 26, 153